DATE DUE

DE 23 '94		
MR 31 '9		
JU 15 '95		
MY 7 '97		

DEMCO 38-296

Mastering NEPA: A Step-by-Step Approach

Ronald E. Bass
Albert I. Herson

Solano Press Books
Point Arena, California

Mastering NEPA: A Step-by-Step Approach

First Edition, January 1993
Solano Press Books
Post Office Box 773
Point Arena, California 95468

Book design by Solano Press Books
Cover design by Canterbury Press
Printed by Canterbury Press, Berkeley, California

ISBN 0-923956-14-X

Trees are one of nature's renewable resources. To
preserve this invaluable resource for future generations,
Solano Press Books makes annual contributions to the
American Forests Global Releaf program. *American Forests*
is the nation's oldest non-profit citizens' conservation
organization.

Notice

Before you rely on the information in this
book, be sure you have the latest edition and
are aware that some changes in statutes,
guidelines or case law may have gone into
effect since the date of publication. The
book, moreover, provides general
information about the law. Readers should
consult their own attorneys before relying on
the representations found herein.

Congressional Declaration of National Environmental Policy (NEPA §101)

"Congress, recognizing the profound impact of man's activity on the interrelations of all components of the natural environment, particularly the profound influences of population growth, high-density urbanization, industrial expansion, resource exploitation, and new and expanding technological advances, and recognizing further the critical importance of restoring and maintaining environmental quality to the overall welfare and development of man, declares that it is the continuing policy of the federal government, in cooperation with state and local governments and other concerned public and private organizations, to use all practicable means and measures, including financial and technical assistance, in a manner calculated to foster and promote the general welfare, to create and maintain conditions under which man and nature can exist in productive harmony, and fulfill the social, economic, and other requirements of present and future generations of Americans." 42 U.S.C. 4331.

PREFACE

The National Environmental Policy Act (NEPA) is the nation's broadest environmental law. NEPA applies to all federal agencies and most of the activities they manage, regulate, or fund that affect the environment. It requires all agencies to disclose and consider the environmental implications of their proposed actions.

NEPA requires the preparation of environmental impact statements (EISs) to ensure that federal agencies accomplish the law's purposes. The President's Council on Environmental Quality (CEQ) has adopted regulations and other guidance that provide detailed procedures federal agencies must follow to implement NEPA. A fundamental first step to successful NEPA compliance is understanding the environmental review process established by the statute, the regulations, and relevant court decisions. The key to NEPA's success is the ability to integrate NEPA into federal agency decision-making.

NEPA's reach is pervasive throughout the federal government. It applies to virtually any activity undertaken, funded, or permitted by a federal agency that affects the environment. For example, NEPA may apply to diverse federal actions and agencies, such as a new highway in Boston (Federal Highway Administration), the filling of wetlands for housing development in Florida (U.S. Army Corps of Engineers), timber sales on National Forest land in Alaska (U.S. Forest Service), and the sale of water for agricultural purposes in California (U.S. Bureau of Reclamation). In these and thousands of other federal decisions, agency officials and their staffs must have a working knowledge of NEPA's purposes and procedural requirements.

NEPA's success also depends on informed participation by private organizations, public-interest groups, and citizens concerned about the environment. Citizen participation is an integral part of NEPA's procedural requirements; the more the public understands about the environmental review process, the more effectively they can participate. This handbook is designed to help citizens participate effectively in the government decision-making process by educating them on NEPA implementation.

Mastering NEPA: A Step-by-Step Approach is designed to provide the users a simplified framework for understanding NEPA and incorporating it into their agency's day-to-day activities, thus helping them obtain maximum benefit from the environmental review process. However, because it is intended as a user's handbook rather than a comprehensive legal analysis, case law is cited only on a limited basis. The legal citations in this book are not exhaustive, but rather refer primarily to NEPA, CEQ's NEPA regulations, and CEQ's other guidance on NEPA implementation. Although this handbook emphasizes the law and regulations, it also includes the authors' recommendations for successful NEPA compliance. For detailed legal treatment, users should consult additional NEPA publications, listed in Appendix 7.

The authors were inspired to write this handbook after listening to the comments of participants at professional workshops on environmental impact assessment. NEPA has been in effect since 1970, and although numerous publications have focused on the legal aspects of NEPA, none has presented NEPA in a simplified, user-friendly format. *Mastering NEPA: A Step-by-Step Approach* is designed to meet this need.

ABOUT THE AUTHORS

Ronald E. Bass is a Vice President of Jones & Stokes Associates, Inc., a Sacramento-based consulting firm providing services in environmental planning and natural resource management. He was formerly the Director of the State Clearinghouse in California's Office of Planning and Research, where he coordinated the review of NEPA documents for state agencies and was responsible for administration of the California Environmental Quality Act (CEQA). Mr. Bass is a past President of the California Chapter of the American Planning Association and the Association of Environmental Professionals. He is a well-known authority on NEPA and CEQA and teaches professional seminars throughout the U.S. and abroad on environmental impact assessment procedures.

Mr. Bass received a J.D. from the Washington College of Law at American University, an M.A. in environmental planning from California State University, Sacramento, and a B.A. in anthropology from Ohio State University. He is a member of the Bar in the District of Columbia and Maryland.

Mr. Bass and Mr. Herson are coauthors of *Successful CEQA Compliance: A Step-by-Step Approach*, published by Solano Press Books; contributing authors of *California Environmental Law and Land Use Practice*, published by Mathew Bender and Company, Inc.; members of the editorial board of *California Environmental Law Reporter*; and authors of numerous articles on environmental impact assessment.

Albert I. Herson is Senior Vice-President and Legal Counsel of Jones & Stokes Associates, Inc. He was previously a regional planner with the Southern California Association of Governments and in private law practice, where he specialized in water and environmental issues. He is a frequent speaker and author on NEPA, CEQA, and other environmental laws. Mr. Herson is a past President of the California Chapter of the American Planning Association.

Mr. Herson received a J.D. from the University of the Pacific McGeorge School of Law; an M.A. in urban planning from the University of California, Los Angeles; and a B.A. in psychology from the University of Illinois. He is a member of the California Bar and the American Institute of Certified Planners (AICP).

ACKNOWLEDGEMENTS

The preparation of this handbook was a collaborative effort of many people at Jones & Stokes Associates, the authors' employer. The authors wish to thank the following staff members for their assistance: Christy Anderson, graphics coordinator; Joanne Gorbach and Nancy Hartwick, graphic artists; Amy Rucker, landscape architect and contributing artist; David Haining and Judy Bell, production assistants; Karen Rusk and Nick Kroska, technical editors; and Brad Norton, research assistant. Kelly Burnette and Larry Hughston were also contributing graphic artists.

The authors also wish to thank Lucinda Swartz, Deputy General Counsel, President's Council on Environmental Quality and William Dickerson, Deputy Director, Office of Federal Activities, U.S. Environmental Protection Agency for their review and comment. Also, the intellectual insight and conceptual models of NEPA provided by Owen Schmidt are gratefully acknowledged.

TABLE OF CONTENTS

List of Figures and Sidebars

List of Figures

#	Figure	Page

CHAPTER 3

CHAPTER 4

#	Figure	Page

LIST OF SIDEBARS

Sidebar	Page

CHAPTER 1   BACKGROUND AND IMPLEMENTATION OF NEPA

A. INTRODUCTION AND OVERVIEW OF THE LAW

1. Purposes

The National Environmental Policy Act (NEPA) was signed into law on January 1, 1970, in response to an overwhelming national sentiment that federal agencies should take a lead in providing greater protection for the environment. NEPA is our country's basic national charter for protection of the environment. It establishes environmental policy for the nation, provides an interdisciplinary framework for federal agencies to prevent environmental damage, and contains "action-forcing" procedures to ensure that federal agency decision-makers take environmental factors into account. 42 U.S.C. 4321; 40 C.F.R. 1500.1.

Under NEPA, Congress authorizes and directs that, to the fullest extent possible, federal agencies carry out their regulations, policies, and programs in accordance with NEPA's policies of environmental protection. 42 U.S.C. 4322; 40 C.F.R. 1500.2.

There are four stated purposes of NEPA. 42 U.S.C. 4321 (Figure 1-1).

2. Environmental Policies

Section 101 of NEPA expresses several broad environmental policies for the nation (Figure 1-2). The policies have played an important role in federal agency implementation and in judicial interpretations of NEPA.

Purposes of NEPA

◆ Declare a national policy which will encourage productive and enjoyable harmony between people and the environment

◆ Promote efforts which will prevent or eliminate damage to the environment and biosphere and stimulate health and welfare

◆ Enrich the understanding of the ecological system and natural resources important to the nation

◆ Establish a Council on Environmental Quality

42 U.S.C. 4321

Figure 1-1

Environmental Policies Stated in NEPA

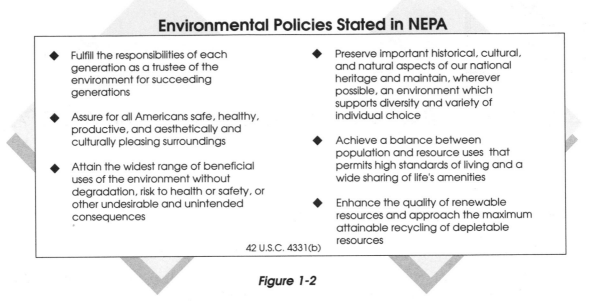

- ◆ Fulfill the responsibilities of each generation as a trustee of the environment for succeeding generations

- ◆ Assure for all Americans safe, healthy, productive, and aesthetically and culturally pleasing surroundings

- ◆ Attain the widest range of beneficial uses of the environment without degradation, risk to health or safety, or other undesirable and unintended consequences

- ◆ Preserve important historical, cultural, and natural aspects of our national heritage and maintain, wherever possible, an environment which supports diversity and variety of individual choice

- ◆ Achieve a balance between population and resource uses that permits high standards of living and a wide sharing of life's amenities

- ◆ Enhance the quality of renewable resources and approach the maximum attainable recycling of depletable resources

42 U.S.C. 4331(b)

Figure 1-2

3. Interdisciplinary Framework for Environmental Protection

Unlike other single-topic environmental laws, NEPA encourages the protection of all aspects of the environment. Specifically, NEPA requires federal agencies to utilize a systematic, interdisciplinary approach to agency decision-making, which will ensure the integrated use of the natural sciences, social sciences, and the environmental design arts. It also requires agencies to identify and develop methods and procedures which will ensure that agency decision-making takes into consideration unquantifiable environmental amenities and values as well as economic and technical factors. 42 U.S.C. 4332.

4. "Action-Forcing" Procedures

To ensure that the stated environmental policies are achieved, Section 102 of NEPA establishes a series of "action-forcing" procedures that require federal agencies to consider environmental factors. The key concept of NEPA, and the one most closely associated with the law, is the requirement for every federal agency to prepare an environmental impact statement (EIS) for proposed legislation or other major federal actions significantly affecting the quality of the human environment. 42 U.S.C. 4332; 40 C.F.R. 1501.

The EIS is a detailed statement that describes the environmental impacts of a proposed action and its alternatives. The EIS and the procedures surrounding its preparation and review form the cornerstone of NEPA's system of environmental protection. The detailed content requirements of an EIS and the process for preparing it are described in Chapter 3.

5. Substantive Effect

For many years after NEPA was enacted, a debate existed as to whether NEPA had a substantive effect on agency decision making by requiring agencies to reject environmentally damaging proposals. The Supreme Court resolved the debate in 1978 by declaring that NEPA's mandate to agencies is "essentially procedural," even though it sets forth significant national goals for protecting the environment. *Vermont Yankee Nuclear Power Corporation v. Natural Resources Defense Council*, 435 U.S. 519, 558 (1978). In a 1980 decision, the U.S. Supreme Court affirmed that once an agency has made a decision subject to NEPA's requirements, the judicial role is limited to whether the agency has "considered" environmental consequences of its action. *Strycker's Bay Neighborhood Council, Inc. v. Karlen*, 444 U.S. 223, 227 (1980).

THE CONGRESSIONAL DEVELOPMENT OF NEPA

NEPA was developed in Congress through a lengthy discourse on the need for a national environmental policy. The act evolved over a period of more than 10 years and was modeled after the concept of a national employment policy in the Employment Act of 1946. This legislation inspired Senator Murray to propose the creation of a Council on Environmental Quality as early as 1959. However, it was not until 1969 that Senator Henry Jackson and Congressman John Dingell authored the legislation that would become NEPA.

The first House of Representatives drafts of NEPA contained two primary objectives: preventing environmental damage and ensuring that agency decision-makers take environmental factors into account. The inclusion of individual environmental rights, the reporting of impacts, and the limitation of agency power were key topics in the debate that transpired during the legislative drafting process.

The draft Senate bill was more comprehensive than the House bill, but it did not contain a statement of environmental policy. One of the first amendments proposed by Senator Jackson added ". . . each person has a fundamental and inalienable right to a healthful environment." This amendment would have created a judicially enforceable right to environmental protection. Another amendment proposed by Jackson required federal agencies to report written "findings" on the environmental impacts of agency actions. In his Congressional testimony, Professor Lynton Caldwell, an Indiana University professor, promoted this concept, which eventually evolved into the EIS. The House of Representatives made one significant amendment to substantively limit the act by adding: "nothing in this Act shall increase, decrease or change any responsibility of any Federal official or agency."

(continued)

> These additions were disputed in the conference committee and replaced or removed. The concept of "findings" was replaced with "detailed statements" to avoid incomplete agency disclosure, and the phrase "has a fundamental and inalienable right to a healthful environment" was replaced with "should enjoy a healthful environment" to avoid a judicially enforceable right. The House of Representatives amendment limiting NEPA's effect on agency decision-making was also removed. Finally, the conference committee added several additional items, including the requirement for external review to avoid internal agency bias. At the time of NEPA's final passage, Senator Henry Jackson referred to NEPA as "the most important and far-reaching environmental and conservation measure ever enacted...."

B. PARTICIPANTS IN THE NEPA PROCESS

1. General

Although NEPA applies only to federal agencies, its implementation involves a variety of participants, including state agencies, local governments, Native American tribes, third-party contractors, interest groups, and concerned citizens. Figure 1-3 shows the key participants in the NEPA process. The roles of each of these participants are described throughout this manual.

Key Participants in the NEPA Process

Figure 1-3

2. NEPA Administration and Oversight

Two federal agencies have responsibility for administering, overseeing and reviewing the implementation of NEPA by other agencies: the President's Council on Environmental Quality (CEQ) and the U.S. Environmental Protection Agency (EPA).

3. Council on Environmental Quality

a. General Responsibilities

CEQ was created by NEPA and given the responsibility for environmental policy development and the oversight of federal agencies implementing NEPA. According to NEPA, CEQ is supposed to be a three-member council appointed by the President. However, to increase the operating efficiency of the Council, during the past few years the President has appointed only one member.

CEQ was made a part of the Executive Office of the President to ensure that environmental policy received high-level consideration within the federal government. NEPA gives CEQ eight stated duties and purposes. 42 U.S.C. 4344 (Figure 1-4). In addition, Executive Order No. 11991 authorizes CEQ to issue NEPA regulations to federal agencies.

CEQ: Duties & Functions

◆ Assist and advise the President in preparing an annual environmental quality report	◆ Conduct investigations, studies, surveys, research, and analysis relating to ecological systems and environmental quality
◆ Gather, analyze, and interpret information on conditions and trends in the quality of the environment	◆ Document and define changes and trends in the natural environment and their underlying causes
◆ Review and appraise federal agency compliance with the environmental policies of NEPA	◆ Report at least once each year to the President on the condition of the environment
◆ Develop and recommend to the President national policies to foster and promote the improvement of environmental quality	◆ Make recommendations to the President with respect to environmental policies and legislation

42 U.S.C. 4344

Figure 1-4

b. Specific NEPA Responsibilities

In addition to the general duties and functions of CEQ for developing and overseeing environmental policy, CEQ has been given several specific responsibilities relating to the administration of NEPA (Figure 1-5).

CEQ: Specific NEPA Responsibilities

◆ Issue regulations and other guidance regarding NEPA

◆ Resolve lead agency disputes

◆ Mediate interagency disputes over environmental policy

◆ Provide training and advice to federal agencies regarding NEPA compliance

E.O. 11514 as amended by E.O. 11991

Figure 1-5

As a branch of the Executive Office of the President, CEQ's involvement with NEPA and its effectiveness in overseeing NEPA compliance has reflected the environmental policies of each respective President. CEQ's NEPA responsibilities have fluctuated greatly from administration to administration. CEQ had its heyday during the Carter Administration (1976-1980). During that period, it took an active role in establishing NEPA as an important element of federal environmental policy. An abrupt turnaround occurred during the Reagan Administration (1980-1988); CEQ's budget, staff, and role were reduced drastically. Little guidance or assistance on NEPA occurred under Reagan's leadership. Under President Bush (1988-1992), CEQ staffing and budget were increased; the staff maintained a helpful but cautious role in NEPA. Figure 1-6 shows the fluctuation in staffing and budgeting between 1970 and 1992. In its annual report to the President, CEQ generally includes a section dealing with its NEPA activities and the current trends in NEPA implementation by federal agencies.

Council on Environmental Quality:
Historical Funding and Staffing
(Source: CEQ)

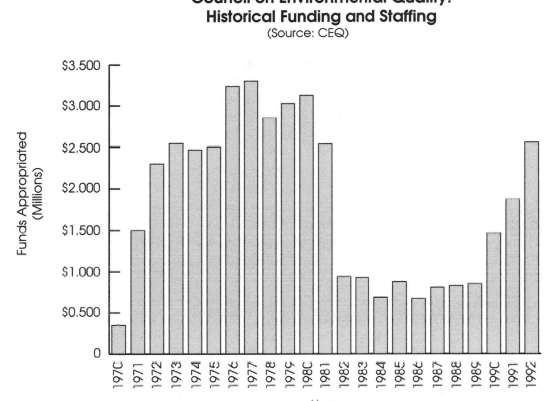

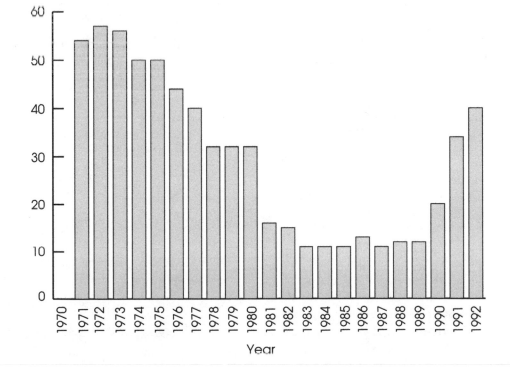

Figure 1-6

c. CEQ's NEPA Regulations

i. Background

In 1978, CEQ issued the first set of binding regulations concerning the implementation of NEPA. These regulations became effective in 1979. Prior to that, NEPA implementation followed a set of nonbinding guidelines issued by CEQ. Because they were not binding and were limited primarily to EIS preparation, the guidelines were interpreted very differently from agency to agency, resulting in inconsistent compliance with NEPA.

In 1977, President Jimmy Carter signed Executive Order No. 11991, giving CEQ the authority to issue binding regulations and expand the scope of the regulations to cover all of the procedural provisions of NEPA. This executive order led to CEQ's 1978 regulations, which have been amended only once. The amendment, adopted in 1986, deleted the requirement to conduct a worst-case analysis under Sec.1502.22. The regulations are included as Appendix 2 to this guidebook.

ii. Objectives and Organization of the Regulations

In addition to bringing consistency to agency practice, the stated objectives of the regulations are to reduce paperwork and delay in the environmental review process under NEPA. 40 C.F.R. 1500.4, 1500.5. The regulations are organized into various parts (Figure 1-7).

iii. Legal Effect of Regulations

The regulations are binding on all federal agencies, including independent regulatory commissions, except where compliance would be inconsistent with other federal laws. Therefore, the statute and regulations must be read together as a whole to comply with the letter

Organization of the CEQ NEPA Regulations

◆ Part 1500 -	Purpose, policy, and mandate
◆ Part 1501 -	NEPA and agency decisions
◆ Part 1502 -	Environmental Impact Statement
◆ Part 1503 -	Commenting
◆ Part 1504 -	Predecision referrals to CEQ of proposed federal actions determined to be environmentally unsatisfactory
◆ Part 1505 -	NEPA agency decision-making
◆ Part 1506 -	Other requirements of NEPA
◆ Part 1507 -	Agency compliance
◆ Part 1508 -	Terminology and index

Figure 1-7

and spirit of NEPA. A violation of the regulations may give rise to a cause of action for violating NEPA. The federal courts give CEQ's interpretation of NEPA "substantial deference," *Andres v. Sierra Club*, 442 U.S. 347, 358 (1979). 40 C.F.R. 1500.3; Forty Questions No. 12(c).

iv. Other NEPA Guidance

In addition to NEPA Regulations, CEQ has issued other guidance concerning the implementation of NEPA (Figure 1-8). The most frequently cited guidance is entitled *Forty Most Asked Questions Concerning CEQ's NEPA Regulations* (Forty Questions). Other than regulations and relevant federal court decisions, Forty Questions is the best source of NEPA interpretation. (Forty Questions is referenced where applicable in this guidebook and included as Appendix 3.) The courts do not, however, give CEQ's guidance (e.g., Forty Questions) the same deference as CEQ's NEPA Regulations.

NEPA Regulations and Guidance Issued by CEQ

◆ Regulations for implementing the Procedural Provisions of NEPA. 40 C.F.R. 1500.

◆ Forty Most Asked Questions Concerning CEQ's NEPA Regulations. 46 Fed. Reg. 18028. (March 23, 1981)

◆ Council on Environmental Quality Memorandum: Scoping Guidance. (April 30, 1981)

◆ Council on Environmental Quality Memorandum: Guidance Regarding NEPA Regulations. 48 Fed. Reg. 34263. (July 28, 1983)

Figure 1-8

4. U.S. Environmental Protection Agency

a. General

The U.S. Environmental Protection Agency (EPA) has three important roles in the NEPA process: a reviewing role, a filing and noticing role, and a cooperating agency role (Figure 1-9). In its regulatory capacity, EPA rarely prepares EISs because many of its regulatory functions are considered "functionally equivalent" to those of NEPA. See Chapter 2 for a discussion of this concept.

EPA: NEPA Responsibilities

♦ Reviewing Agency Role

EPA reviews all EISs for document adequacy and environmental quality of the proposal

♦ Filing and Noticing Role

EPA receives all EISs and provides notice in the *Federal Register*

♦ Cooperating Agency Role

EPA cooperates with lead agencies concerning EPA environmental programs

Figure 1-9

b. Reviewing Role

EPA's authority for reviewing EISs does not derive from NEPA but from Section 309 of the Clean Air Act. 42 U.S.C. 7609. Under Section 309, EPA is given the authority to review and comment in writing on the environmental impact of proposed legislation, regulations, or major federal actions for which an EIS is prepared under NEPA. If, as a result of this review, EPA determines that the proposed activity is unsatisfactory from the standpoint of public health, welfare, or environmental quality, EPA is authorized to refer the matter to CEQ for resolution.

The Office of Federal Activities within EPA is responsible for the review of EISs under NEPA. The office has developed detailed criteria for evaluating the extent of a proposal's impacts and for the quality of an EIS analysis. EPA's review of EISs is discussed in detail in Chapter 3.

c. Filing and Noticing Role

EPA's second unique role in the NEPA process is to officially file all EISs and publish notices of their availability and comment date in the *Federal Register*. The requirements for filing notices in the *Federal Register* are described in greater detail in Chapter 3.

d. Cooperating Agency Role

EPA's authority to review EISs under Section 309 of the Clean Air Act is independent of the role that it sometimes plays as a cooperating agency or agency with jurisdiction by law or special expertise. In this capacity, EPA often participates in EIS preparation by other agencies because of jurisdiction over, and expertise in, water quality, air quality, solid waste, toxic substances, and other areas of pollution control. Forty Questions No. 15.

C. NEPA IMPLEMENTATION BY OTHER FEDERAL AGENCIES

1. Application to Federal Agencies

NEPA applies to all agencies of the federal government, including independent regulatory agencies. It does not, however, apply to Congress, the Judiciary, the President, or the President's immediate staff. 40 C.F.R. 1500.3, 1508.12; Forty Questions No. 31(a).

2. Agency Authority

Every federal agency must interpret NEPA as a supplement to its existing authority and is required to view its traditional policies and missions in light of NEPA's environmental objectives. Agencies must review and revise their policies, procedures, and regulations, as necessary, to ensure full compliance with NEPA. 40 C.F.R. 1500.6.

3. Agency Compliance

Every federal agency must comply with NEPA and maintain sufficient personnel and other resources to do so. Each agency must also designate a person to be responsible for overall review of agency NEPA compliance. The list of agency NEPA liaisons is included as Appendix 6 of this guidebook. 40 C.F.R. 1507.1, 1507.2.

4. Supplemental Agency Procedures

a. Preparation of Procedures

Every federal agency must prepare procedures to supplement NEPA and the CEQ NEPA Regulations. Prior to adopting or revising their procedures, agencies must consult with CEQ and publish the procedures in the *Federal Register* for public comment. 40 C.F.R.1507.3(a). Agencies must make diligent efforts to involve the public in preparing, implementing, and amending their NEPA procedures. 40 C.F.R. 1506.6(a).

b. Contents

Agency procedures shall comply with CEQ NEPA Regulations except where compliance would be inconsistent with statutory requirements. The required and recommended contents of an agency's procedures for complying with NEPA are shown in Figure 1-10. 40 C.F.R. 1507.3(b)(c).

Federal Agency NEPA Procedures

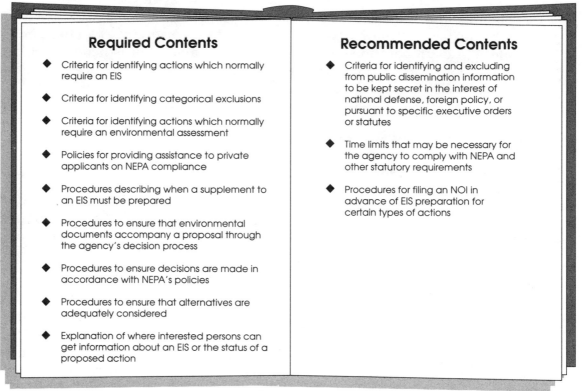

Required Contents

◆ Criteria for identifying actions which normally require an EIS

◆ Criteria for identifying categorical exclusions

◆ Criteria for identifying actions which normally require an environmental assessment

◆ Policies for providing assistance to private applicants on NEPA compliance

◆ Procedures describing when a supplement to an EIS must be prepared

◆ Procedures to ensure that environmental documents accompany a proposal through the agency's decision process

◆ Procedures to ensure decisions are made in accordance with NEPA's policies

◆ Procedures to ensure that alternatives are adequately considered

◆ Explanation of where interested persons can get information about an EIS or the status of a proposed action

Recommended Contents

◆ Criteria for identifying and excluding from public dissemination information to be kept secret in the interest of national defense, foreign policy, or pursuant to specific executive orders or statutes

◆ Time limits that may be necessary for the agency to comply with NEPA and other statutory requirements

◆ Procedures for filing an NOI in advance of EIS preparation for certain types of actions

Figure 1-10

c. Time Limits

Although CEQ NEPA Regulations do not prescribe universal time limits for completing the NEPA review process, each federal agency is encouraged to set time limits for completing the entire NEPA process or constituent parts of the process that are appropriate to individual actions. The CEQ NEPA Regulations do, however, contain certain interim time periods, such as minimum requirements for public notice and review, that must be factored into any overall time limits that an agency adopts. Additionally, an agency must set time limits if an applicant for a proposed action requests them. The CEQ NEPA Regulations provide a variety of factors that must be considered by an agency when it establishes time limits. 40 C.F.R. 1501.8. In practice, very few federal agencies establish standard time limits for EIS preparation under NEPA.

d. Other Agency Guidance

In addition to adopting formal NEPA procedures, many federal agencies have developed informal NEPA guidance in the form of manuals or handbooks. These handbooks generally outline internal procedures for the management and preparation of NEPA documents.

e. Differences Among Agency NEPA Regulations

While the fundamental NEPA procedures differ little from agency to agency, each agency has its own unique provisions for implementing NEPA. Some federal agencies have very short NEPA regulations and others, such as the Department of the Interior, have extensive department-wide NEPA regulations supplemented by specific NEPA procedures for individual agencies within the department, such as the U.S. Fish and Wildlife Service, the U.S. Bureau of Reclamation, and the U.S. Bureau of Land Management. In addition to publishing their NEPA procedures in the *Federal Register*, some agencies publish their NEPA procedures in the Code of Federal Regulations, and others make them part of their department manuals. Persons involved in the NEPA process must, therefore, not only be familiar with CEQ NEPA Regulations, but also with the regulations and manuals of individual agencies.

5. Lead and Cooperating Agency Roles

a. Lead Agency

i. Determining a Lead Agency

A lead agency is the federal agency with primary responsibility for preparing an EIS. 40 C.F.R. 1508.16; 1508.17; Forty Questions No. 14(a). If more than one federal agency is involved in a project, the lead agency is determined by considering the factors shown in Figure 1-11. 40 C.F.R. 1501.5(c).

Factors Used to Determine the Lead Agency

- ◆ Magnitude of the agency's involvement
- ◆ Approval or disapproval authority over the proposed action
- ◆ Expertise with regard to environmental effects
- ◆ Duration of the agency's involvement
- ◆ Sequence of the agency's involvement

Figure 1-11

ii. Resolving Lead Agency Disputes

Disputes over lead agency status may be referred to CEQ for resolution. A request for lead agency designation must include a description of the proposed action and a detailed statement as to why each disputing agency should or should not serve as the lead agency. CEQ is required to resolve the dispute within 20 days. 40 C.F.R. 1501.5(e); Forty Questions No. 14(b).

b. Cooperating Agencies

i. Definition

A cooperating agency may be any federal agency other than the lead agency that has jurisdiction by law or special expertise with respect to the environmental impacts expected to result from a proposal. 40 C.F.R. 1508.5; 1501.6; Forty Questions No. 14(a), 14(b), 14(c). An agency has "jurisdiction by law" if it has the authority to approve, veto, or finance all or part of the proposal. 40 C.F.R. 1508.15. An agency has "special expertise" if it has statutory responsibility, agency mission, or related program experience with regard to a proposal. 40 C.F.R. 1508.26.

ii. Identifying Cooperating Agencies

On the lead agency's request, any other federal agency with jurisdiction by law or special expertise shall be a cooperating agency. In addition, the lead agency may request any other federal agency with special expertise regarding any environmental issue to become a cooperating agency. 40 C.F.R. 1501.6. A lead agency may designate a state or local agency as a cooperating agency. 40 C.F.R. 1508.5.

iii. Lead Agency Responsibilities Regarding Cooperating Agencies

A lead agency must request the participation of cooperating agencies as early as possible in the NEPA process, use the environmental analyses and proposals prepared by cooperating agencies as much as possible, and meet with cooperating agencies at their request. 40 C.F.R. 1501.6(a).

iv. Cooperating Agency Responsibilities

A cooperating agency must participate in the NEPA process as early as possible, participate in the scoping process, and, on the lead agency's request, develop information to be included in the EIS and provide staff support in its preparation. 40 C.F.R. 1501.6(b). If a cooperating agency determines that resource limitations will limit its involvement in the EIS process, it must inform the lead agency in writing. 40 C.F.R. 1501.6(c).

v. Disagreements Among Lead and Cooperating Agencies

Disagreements among the lead agency and cooperating agencies must be resolved among the agencies themselves. If, however, a lead agency fails to include information requested by a cooperating agency in an EIS, the cooperating agency may later determine that the EIS is inadequate or insufficient for its decision-making. Forty Questions No. 14(b).

D. Overview of the Steps in the NEPA Process

The environmental review process established under NEPA involves three key phases: the review for categorical exclusions or other exemptions, the preparation of an Environmental Assessment (EA), and the preparation of an EIS. The key steps in the NEPA process are shown in Figure 1-12. These phases and the detailed steps under each are explained throughout this manual.

NEPA Environmental Review Process: An Overview

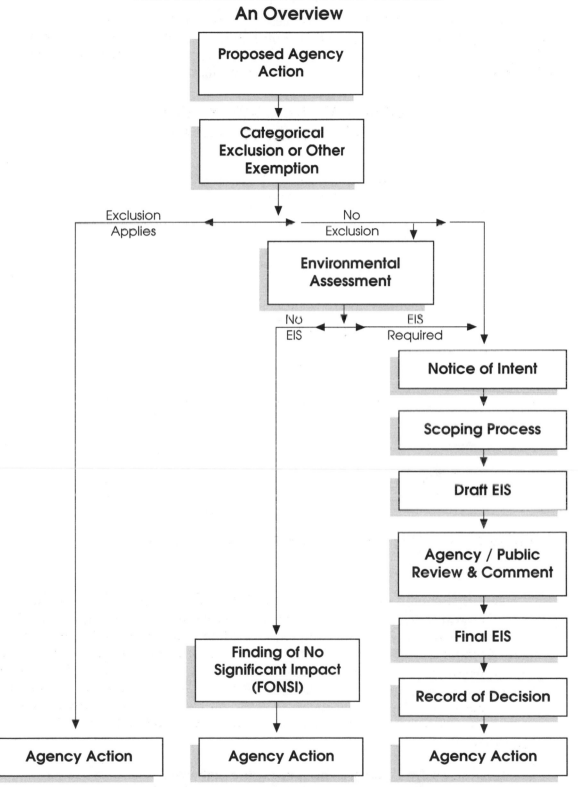

Figure 1-12

E. WHEN TO COMMENCE NEPA REVIEW

Agencies must integrate the NEPA process with their activities at the earliest possible time. Early application of NEPA will accomplish the objectives listed in Figure 1-13. 40 C.F.R. 1501.1; 1501.2; Forty Questions No. 8. Specific requirements for integrating NEPA review with agency planning are discussed in Chapter 3.

Advantages of Complying with NEPA as Early as Possible

◆ Ensures that federal agency planning reflects environmental values

◆ Avoids delays later in the planning process

◆ Avoids conflicts over environmental issues

◆ Contributes to environmental decision-making throughout project evaluation

◆ Avoids the use of the EIS for rationalizing projects

◆ Allows for cooperative consultation among agencies before the EIS is prepared

◆ Identifies key environmental issues early in the planning process

Figure 1-13

F. INTEGRATION OF NEPA WITH OTHER ENVIRONMENTAL LAWS

1. General

Federal agencies must integrate the NEPA process with other environmental laws. Generally, proposed federal actions that trigger review under NEPA also require compliance with a variety of other federal, and often state, environmental laws. Each federal agency has an obligation to inquire as to which other environmental requirements may be applicable to an action and to list, in the EIS, all federal permits, licenses, and other entitlements that are needed in the EIS. To the fullest extent possible, agencies are encouraged to integrate the NEPA process with the review processes established by these other laws. 40 C.F.R. 1502.25(a); Forty Questions No. 9.

2. Which Federal Laws Must Be Integrated with NEPA

Each proposed federal action will trigger a different set of related environmental requirements, depending on the type of activities being proposed and the location of the project or action. In practice, every agency should maintain a list of those requirements that generally apply to its activities. However, certain federal environmental requirements apply more commonly because of their general application. These are listed in Figure 1-15.

3. Is Comprehensive Environmental Response Compensation and Liability Act Integration Required?

Legal opinions differ over whether the integration of the Comprehensive Environmental Response Compensation and Liability Act of 1980 (CERCLA) and NEPA is required. Although integration has been encouraged by CEQ, EPA does not have an official position. In fact, within EPA there is a difference of opinion whether a Remedial Investigation/Feasibility Study (RI/FS) performed under CERCLA is "functionally equivalent" to an EIS under NEPA, and therefore, exempt from NEPA compliance. Additionally, EPA believes that the concept of "functional equivalence" only applies to EPA. On the other hand, some federal agencies, such as the Department of Energy, have formal guidance on integrating NEPA with CERCLA. Until this issue is resolved, agencies undertaking certain remediation activities should comply, to the extent possible, to avoid duplication of effort and legal challenges.

4. Interaction of NEPA with State and Local Laws

Numerous states have adopted environmental impact assessment laws modeled after NEPA. Although these laws incorporate many of NEPA's general concepts, each has different thresholds of applicability and different procedures for preparing EISs. Figure 1-14 shows the states with environmental impact assessment laws. Federal

States with Environmental Impact Assessment Laws

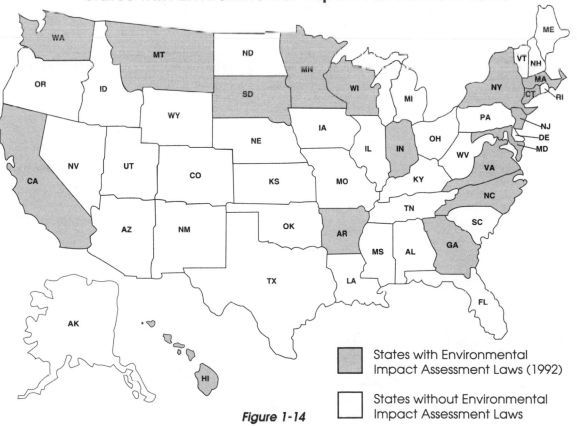

Figure 1-14

Federal Environmental Review and Consultation Requirements Which May Have to Be Integrated into the NEPA Process

Activities Requiring Review or Consultation	Agency	Legal Authority
Discharges into "waters of the U.S." (including wetlands)	U.S. Army Corps of Engineers	Section 404 of the Clean Water Act, 33 U.S.C. 1344, Executive Order 11990
Construction activities in "navigable waters"	U.S. Army Corps of Engineers	Section 10 of the Rivers and Harbors Act of 1899, 33 U.S.C. 403
Activities proposed in floodplains	Federal Emergency Management Agency	Executive Order 11988, Floodplain Management
Activities affecting endangered species	U.S. Fish and Wildlife Service or the National Marine Fisheries Service	Endangered Species Act, 16 U.S.C. 1536
Activities affecting historical and archaeological resources	Advisory Council on Historic Preservation	Section 106 of the National Historic Preservation Act, 16 U.S.C. 470
Transportation projects proposed in recreation areas and parks	Federal Highway Administration	Section 4(f) of the Transportation Act of 1966, 49 U.S.C. 303
Activities resulting in the conversion of farmlands	U.S. Department of Agriculture, Soil Conservation Service	Farmlands Protection Policy Act of 1981, 7 U.S.C. 4201
Projects in the coastal zone	National Oceanic and Atmospheric Administration	Coastal Zone Management Act, 16 U.S.C. 1451
Cleanup of hazardous waste sites	U.S. Environmental Protection Agency	Comprehensive Environmental Response, Compensation and Liability Act of 1980 (CERCLA), 43 U.S.C. 9601
Solid or hazardous waste generation, storage, transportation, or disposal	U.S. Environmental Protection Agency	Resource Conservation and Recovery Act of 1976 (RCRA), 42 U.S.C. 692

Figure 1-15

agencies are encouraged to cooperate with state and local agencies to integrate their respective environmental impact assessment requirements.

5. Environmental Impact Assessment Abroad

NEPA has not only been copied by many states in the United States, but it has also served as a model for environmental impact assessment rules throughout the world. For example, in addition to the states that have copied NEPA, the European Community has required its member nations to adopt environmental impact assessment (EIA) procedures. Similarly, the World Bank and its affiliated lending institutions are requiring funding recipients to evaluate the environmental impacts of their projects throughout the world.

To assist other nations in implementing their programs, the World Bank and the United Nations Environment Program have published two manuals on the fundamentals of EIA: *Environmental Impact Assessment: Basic Procedures for Developing Countries*, United Nations Environmental Program (1988), Bangkok, Thailand and *Environmental Assessment Sourcebook*, The World Bank (1991), World Bank Technical Papers Number 139, 140 and 154, Washington D.C.

ENVIRONMENTAL IMPACT ASSESSMENT: A UNIVERSAL MODEL FOR ENVIRONMENTAL MANAGEMENT

NEPA introduced several entirely new concepts of environmental management to government agencies. Prior to the enactment of NEPA, agency decision-making was generally mission-oriented and one-dimensional and often occurred with little or no public or interagency involvement. The NEPA model for review and evaluation of projects has been copied by jurisdictions throughout the United States and around the world. Although the specifics of environmental impact assessment differ from agency to agency, state to state, and nation to nation, NEPA contains certain fundamental principles that are becoming universal; these are summarized below.

- Full and open disclosure of environmental consequences prior to agency action

- Interdisciplinary approach to project evaluation

- Focus on key issues relating to the agency decision

- Objective consideration of all reasonable alternatives

- Application of measures to avoid or reduce adverse impacts

- Encouragement of public participation

- Consultation and coordination among agencies

Through the application of these general principles by government agencies throughout the nation and the world, the consideration of environmental factors has been elevated in importance as a public policy concern.

G. PUBLIC INVOLVEMENT

1. Importance

Public involvement is an important part of the NEPA process. The success of NEPA as an environmental disclosure and problem-solving law is based on open decision-making. Therefore, federal agencies must make diligent efforts to involve the public in implementing their NEPA process. 40 C.F.R. 1506(a).

2. Opportunities for Public Involvement

NEPA provides for public involvement at various steps in the environmental review process, particularly when a federal agency prepares an EIS. Opportunities for public involvement exist during scoping and public review of a draft EIS. Additionally, public hearings on environmental documents are often held if a project is controversial or when otherwise requested. 40 C.F.R. 1506.6(c). In preparing EAs, federal agencies must involve environmental agencies, applicants, and the public, to the extent practicable. 40 C.F.R. Sec. 1501.4(b). The detailed requirements for involving the public in EIS preparation are discussed in Chapter 3.

3. Citizens as the Enforcers of NEPA

Other than the mediation role CEQ plays in the referral process described earlier, NEPA does not establish a formal enforcement process to ensure agency compliance. Rather, the enforcement of NEPA has come primarily from concerned citizens and public interest groups challenging lead agencies through vigilant public involvement and litigation. The role of NEPA litigation is discussed in greater detail in Chapter 6.

TIPS FOR EFFECTIVE CITIZEN PARTICIPATION IN THE **NEPA** PROCESS

According to the CEQ NEPA Regulations, public participation is a cornerstone of the NEPA process. However, in practice, it is not easy for a private citizen to get involved in the process and influence the outcome of federal agency decisions, for several reasons: most federal agencies are large and have multiple locations and complex organizational structures, public notice is often limited, and hearings are sometimes held in agency headquarters offices rather than near the project site. Despite these obstacles, opportunities to participate in the NEPA process are afforded to the public. The following tips will help citizens take advantage of these opportunities.

- Learn the organizational structure and decision-making lines of authority for the agencies of concern

- Identify the key individuals responsible for the decisions that concern you

- Write to those individuals and request to be put on the list of persons to be notified of NEPA actions

- Join forces with established environmental organizations or interest groups with an interest in similar issues

- Regularly monitor local newspapers for any formal announcements of, or articles about, federal agency activities in your community

- Review the *Federal Register* (available in public libraries) for NEPA notices

- Submit comments at every possible opportunity afforded by the agency; these may include:

    – the Notice of Intent

    – public scoping meetings

    – public comment period on the draft EIS

    – public hearings on the draft EIS

    – the final EIS

- Make sure that your comments are substantive, well-written or presented, and supported by relevant data

- Be willing to meet with agency staff to discuss your views about their proposed actions

A vigilant, informed, and well-prepared public (including interest groups) is the key to the enforcement of NEPA and better environmental decision-making by federal officials.

CHAPTER 2   DETERMINING WHETHER TO PREPARE AN EIS

A. SUMMARY OF THE NEPA PROCESS

1. Three-Phase Process

NEPA requires EIS preparation only for "proposals for legislation and other major federal actions significantly affecting the quality of the human environment." A federal agency must, therefore, evaluate and screen each proposed action to determine whether NEPA applies, and if it does, whether an EIS must be prepared. Although not expressly set forth by NEPA or the CEQ NEPA Regulations, the authors have found it helpful to describe the NEPA process in three phases (Figure 2-1).

First, the agency must determine whether NEPA applies to the proposed action. During this step, the agency must determine whether the action is categorically excluded or otherwise exempt from NEPA.

Second, if the action is not categorically excluded or exempt, the agency must determine whether the proposed action may "significantly affect the quality of the human environment." This step generally involves preparing an Environmental

Three-Step NEPA Process

Phase 1

Determine whether NEPA applies to the proposed action

- ◆ Is the proposed action a "proposal"?
- ◆ Is the proposal "federal"?
- ◆ Does a categorical exclusion apply?
- ◆ Has Congress exempted the action from NEPA?

Phase 2

Determine whether an EIS is required (the Environmental Assessment)

- ◆ Will the proposed action cause any effects on the "quality of the human environment"?
- ◆ Are those effects "significant"?

Phase 3

Prepare EIS or FONSI

Figure 2-1

Assessment (EA) to determine whether the proposed action would result in any significant environmental effects.

During the third phase of the NEPA process, the federal agency either prepares a Finding of No Significant Impact (FONSI) or an EIS. A FONSI is prepared if the agency determines that no significant effects would occur from the proposed action. An EIS is prepared if the agency determines that the proposed action may have significant effects on the human environment.

2. Trends in EIS Preparation

Despite NEPA's emphasis on the EIS, in practice, most federal agency proposals do not require an EIS because they are categorically excluded from NEPA documentation under agency regulations, or because an EA indicates no significant effects on the human environment would occur. In 1990, for example, federal agencies prepared only 477 environmental impact statements, despite the approval or authorization of thousands of proposed actions. The total number of EISs prepared by federal agencies through 1979-1990 is shown in Figure 2-3.

3. Elements of Section 102(2)(C) Language

The specific elements of Section 102(2)(C) of NEPA (42 U.S.C. 4332(2)(c)) have played a prominent role in defining when NEPA applies and whether an EIS must be prepared. This section states that all agencies of the federal government must

> ". . . include in every recommendation or report on proposals for legislation and other major Federal actions significantly affecting the quality of the human environment, a detailed statement .. . ."

Each element of this section has been extensively interpreted by the courts as a threshold for NEPA compliance and must be considered in determining whether NEPA applies and whether to prepare an EIS. The key elements from Section 102(2)(C) are listed in Figure 2-2 and discussed below in detail.

B. Determining Whether NEPA Applies to a Proposed Activity

1. Is There a "Proposal"?

NEPA applies to a federal activity only when it becomes a recommendation or report on a "proposal" for legislation

Key Terms That Determine Whether an EIS Must Be Prepared

- ◆ "Proposal"
- ◆ "Legislation"
- ◆ "Major Federal Action"
- ◆ "Significantly"
- ◆ "Affecting the Quality of the Human Environment"

Figure 2-2

ENVIRONMENTAL IMPACT STATEMENTS FILED BY FEDERAL AGENCIES*
(1979-1991)

AGENCY	1979	1980	1981	1982	1983	1984	1985	1986	1987	1988	1989	1990	1991
Department of Agriculture	172	104	102	89	89	65	117	118	75	68	89	136	145
Department of Commerce	54	53	36	25	14	24	10	8	9	3	5	8	13
Department of Defense	1	1	1	1	1	0	0	0	2	0	0	0	0
Air Force	8	3	7	4	6	5	7	8	9	6	11	19	20
Army	40	9	14	3	6	5	5	2	10	8	9	9	21
Corps of Engineers	182	150	186	127	119	116	106	91	76	69	40	46	45
Navy	11	9	10	6	4	9	8	13	9	6	4	19	9
Department of Energy	28	45	21	24	19	14	4	13	11	9	6	11	2
Environmental Protection Agency	84	71	96	63	57	42	16	18	19	23	25	31	16
General Services Administration	13	11	13	8	1	0	4	0	1	3	0	4	3
Housing and Urban Development	170	140	140	93	42	13	15	18	6	2	7	5	7
Department of Interior	126	131	107	127	146	115	105	98	110	117	61	68	64
Department of Transportation	277	189	221	183	159	147	126	110	101	96	90	100	87
Tennessee Valley Authority	9	6	4	0	2	1	0	1	0	0	0	3	0
Other	98	44	76	55	22	21	26	15	17	20	23	18	24
TOTAL	1,273	966	1,033	808	677	577	549	521	455	430	370	477	456

Figure 2-3

* **Source:** U.S. Environmental Protection Agency. Office of Federal Activities, Washington, D.C.

or other major federal action. A proposal exists at that stage in the planning of an action when the agency has a goal and is actively proposing to make a decision on one or more alternative means of accomplishing that goal. See Figure 2-4 for an illustration. A "proposal" may exist even though an agency has not formally declared that one exists. 40 C.F.R.1508.2.

When Does a Federal Activity Become a "Proposal" Subject to NEPA?

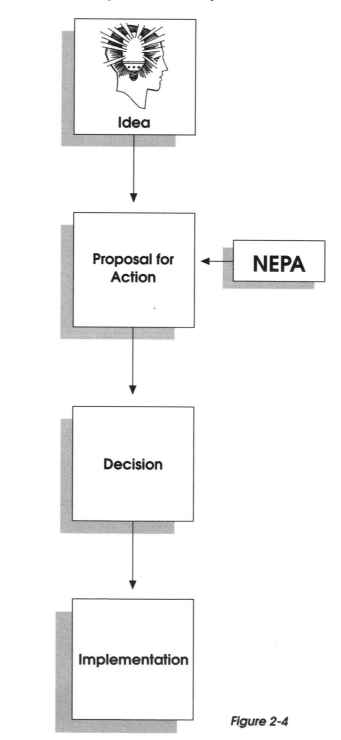

Figure 2-4

2. What Is a Proposal for "Legislation"?

NEPA applies to proposals made by federal administrative agencies for "legislation" that significantly affects the quality of the human environment. "Legislation" includes a bill or legislative proposal submitted to Congress developed by, or with the significant cooperation and support of, a federal agency, but it does not include requests for appropriations. Proposed legislation initiated by Congress is not subject to NEPA. An agency is considered to significantly cooperate in proposed legislation when it is the primary proponent of the legislation. Drafting does not, by itself, constitute significant cooperation. Proposals for legislation include ratification of treaties. 40 C.F.R. 1508.17. Legislative proposals are subject to special legislative EISs, described in greater detail in Chapter 3.

3. What Is a "Major Federal Action"?

"Major federal action" includes actions that are potentially subject to federal control and responsibility if these actions have effects that may be significant. The term "major" does not refer to the size of the action but to the significance of its impact. Thus, the term "major" has no independent meaning, and the focus of this threshold element is on the term "federal action." To trigger NEPA, the proposed activity must be an "action" and it must be "federal." 40 C.F.R. 1502.4, 1508.18(a).

a. Types of "Actions"

The types of actions that are subject to NEPA are listed in Figure 2-5. 40 C.F.R. 1508.18; Forty Questions No. 24(a).

Types of Actions Subject to NEPA

◆ **Actions are defined as:**

– New and continuing federal activities that are either financed, assisted, conducted, or approved by a federal agency

– New or revised agency rules, regulations, plans, policies, or procedures

– Legislative proposals

◆ **Actions typically consist of:**

– Adoption of official policies, rules, and regulations

– Adoption of plans

– Adoption of programs

– Approval of specific projects, including private undertakings approved by agency permit or regulatory decision

Figure 2-5

Federal action includes *inaction* by a federal official if such inaction is reviewable by law. 40 C.F.R. 1508.18(b). Actions do not include federal funding assistance that is solely in the form of general revenue sharing where there is no federal control over the use of such funds. Additionally, judicial or administrative civil or criminal enforcement activities do not constitute actions. 40 C.F.R. 1508.18(a).

b. When Is an Activity "Federalized"?

NEPA applies only to "federal" actions. However, a nonfederal activity may be subject to NEPA when it requires a permit, regulatory decision, or funding from a federal agency. Thus, a state, local, or private activity may be subject to NEPA if federal approval, contract, or funding is involved. 40 C.F.R. 1508.18(b)(4). The extent of federal involvement needed to transform a nonfederal action to a federal action subject to NEPA is unclear, and therefore, agencies have developed their own standards. For example, the U.S. Army Corps of Engineers' (Corps') NEPA regulations provide that if the federal involvement in a nonfederal activity is a small component of the entire activity, the Corps' NEPA document need not cover the entire activity. Thus, under the Corps' regulations, if a private applicant requires a Corps permit (e.g., for construction of a pipeline crossing within a navigable water), which is merely one component of a larger project (e.g., a pipeline crossing miles of upland area), the federal permit will not "federalize" the entire project for purposes of NEPA. Rather, NEPA will only apply to the portion of the project over which the Corps exercises control and responsibility. 53 F.R. 3127 (February 3, 1988).

4. Categorical Exclusions

a. Definition

A "categorical exclusion" means a category of proposed actions, which a federal agency identifies in its NEPA procedures, that do not individually or cumulatively have a significant effect on the environment. Typically, excluded activities are small, routine undertakings with no potential significant environmental effect. 40 C.F.R. 1508.4.

b. Effect of Exclusion

If a proposed action is described in an agency's list of categorical exclusions, neither an EA nor an EIS is required. 40 C.F.R. 1508.4. Some agencies, however, do prepare an internal memorandum documenting the determination that a proposed action is categorically excluded from NEPA documentation.

c. Exceptions to Categorical Exclusions

An agency must, in its NEPA procedures, provide for exceptions to categorical exclusions in extraordinary circumstances such as when a proposed action would affect wetlands or threatened and endangered species. Additionally, an agency may prepare an EA even though one is not required for categorically excluded actions. 40 C.F.R. 1501.3(b), 1508.4.

5. Other Circumstances When NEPA Does Not Apply

a. Express Statutory Exemptions

In certain rare circumstances, Congress expressly exempts federal programs or activities from NEPA. In those situations, the agency need not comply with NEPA even if its actions would have significant environmental effects. For example, in the Defense Base Closure and Realignment Act of 1991, PL 101-510 Sec. 2906, Congress exempted from NEPA documentation the decision to close certain military bases.

b. Statutory Conflicts

NEPA's requirements are not applicable to federal agencies if there are clear and unavoidable conflicts of statutory authority. For example, in some circumstances, Congress has enacted other legislation that requires federal agencies to act in a time frame that does not permit compliance with NEPA. Courts have required agencies to show that it is "impossible" and not just "difficult" to comply with NEPA under such circumstances.

c. Emergencies

Where emergency circumstances make it necessary to take an action with significant environmental impacts that would conflict with normal NEPA compliance, the federal agency taking the action should consult with CEQ about alternative arrangements. In these situations, CEQ is authorized to limit such arrangements to actions necessary to control the immediate impacts of the emergency. 40 C.F.R. 1506.11.

CEQ ESTABLISHES EMERGENCY NEPA PROCEDURES FOR OPERATION DESERT STORM

Following Iraq's invasion of Kuwait in August 1990, the President directed the rapid deployment of over 400,000 troops and the needed supplies and weaponry to support Operation Desert Shield and Operation Desert Storm. Because there is no exemption from NEPA for national defense actions, the Department of Defense (DOD) requested that CEQ develop alternative procedures under the "emergency" provisions of the CEQ NEPA Regulations. CEQ concurred with the DOD that activities in support of national security interests in the Middle East constituted an "emergency" situation, allowing DOD to establish alternative NEPA procedures. 40 C.F.R. 1506.11.

Using this authority, DOD twice used alternative NEPA arrangements for domestic operations, with close participation and oversight by CEQ. These situations involved limited testing of fuel-air explosives in Nevada and changing flight operations at Westover Air Force Base in Massachusetts. NEPA emergency procedures did not relieve the military branches of their duty to conduct all other operations in full compliance with applicable federal, state, and local environmental laws.

Source: CEQ 22nd Annual Report of the Council on Environmental Quality (1992).

d. Functional Equivalency

EPA is exempt from compliance with NEPA when it engages in most regulatory activities designed to protect the environment. This exemption has been developed by the courts on the theory that EPA's regulatory programs are "functionally equivalent" to the requirements of NEPA, thus making compliance with NEPA duplicative. The functional equivalence doctrine has been applied only to EPA regulatory activities under the Clean Air Act; the Federal Insecticide, Fungicide, and Rodenticide Act; the Toxic Substances Control Act; and certain sections of the Clean Water Act. There is legal disagreement, however, as to whether the doctrine also applies to CERCLA and RCRA. The courts have only allowed the "functionally equivalent" doctrine for EPA, and expressly disallowed it for actions of other agencies.

e. Extraterritorial Application of NEPA

The courts have held that NEPA does not apply to activities of United States federal agencies in other nations. However, Executive Order No. 12114 requires agencies to implement procedures for considering the environmental effects of major federal actions that occur outside the boundaries of the United States. The only type of action that may require an EIS is one that affects the global commons outside the jurisdiction of any nation (e.g., the oceans or Antarctica). For other federal actions, agencies may prepare EISs, EAs, or bilateral or multilateral environmental studies with other nations or other types of environmental reviews. Executive Order No. 12114, Environmental Effects Abroad of Major Federal Actions, 3 C.F.R. 356 (1980).

CEQ Oversees Extraterritorial Application of Environmental Impact Assessment

Although application of NEPA has been confined to the United States, the federal government recognizes that environmental problems cross international borders. Executive Order 12114, which took effect in 1979, mandates analysis of the environmental effects of major federal actions abroad. CEQ leads an interagency task force that is reviewing the effectiveness of the Executive Order. Additionally, in February 1991, the United States signed a Convention on Environmental Impact Assessment with European countries, obligating the signatories to consult with each other when an activity is likely to cause adverse transboundary environmental impacts. The Department of State, EPA, and CEQ are devising an implementation strategy for the convention.

Source: CEQ 22nd Annual Report of the Council on Environmental Quality (1992).

---

f. Classified Information

There is no national defense exemption under NEPA. However, environmental documents addressing classified proposals may be restricted from public dissemination. 40 C.F.R. 1507.3(c). In such cases, agencies should attempt to put classified information in appendices and release as much of this information as reasonably possible.

C. ENVIRONMENTAL ASSESSMENTS AND THE THRESHOLD DECISION

1. When Must an EIS Be Prepared?

After a federal agency determines that no exclusions apply to a proposed action, it must then decide whether to prepare an EIS. An EIS is required if the proposed federal action has the potential to "significantly affect the quality of the human environment." The primary tool used to make this determination is the EA.

An agency may, however, bypass the preparation of an EA for certain types of proposed actions that it determines normally require an EIS. Each federal agency must identify, in its NEPA regulations, specific criteria for identifying those classes of actions that normally require an EIS. In those situations, an agency need not prepare an EA. 40 C.F.R. 1507.3.

2. Environmental Assessments

a. Definition and Purposes

An EA is a concise public document that a lead agency prepares when a project is not covered by a categorical exclusion, and the lead agency does not know whether the impacts will be significant. 40 C.F.R. 1508.9(a). The EA has three purposes, which are listed in Figure 2-6. The EA is the primary tool used by an agency to determine whether to prepare an EIS. During the preparation of an EA, the agency should carefully evaluate the proposal to determine if it would result in significant effects on the human environment.

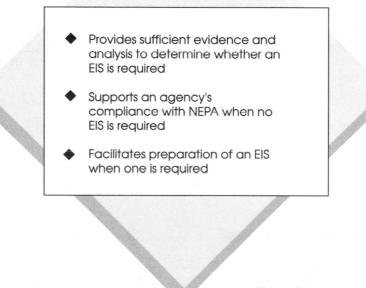

Purposes of an Environmental Assessment

◆ Provides sufficient evidence and analysis to determine whether an EIS is required

◆ Supports an agency's compliance with NEPA when no EIS is required

◆ Facilitates preparation of an EIS when one is required

Figure 2-6

In practice, the EA is commonly used to document and justify the use of a FONSI. When used for this purpose, the EA should contain the supporting data and references to convincingly demonstrate that there would be no significant effects on the human environment.

b. When Must an EA Be Prepared?

An agency must prepare an EA unless the agency's NEPA procedures provide that the proposed action is covered by a categorical exclusion or normally requires an EIS. 40 C.F.R. Sec. 1501.4(b). An agency may, however, prepare an EA on any action at any time to assist in agency planning and decision-making. 40 C.F.R. 1501.3. An agency may rely on an EA prepared by a project applicant, consultant, or other agency, provided that it has independently reviewed the EA, exercised independent judgment, and verified that it meets the requirements of NEPA and the CEQ NEPA Regulations.

c. Format and Content

An EA must briefly discuss the need for the proposed action, reasonable alternatives, the probable environmental impacts, and the agencies and persons consulted (Figure 2-7). 40 C.F.R. Sec. 1508.9(b); Forty Questions No. 36(a).

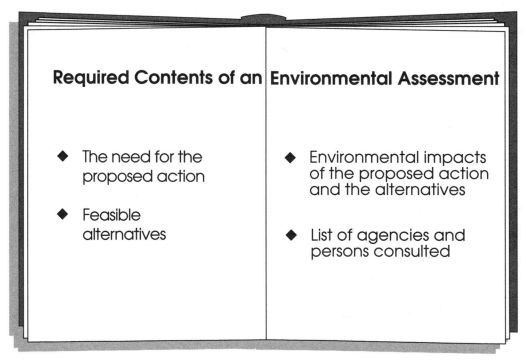

Required Contents of an Environmental Assessment

◆ The need for the proposed action

◆ Feasible alternatives

◆ Environmental impacts of the proposed action and the alternatives

◆ List of agencies and persons consulted

Figure 2-7

d. Length and Level of Detail

The CEQ NEPA Regulations do not contain page limits for an EA. However, CEQ has advised agencies to keep the length of an EA to approximately 10 to 15 pages. To avoid unnecessary length, an EA may incorporate background data by

ORIGINS OF THE MATRIX SYSTEM OF IMPACT ASSESSMENT

One of the earliest approaches to conducting environmental impact assessment under NEPA was developed by the U.S. Geological Survey in 1971 under the guidance of Luna B. Leopold. Leopold, a noted professor at the University of California, Berkeley, developed a matrix system of assessment that set an important precedent throughout the federal government for conducting impact assessments to comply with NEPA.

In a publication entitled *A Procedure for Evaluating Environmental Impact*, Leopold and his colleagues developed a system in which a detailed matrix is used as a reference checklist covering the full range of proposed actions and impacts on the environment. The use of the matrix involved not only identifying potential impacts but also classifying them numerically by their "magnitude" and "importance." The concepts of "magnitude" and "importance" are similar to the concepts of "context" and "intensity" that are now a part of the CEQ NEPA Regulations. Although the original matrix approach recommended by Leopold was not universally adopted during the past 20 years, many federal agencies still use a matrix as a reference guide. A sample matrix is shown below.

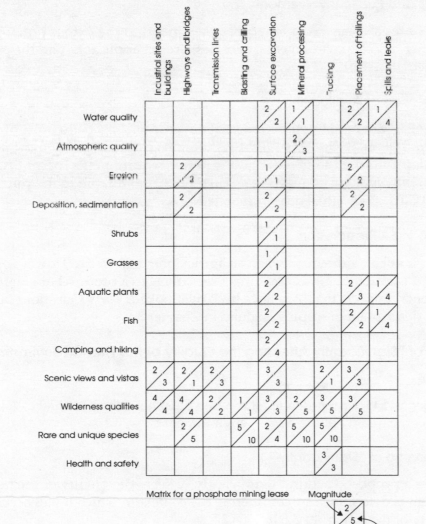

Matrix for a phosphate mining lease

reference to support its precise discussion of the proposal and relevant environmental issues. Agencies should avoid lengthy EAs, except in unusual circumstances, when it is necessary to determine whether the proposal could have significant environmental effects. Forty Questions No. 36.

Despite CEQ's advice, in practice EAs usually exceed 15 pages and are generally much longer. In fact, an agency will often use an expanded EA as a surrogate for an EIS for a large, complex project. However, in general, an EA cannot legally substitute for an EIS if the proposed action may have significant environmental effects. Exceptions to this standard are those situations where an EA is used to document and justify a mitigated FONSI (see Section D).

e. Consideration of Cumulative Effects

An EA must consider cumulative impacts when determining whether an action significantly affects environmental quality. If it is reasonable to anticipate cumulatively significant impacts, an EIS must be prepared. 40 C.F.R. Sec. 1508.25(c).

f. Agency and Public Involvement

When it prepares an EA, a federal agency must, to the extent practicable, involve other federal environmental agencies, project applicants, and the public. 40 C.F.R. Sec. 1501.4(b).

g. Public Notice of Availability

Because EAs are "public environmental documents," agencies must provide notice of their availability. The NEPA regulations of each agency must be followed in determining the specific public notice requirements for an EA. At a minimum, however, an agency must make the EA available to the public on request. 40 C.F.R. 1506.6(b); Forty Questions No. 38.

h. Scoping in EA Preparation

Scoping is not a requirement when an agency prepares an EA. However, scoping can be a useful tool for discovering alternatives to a proposal or significant environmental impacts that may have been overlooked. Forty Questions No. 13. A detailed description of scoping is found in Chapter 3.

3. Definition of "Significantly Affecting the Quality of the Human Environment"

a. General

To trigger an EIS, a proposed federal action must have the potential to "significantly affect the quality of the human environment."

b. The Meaning of "Significantly"

Whether a proposed action "significantly" affects the quality of the human environment is determined by considering the context in which it will occur and the intensity of the action. 40 C.F.R. 1508.27.

i. Context

The significance of the action must be analyzed based on society as a whole, affected interests, the affected region, and the locality in which it would occur (Figure 2-8). Significance, therefore, will vary depending on the setting of the proposed action. 40 C.F.R. 1508.27(a).

Determining the "Context" of an Action

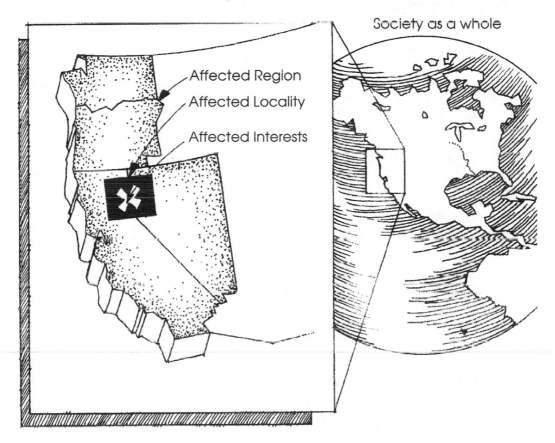

Figure 2-8

ii. Intensity

Intensity refers to the severity of the impact. In determining the intensity of an impact, the federal agency should consider the factors shown in Figure 2-9. 40 C.F.R. 1508.27(b).

c. The Meaning of "Affecting"

A federal activity is considered to be "affecting" the environment when it has an "effect" on it. 40 C.F.R. 1508.3. Effects and "impacts" are synonymous under NEPA. Effects may be ecological, aesthetic, historical, cultural, economic, social, or health-related. 40 C.F.R. 1508.8. For the action to be thought of as affecting the environment, it must have a causal relationship with the environment. Effects can be direct, indirect, and cumulative (Figure 2-10).

Determining the "Intensity" of an Impact

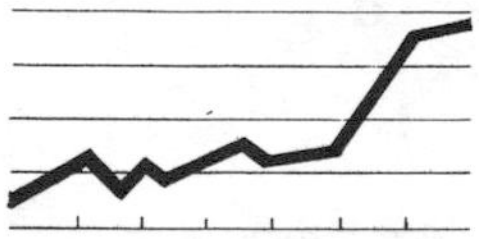

Beneficial effects: A significant environmental effect may exist even though the proposed action has an overall beneficial effect.

Public health: The degree to which the proposed action affects public health or safety.

Unique characteristics: Unique characteristics of the geographical area, such as proximity to historical or cultural resources, parklands, prime farmlands, wetlands, wild and scenic rivers, or ecologically critical areas.

Degree of controversy: The degree to which the effects on the quality of the human environment are likely to be controversial.

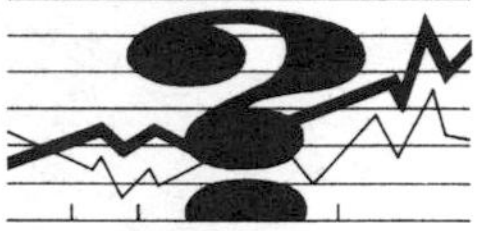

Degree of unique or unknown risk: The degree to which the possible effects on the human environment are highly uncertain or involve unique or unknown risks.

Precedent-setting effect: The degree to which the action may establish a precedent for future actions with significant effects.

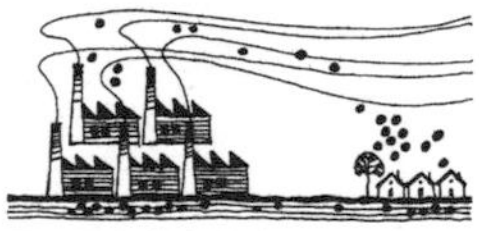

Cumulative effect: Whether the action is related to other actions with individually insignificant, but cumulatively significant, impacts.

Cultural or historical resources: The degree to which the action may adversely affect districts, sites, highways, structures, or objects listed in, or eligible for listing in, the National Register of Historic Places.

Special-status species: The degree to which the action may adversely affect an endangered or threatened species or its habitat.

Violations of federal, state, or local environmental law: Whether the action threatens a violation of federal, state, or local law, or a requirement imposed for the protection of the environment.

Figure 2-9

Types of Environmental Effects

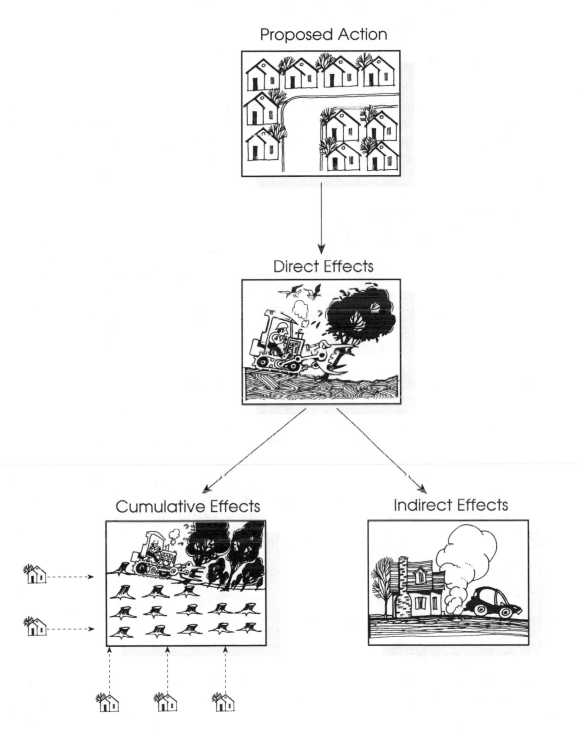

Figure 2-10

i. Direct Effects

Direct effects are caused by the action and occur at the same time and place. 40 C.F.R. 1508.8(a).

ii. Indirect Effects

Indirect effects are caused by the action but occur later in time or are further removed in distance, but must be reasonably foreseeable. Indirect effects may include growth-inducing effects and other effects related to induced changes in the pattern of land use; population density or growth rate; and related effects on air, water, and other natural systems or ecosystems. 40 C.F.R. 1508(b).

iii. Cumulative Effects

Cumulative effects are those that result from the incremental impacts of the action when added to other past, present, and reasonably foreseeable future actions regardless of which agency (federal or nonfederal) or person undertakes such actions. Cumulative impacts can result from individually minor but collectively significant actions taking place over a period of time. 40 C.F.R. 1508.7. A more detailed discussion of the types of environmental effects included in NEPA is found in Chapter 3.

d. The Meaning of "Quality of the Human Environment"

An EIS need only be prepared when federal action significantly affects "the quality of the human environment." "Human environment" is a comprehensive phrase that includes the natural and physical environments and the relationship of people with those environments. 40 C.F.R. 1508.14. Economic and social effects are not, by themselves, intended to require preparation of an EIS. However, when an EIS is prepared and economic, social, natural, or physical effects are interrelated, the EIS must discuss all of these effects on the human environment. 40 C.F.R. 1508.14. For example, urban blight caused by abandonment of a downtown area would be analyzed in a NEPA document, but the resulting loss of property values, increased unemployment, or increased crime would not.

D. FINDINGS OF NO SIGNIFICANT IMPACT

1. Definition and Purpose

A FONSI is a public document that briefly describes why an action that is otherwise not excluded from NEPA will not have any significant environmental effects and will not, therefore, require an EIS. An agency preparing an EA must write a FONSI if it decides not to prepare an EIS. 40 C.F.R. 1501.4(e), 1508.13.

2. Contents

A FONSI must include an explanation of why an action will not have a significant effect on the human environment. The finding itself need not be detailed but must succinctly state the reasons for deciding that the action will not have significant effects, and if relevant, must show which factors were weighed most heavily in the determination. In addition, a FONSI must include, summarize, attach, or incorporate the EA by reference (Figure 2-11). 40 C.F.R. 1508.13; Forty Questions No. 37(a).

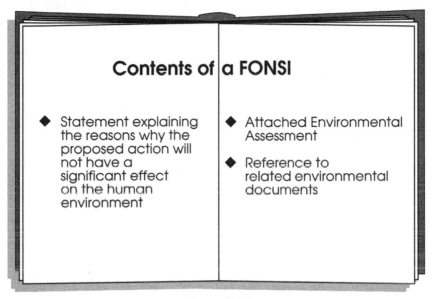

Figure 2-11

3. Public Notice of Availability

a. General

Because FONSIs are "public environmental documents," agencies must provide notice of their availability. A federal agency must make a FONSI available to the affected public. However, the CEQ NEPA Regulations do not prescribe any particular public notice requirements for a FONSI. Rather, each federal agency has developed its own unique public notice requirements for the review of FONSIs. The NEPA regulations of each federal agency must be evaluated to determine these requirements. 40 C.F.R. 1501.4(e)(1), 1506.6(a). At a minimum, however, an agency must make the FONSI available to the public on request. 40 C.F.R. 1506.6(b); Forty Questions No. 38.

b. Public Review Period

The CEQ NEPA Regulations do not generally prescribe a public review period for a FONSI. Each agency has developed its own review periods. However, in certain limited circumstances, a federal agency must make the FONSI available for public review for at least 30 days before making its final determination (Figure 2-12). 40 C.F.R. 1501.4(e)(2); Forty Questions No. 37(b).

4. Mitigated FONSIs

a. Definition

A "mitigated FONSI" is one that is prepared when an EA indicates that environmental effects of a proposal are potentially significant but that, with mitigation, those effects will be reduced to less-than-significant levels.

When a FONSI Must Be Made Available for a 30-Day Public Review Period

◆ The proposal is a borderline case when there is a reasonable argument that an EIS could have been prepared

◆ The proposal is an unusual case, a new kind of action, or will be precedent-setting

◆ There is a scientific or public controversy over the proposal

◆ The proposal is similar to one that normally requires an EIS

◆ The proposed action would be located in a floodplain or wetland

Figure 2-12

b. Judicial Response

Most courts have approved the use of mitigated FONSIs, provided that the conditions shown in Figure 2-13 are satisfied.

c. Some Advantages of Mitigated FONSIs

The use of a mitigated FONSI encourages the adoption of environmentally acceptable projects. When an agency relies on a mitigated FONSI, it must reduce all of the significant environmental impacts of the proposed action to less-than-significant levels; with an EIS, the impacts need not be mitigated. Another advantage is that NEPA compliance with a mitigated FONSI is generally less expensive and of shorter duration than

Criteria for Legally Adequate Mitigated FONSIs

◆ The agency can demonstrate that it has taken a ''hard look'' at the environmental consequences of the proposed action

◆ The agency can convincingly show that mitigation measures will reduce impacts to less-than-significant levels

◆ Mitigation on which the mitigated FONSI is based is specific and project-related, and the agency or applicant has committed to it

◆ The mitigated FONSI is supported by an adequate EA

Figure 2-13

with the preparation of an EIS. Figure 2-14 shows some of the advantages of mitigated FONSIs.

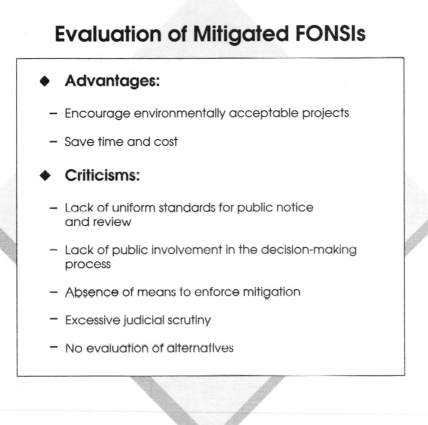

Evaluation of Mitigated FONSIs

◆ **Advantages:**

   – Encourage environmentally acceptable projects

   – Save time and cost

◆ **Criticisms:**

   – Lack of uniform standards for public notice
     and review

   – Lack of public involvement in the decision-making
     process

   – Absence of means to enforce mitigation

   – Excessive judicial scrutiny

   – No evaluation of alternatives

Figure 2-14

d. Some Criticisms of Mitigated FONSIs

When CEQ first issued the Forty Questions it discouraged the use of mitigated FONSIs because of the lack of uniform standards for public notice and review and the absence of means for enforcing mitigation measures (Forty Questions No. 40). However, Question 40 has been effectively overruled by the courts, as well as publicly disavowed by CEQ.

Additionally, critics of mitigated FONSIs cite several other problems with their use (Figure 2-14).

e. Importance of Adequate Mitigation Measures

Reviewing courts have insisted that mitigation measures used to justify FONSIs be tangible and specific, not vague or illusory. Chapter 4 includes a discussion of the types of mitigation measures that would typically be adequate versus those that would be ineffective to support a mitigated FONSI.

CHAPTER 3   PREPARATION AND REVIEW OF AN EIS

A. PURPOSE OF THE EIS

1. Action-Forcing Mechanism

The primary purpose of an EIS is to serve as an action-forcing device to ensure that the policies and goals of NEPA are incorporated into and considered during the ongoing programs and actions of federal agencies. An EIS is more than a disclosure document; it must be used by federal officials in conjunction with other relevant information to plan actions and make decisions. 40 C.F.R. 1502.1.

2. Informative Emphasis

An EIS must provide a full and fair discussion of significant environmental impacts and must inform the decision-makers and the public of reasonable alternatives that would avoid or minimize adverse impacts. In preparing an EIS, an agency must focus on significant environmental issues and alternatives and must reduce paperwork and the accumulation of extraneous background data. The EIS must be concise, clear, to the point, and supported by evidence that the agency has made the necessary environmental analysis. 40 C.F.R. 1502.1.

B. TYPES OF ENVIRONMENTAL IMPACT STATEMENTS

1. General

The CEQ NEPA Regulations provide for the preparation of three different types of EISs. The type of EIS prepared by a federal agency should correspond in focus and level of specificity to the proposed federal action.

2. EIS on an Individual Proposed Action

An action-specific EIS is an EIS prepared for an individual undertaking, such as a federal construction project or a private activity, subject to a federal permit or other entitlement.

3. Programmatic EIS on Broad Federal Actions

a. Definition

A programmatic EIS is one prepared on a "broad federal action," such as the adoption of a regulation, policy, plan, or program. 40 C.F.R. 1502.4(b).

b. Evaluation Methods

When preparing an EIS for a "broad federal action," the lead agency may evaluate the proposal based on common geographic locations, similarities of impacts, or by stages of development. Preparation of a programmatic EIS presents the opportunity for the federal agency to evaluate the potential cumulative impacts of the reasonably foreseeable actions under that program or within that geographical area. 40 C.F.R. 1502.4(c); Forty Questions No. 24(b).

c. Use in Tiering

The preparation of a programmatic EIS facilitates and expedites the preparation of subsequent project-specific NEPA documents through the use of tiering. Subsequent documents need only incorporate by reference and summarize issues discussed in the programmatic EIS, and they must concentrate only on site-specific issues. 40 C.F.R. 1500.4(c), 1502.4(d). See the discussion on tiering later in this chapter.

4. Legislative EIS

A legislative EIS is prepared by a federal agency on proposals for legislation. It is an abbreviated version of the normal EIS and may be prepared on an expedited timetable to ensure proper consideration in Congressional hearings and deliberations. Special rules apply to the preparation and review of legislative EISs. 40 C.F.R. 1506.8.

C. WHO MAY PREPARE AN EIS?

1. Lead Agency Responsibility for Preparation

An EIS must be prepared directly by the lead agency or a contractor (consultant) selected by the lead agency (Figure 3-1). A cooperating agency may also participate in the preparation of an EIS at the request of the lead agency. The lead agency is responsible for the scope, contents, and legal adequacy of the EIS. 40 C.F.R. 1506.5(c).

2. Preparation by Contractors

a. Guidance to Contractors

If a contractor is used, the lead agency must select the contractor. Additionally, the lead agency must furnish guidance to the contractor and participate in the preparation of the EIS. The lead agency must also independently evaluate the EIS prior to its approval and is responsible for its scope and content. 40 C.F.R. 1506.5(c); Forty Questions No. 16.

Who May Prepare the Draft EIS?

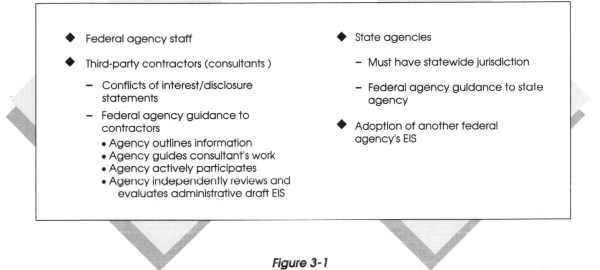

- ◆ Federal agency staff
- ◆ Third-party contractors (consultants)
    - – Conflicts of interest/disclosure statements
    - – Federal agency guidance to contractors
        - • Agency outlines information
        - • Agency guides consultant's work
        - • Agency actively participates
        - • Agency independently reviews and evaluates administrative draft EIS

- ◆ State agencies
    - – Must have statewide jurisdiction
    - – Federal agency guidance to state agency
- ◆ Adoption of another federal agency's EIS

Figure 3-1

b. Conflicts of Interest and Disclosure Statements

If a contractor is used to prepare an EIS, the contractor must first execute a disclosure statement specifying that the contractor has no financial or other interest in the outcome of the project. Financial interests may include the promise of future design or construction work on the project. The purpose of the disclosure statement is to preserve the objectivity and integrity of the NEPA process. 40 C.F.R. 1506.5(c); Forty Questions Nos. 17(a) and 17(b).

c. Information Submitted by Applicants

If an agency requires an applicant to submit information for use in preparing an EIS, the agency should assist the applicant by outlining the types of information required and must independently evaluate the information submitted. The agency is responsible for the accuracy of the information. 40 C.F.R. 1506.5(a).

3. Adoption of Another Federal Agency's EIS

A federal agency may adopt an EIS prepared by another federal agency rather than preparing another EIS. If the proposed action is substantially the same, the agency adopting another agency's statement is not required to recirculate it as a draft EIS. 40 C.F.R. 1506.3.

4. Preparation by State Agencies

In certain limited situations involving federal grants to states, an EIS may be prepared by a state agency. For example, the Federal Highway Administration allows state highway departments to prepare EISs for certain jointly funded transportation projects.

Preparation by a state agency is allowed only if:

- the agency has statewide jurisdiction and has the responsibility for the proposed action,

- the responsible federal official furnishes guidance to the state agency and participates in the preparation of the EIS, and

- the responsible federal official independently evaluates the EIS prior to its approval and adoption. 42 U.S.C. 4332(2)(D).

5. Preparation by HUD CDGB Applicants

Applicants for Community Development Block Grants (CDBGs) from the U.S. Department of Housing and Urban Development (HUD) may assume HUD's NEPA obligations if the applicant agrees to assume the status of responsible federal official. 42 U.S.C. 5304(g).

D. INTEGRATION OF THE EIS WITH OTHER FEDERAL ENVIRONMENTAL REQUIREMENTS

To the fullest extent possible, a federal agency must prepare the EIS concurrently and integrated with the environmental analysis required by other federal environmental laws. An EIS should be combined with the documents required by other laws to reduce paperwork and delay. 40 C.F.R. 1502.25, 1506.4; Forty Questions No. 21. See Figure 1-13.

E. INTEGRATION OF THE EIS WITH STATE AND LOCAL PROCEDURES

Numerous states have adopted environmental impact assessment requirements modeled after NEPA (Figure 1-15). The CEQ NEPA Regulations strongly encourage federal agencies to cooperate with state and local agencies to reduce duplication between NEPA and state and local requirements. 40 C.F.R. 1506.2; Forty Questions No. 22. In particular, the activities shown in Figure 3-2 should be combined.

Where a state or local agency and a federal agency work together to prepare one environmental review document under both NEPA and a state

Elimination of Duplication between NEPA and State and Local EIS Requirements

◆ **The CEQ regulations encourage the following:**

– Joint planning processes

– Joint environmental research

– Joint public hearings

– Joint environmental documents

Figure 3-2

or local law, the federal agency must be the lead agency or act as co-lead agency with the state or local lead agency. Where state laws or local ordinances have requirements in addition to, but not conflicting with, those in NEPA, the federal agency must fulfill those requirements. To better integrate an EIS into state or local planning processes, the EIS must discuss any inconsistency of the proposed federal action with any state or local plans or laws and describe the extent to which those inconsistencies would be reconciled.

F. WHEN SHOULD THE EIS BE PREPARED?

1. General

A federal agency must commence preparation of an EIS while it is developing a proposal or, in the case of permit applications, as soon as it receives the application, so that it can be completed in time to accompany any recommendation or report on the proposal (Figure 3-3). The EIS must be prepared early enough so that it can serve as an important contribution to the decision-making process and so that it will not be used to rationalize or justify decisions already made. 40 C.F.R. 1502.5. An EIS need not be prepared until a "proposal" for action exists. *Kleppe v. Sierra Club*, 427 U.S. 390 (1976).

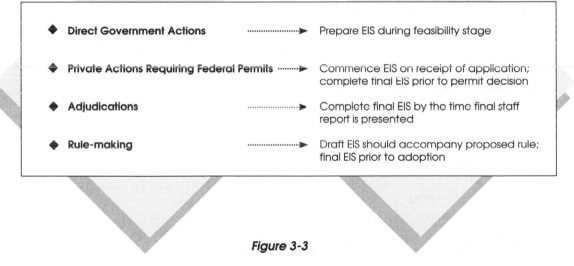

When Should Environmental Evaluation Occur under NEPA?

◆ **Direct Government Actions**	········▶	Prepare EIS during feasibility stage
◆ **Private Actions Requiring Federal Permits**	········▶	Commence EIS on receipt of application; complete final EIS prior to permit decision
◆ **Adjudications**	········▶	Complete final EIS by the time final staff report is presented
◆ **Rule-making**	········▶	Draft EIS should accompany proposed rule; final EIS prior to adoption

Figure 3-3

2. Direct Government Activities

For direct government activities, the EIS must be prepared during the feasibility analysis stage. 40 C.F.R. 1502.5(a).

3. Private Applications

For private applications requiring federal agency approval, draft EIS preparation must commence as soon as possible after the receipt of the application, and the final EIS must be completed prior to the permit decision. 40 C.F.R. 1502.5(b).

4. Adjudications

In adjudications, the final EIS should be completed by the time the final staff report and recommendation are submitted to the decision-making body. 40 C.F.R. 1502.5(c).

5. Rule-making

When adopting rules and regulations, the draft EIS should accompany the proposed rule or regulation, and the final EIS must be completed prior to rule adoption. 40 C.F.R. 1502.5(d).

G. DURATION OF EIS PREPARATION

Because CEQ believes that prescribed, universal time limits for preparing an EIS are too inflexible, each federal agency is encouraged to set time limits appropriate to individual actions. Therefore, the regulations of each agency must be reviewed to determine if any time limits apply to EIS preparation. The CEQ NEPA Regulations list a variety of factors that agencies should consider when establishing time limits for EIS preparation. 40 C.F.R. 1501.8.

CEQ has advised federal agencies that the EIS process should generally require only about 12 months for completion. However, in practice, EIS preparation often takes considerably longer, depending on the complexity of the action, the scope of the alternatives and impacts being evaluated, and the extent of internal agency review. Forty Questions No. 35.

H. STEPS IN THE EIS PREPARATION PROCESS

1. General

The EIS preparation process consists of a series of procedural steps to ensure that adequate analysis of environmental issues occurs (Figure 3-4). The process provides and encourages opportunities for interagency coordination and public involvement. An EIS is prepared in two stages: a draft and a final version. Each of the other steps in the overall EIS process contributes to the preparation of the draft or final EIS. 40 C.F.R. 1502.9.

Typical Steps in EIS Preparation

Determine lead agency

Prepare environmental assessment (optional)

Publish Notice of Intent

Conduct scoping process

Prepare draft EIS

Circulate draft EIS for review

File draft EIS with EPA

Hold public hearing if required or desired

Prepare final EIS

Circulate final EIS

File with EPA

Adopt final EIS

Make agency decision

Prepare Record of Decision

Figure 3-4

2. Notice of Intent

The Notice of Intent to prepare an EIS is the first formal step in EIS preparation. As soon as practical after its decision to prepare an EIS, but before the scoping process begins, the lead agency must publish a Notice of Intent in the *Federal Register*. The Notice of Intent must include the information shown in Figure 3-5. 40 C.F.R. 1508.22.

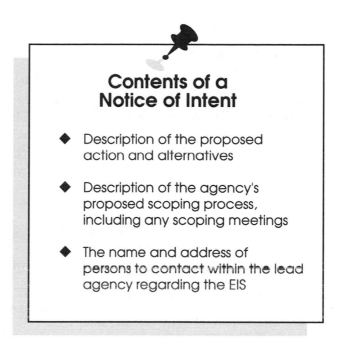

Contents of a Notice of Intent

◆ Description of the proposed action and alternatives

◆ Description of the agency's proposed scoping process, including any scoping meetings

◆ The name and address of persons to contact within the lead agency regarding the EIS

Figure 3-5

Example of a *Federal Register* Notice of Intent

Federal Register / Vol. 57, No. 30 / Thursday, February 13, 1992 / Notices

Environmental Impact Statement: Reuse and Disposal of Fort Ord

AGENCY: Department of the Army, DOD.

ACTION: Notice of intent to prepare an environmental impact statement (EIS) for the reuse and disposal of Fort Ord.

SUMMARY: The action to be evaluated by this EIS is the disposal and reuse of Fort Ord, California, in accordance with the legislative requirements of the Defense Base closure and Realignment Act of 1990, Public Law 101-510.

ALTERNATIVES: Public Law 101-510 exempted the decision-making process, the need to make the realignment, and consideration of alternative installations from the requirements of the National Environmental Policy Act of 1969 (NEPA). This EIS will evaluate alternative methods of implementing the Commission's decision, including alternative reuses of the disposed property. Potential reuse alternatives will be explored as further information about Fort Ord's environmental status is developed. Development of the potential alternative reuses of the disposed property will be made in conjunction with the local community, Office of Economic Adjust-

ment, and the Army. The EIS will also address the socioeconomic effects of the relocation of the Army on Fort Ord. As required by NEPA, the Army will also analyze the "no action" alternative as a baseline for gauging the impacts of the disposal and reuse.

PUBLIC INVOLVEMENT: The public will be invited to participate in the scoping process, review of the draft Environmental Impact Statement, and a public meeting. The location and time of the scoping meeting to be scheduled during the month of March, 1992, will be announced in the local news media. Release of the draft EIS for public comment and the public meeting will also be announced in the local news media, as these dates are established.

POINT OF CONTACT: Mr. Bob Verkade, Sacramento District, Corps of Engineers. 916/557-7423.

Lewis D. Walker,

Deputy Assistant, Secretary of the Army. Environment, Safety and Occupational Health OASA (IL&E).

(FR Doc. 92-3521 Filed 2-12-92; 8:45 a.m.)

BILLING CODE 3710-06-M

3. Scoping

a. Objectives

Scoping is a public process designed to determine the scope of issues to be addressed in the EIS. Scoping should occur as early as possible after a lead agency decides to prepare an EIS. It should be an open process intended to obtain the views of other agencies and the public regarding the scope of the EIS. The objectives of scoping are listed in Figure 3-6. 40 C.F.R. 1501.7(a),(b).

Objectives of Scoping

◆ Invite other agencies to participate

◆ Determine scope and significant issues

◆ Identify and eliminate issues determined to be insignificant

◆ Allocate assignments among agencies

◆ Identify related environmental documents being prepared

◆ Identify other environmental review and consultation requirements

◆ Set page limits

◆ Set time limits

◆ Adopt procedures to combine the environmental analysis process with scoping

Figure 3-6

b. What is Meant by EIS "Scope"?

The scope of an EIS consists of the types of actions to be included, the range of alternatives, and impacts to be considered. 40 C.F.R. 1508.25. Generally, the lead agency should consider three types of actions, three types of alternatives, and three types of impacts. See Figure 3-7. Scoping is also used to determine which specific impacts (e.g., traffic, air quality, and noise) must be evaluated in the EIS.

Determining the Scope of an EIS

◆ **Types of Actions**
- Connected
- Similar
- Cumulative

◆ **Types of Alternatives**
- "No-Action" Alternative
- Other reasonable alternatives
- Mitigation measures

◆ **Types of Impacts**
- Direct
- Indirect
- Cumulative

Figure 3-7

i. Types of Actions to Be Evaluated in an EIS

The scope of the actions to be evaluated in an EIS include "connected" actions, "similar" actions, and "cumulative" actions.

"Connected" actions are those that are closely related. Actions are considered closely related if they:

- automatically trigger other actions,

- cannot proceed unless other actions are taken previously or simultaneously, or

- are interdependent parts of a larger action and depend on the larger action for their justification.

Figure 3-8 lists the circumstances under which actions are considered "connected," thereby requiring that they be evaluated on the same EIS.

Scoping:
Determining the Relationship between Actions

When to Analyze Connected Actions in a Single EIS	When Actions Do Not Have to Be Connected with Same EIS
◆ Action A is justified by Action B	◆ There is a "small federal handle"
◆ Action A "federalizes" Action B	◆ Action B is remote and speculative
◆ It is irrational or unwise to take Action A without taking Action B	◆ The actions are tiered- Action B is later in time, it may not occur, and it can be changed in the interim
◆ Action A triggers Action B	
◆ Action A precludes alternatives to Action B	
◆ Action A is a commitment to Action B	

Figure 3-8

"Cumulative" actions have cumulatively significant impacts when reviewed with other proposed actions and should, therefore, be discussed in the same EIS.

"Similar" actions are those which, when viewed with other reasonably foreseeable proposed actions, have similarities that provide a basis for evaluating their environmental consequences together, but are not necessarily connected.

ii. Types of Alternatives to Be Evaluated in an EIS

The scope of the alternatives to the proposed action include the "No-Action" Alternative, other reasonable courses of actions, and mitigation measures other than those included in the proposed action. A more detailed discussion of alternatives is included in Chapter 4. See Figure 3-7.

iii. Types of Impacts to Be Evaluated in an EIS

The scope of the impacts to be evaluated in an EIS includes direct impacts, indirect impacts, and cumulative impacts (Figure 3-7). A more detailed discussion of the impacts that must be evaluated in an EIS is included in Chapter 4.

c. CEQ's Informal Scoping Guidance

CEQ has prepared guidance to federal agencies on how to conduct an effective scoping process. Among the techniques recommended are scoping meetings and scoping reports. CEQ Memorandum: Scoping Guidance, April 30, 1981.

i. Scoping Meetings

The lead agency may hold scoping meetings, which may be integrated with any other early planning meeting related to a proposed action. 40 C.F.R. 1501.7(b).

ii. Scoping Reports

The lead agency may prepare a scoping report to make public the decisions that have been made during the scoping process. A scoping report generally contains a summary of the issues to be evaluated in the EIS and the views of those participating in the scoping process. CEQ Memorandum: Scoping Guidance, April 30, 1981, II(b)(6).

4. Draft EIS

A draft EIS must be prepared in accordance with the scope decided on in the scoping process. The lead agency must work with the cooperating agencies to obtain their comments regarding the scope of the draft EIS. The draft EIS must contain all of the required contents specified in NEPA and the CEQ NEPA Regulations and must disclose and discuss all major points of view on the environmental impacts of the alternatives. 40 C.F.R. 1502.9(a). A detailed discussion of EIS contents is included in Chapter 4.

5. Public Involvement and Notice Requirements

a. General

A lead agency must make diligent efforts to involve the public in preparing an EIS. The agency must provide public notice of NEPA-related hearings, public meetings, and the availability of environmental documents to inform interested persons and agencies. 40 C.F.R. 1506.6(a),(b).

b. Methods of Public Notice

i. Individual Actions

In all cases, an agency must provide notice to those who have requested it for an individual action. 40 C.F.R. Sec. 1506.6(b)(2).

ii. Actions with Effects of National Concern

For an action with effects of national concern, notice must include publication in the *Federal Register* and notice by mail to national organizations reasonably expected to be interested. An agency engaged in rulemaking may provide notice by mail to national organizations that have requested notice. 40 C.F.R.1506.6(b)(2).

iii. Actions with Effects of Primarily Local Concern

For actions of primarily local concern, several public notice mechanisms may be applicable. 40 C.F.R. 1506.6(b)(3). These are listed in Figure 3-9.

Public Involvement and Notification Methods for Actions of Local Concern

- State and areawide clearinghouses
- Native American tribes
- State public notice requirements
- Publication in local newspapers
- Publication in other local media
- Community and business associations
- Newsletters
- Direct mailing to property owners
- Posting

Figure 3-9

c. Public Hearings

A lead agency must conduct a public hearing on the draft EIS when required by statute or whenever appropriate. Criteria for deciding whether to hold a hearing are listed in Figure 3-10. 40 C.F.R. 1506.6(c).

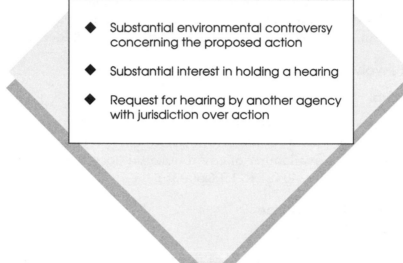

When Must a Public Hearing Be Held?

◆ Substantial environmental controversy concerning the proposed action

◆ Substantial interest in holding a hearing

◆ Request for hearing by another agency with jurisdiction over action

Figure 3-10

d. Availability of Information under the Freedom of Information Act

An agency must make a draft EIS, comments, and any underlying documents available to the public pursuant to the Freedom of Information Act. 5 U.S.C. 552. This must be accomplished without regard to the exclusion for interagency memoranda where such memoranda transmit federal agencies comments on the environmental impacts of the proposal. Materials must be provided without charge, if practicable, or at a fee not to exceed reproduction costs. 40 C.F.R. Sec. 1506.6.

6. Consultation and Commenting on the Draft EIS

a. General

NEPA requires the lead agency to consult with federal agencies that have jurisdiction by law or special expertise during EIS preparation. It further requires that copies of the draft EIS and comments of environmental regulatory agencies be made available to the public. 42 U.S.C. 4332(2)(C).

b. Circulation of the Draft EIS

Normally, a lead agency must circulate the entire draft EIS for review. However, if the EIS is unusually long, the summary alone may be circulated, except that the entire draft EIS must be provided to federal agencies with jurisdiction by law or special expertise, environmental regulatory agencies, the project applicant, and those requesting copies of the full EIS. 40 C.F.R. 1502.19.

i. Inviting Comments on the Draft EIS

After preparing a draft EIS, a lead agency must obtain the comments of other federal agencies with jurisdiction by law over, or special expertise with regard to, the proposed action, or agencies which are authorized to develop and enforce environmental standards. Such agencies are required to comment on the draft EIS. The lead agency must also request the comments of the entities shown in Figure 3-11. 40 C.F.R. 1503.1(a), 1503.2.

Circulation of Draft EIS

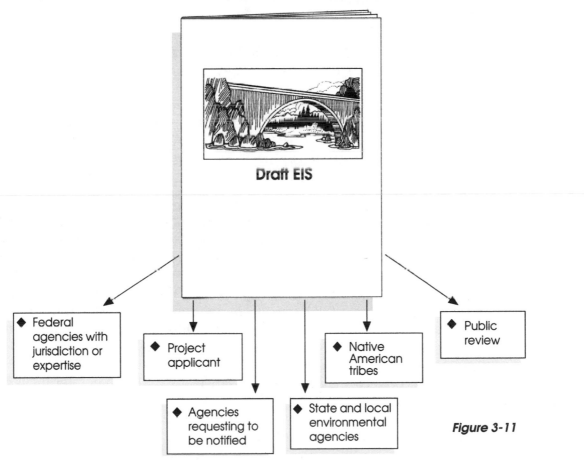

Figure 3-11

ii. Comment Period

Generally, a lead agency must allow at least 45 days for comment on a draft EIS. This period may be extended by the lead agency, however, it may only be shorten by EPA upon a showing that there are compelling reasons of national policy. 40 C.F.R. 1506.10

iii. Specificity of Comments

Comments on the draft EIS or the proposed action must be as specific as possible. A cooperating agency's comments must identify any additional information it needs to fulfill other review and consultation requirements and to take action on the project. 40 C.F.R. 1503.3; Forty Questions No. 14(c).

iv. Securing Views of State and Local Agencies

Each state is required by Executive Order No. 12372 to provide a single point of contact for review of NEPA documents. Executive Order No. 12372, Intergovernmental Review of Federal Programs, July 14, 1982. Under this executive order, states must take the initiative for establishing their own review procedures and priorities for review. In most states, these "clearing-houses" receive the documents and circulate them to appropriate state agencies for review.

7. EPA's Review of Draft EISs

a. Review Authority

Section 309 of the Clean Air Act authorizes EPA to review and comment in writing on the environmental impact of any matter subject to NEPA and to refer to CEQ any matter determined to be unsatisfactory from the standpoint of public health, welfare, or environmental quality. 42 U.S.C. 7609. Additionally, EPA's authority to comment on draft EISs comes from its role as an agency with jurisdiction by law and special expertise concerning environmental impacts of most federal proposals. 40 C.F.R. 1503.1(a).

b. EPA's Review Policies

EPA has issued policy guidance concerning its review of EISs under Section 309 of the Clean Air Act. EPA Policy and Procedures for the Review of Federal Actions Impacting the Environment, October 3, 1984. EPA reviews and rates all EISs submitted to it for review. Additionally, EPA will informally review EAs that it receives if so requested by a lead agency. EPA reviews and comments on the environmental impacts of the proposal and the adequacy of the draft EIS. EPA's rating systems for impacts of the proposal and for EIS adequacy are shown in Figures 3-12 and 3-13, respectively. EPA also conducts detailed reviews of final EISs with emphasis on those that had significant issues raised by EPA at the draft EIS stage. For projects that it rates as unsatisfactory, EPA may refer the issue to CEQ. See Chapter 4.

8. EPA Filing and *Federal Register* Notice

All EISs are formally filed with EPA. 40 C.F.R. 1506; Forty Questions No. 28. Each week, EPA publishes a notice in the *Federal Register* that lists the EISs received during the preceding week. The 45-day minimum time period for public review is calculated from the date of publication in the *Federal Register*. 40 C.F.R 1506.10(a). As part of the filing process, EPA ensures distribution of the draft EIS, reviews a draft EIS format and content, and acts on requests for review time modifications. 40 C.F.R. 1506.10 (d).

EPA Rating System for Review of the Environmental Effects of Proposed Federal Actions

LO: Lack of objection

◆ EPA review has not identified any potential impacts requiring changes to the proposal.

IC: Environmental concerns

◆ EPA review has identified environmental impacts that should be avoided to fully protect the environment.

EO: Environmental objections

◆ EPA review has identified significant impacts that must be avoided to fully protect the environment.

EU: Environmentally unsatisfactory

◆ EPA review has identified adverse impacts of sufficient magnitude that are unsatisfactory from the standpoints of public health and welfare or environmental quality. The proposal will be referred to CEQ unless the unsatisfactory impacts are mitigated.

Figure 3-12

9. Preparation of the Final EIS

The final EIS is prepared after comments on the draft are received and reviewed. The final EIS must contain the lead agency's responses to all comments received and must discuss any opposing views on issues raised. 40 C.F.R. 1502.9(b). The required contents of the final EIS are discussed later in this chapter.

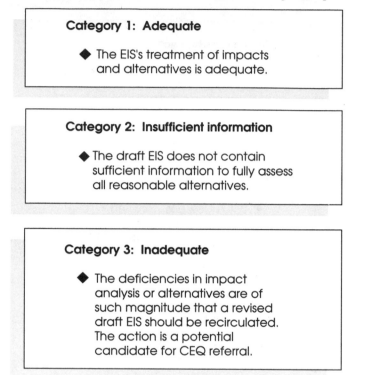

Figure 3-13

10. Circulation of Final EIS

a. General Requirements

The lead agency must circulate the final EIS before making a decision on the proposal. If, however, the final EIS is unusually long, the agency may circulate the summary, except that the entire final EIS must be provided to agencies with jurisdiction by law or special expertise, environmental regulatory agencies, the project applicant and those requesting copies, and those who submitted substantive comments on the draft EIS. Circulation must be made to the entities shown in Figure 3-14. 40 C.F.R. 1502.19.

Circulation of Final EIS

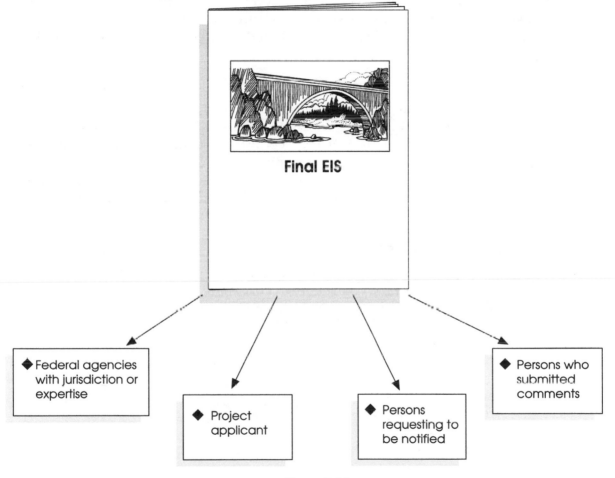

Figure 3-14

b. Filing and *Federal Register* Notice

The lead agency must file the final EIS with EPA's Office of Federal Activities. 40 C.F.R. 1506.9; Forty Questions No. 28. Each week, EPA must publish a notice in the *Federal Register* that lists the final EISs received during the preceding week. 40 C.F.R. 1506.10(a). The 30-day time period for public review of a final EIS is measured from the date of publication in the *Federal Register*.

11. Adoption of Final EIS

a. Adoption by the Lead Agency

When a lead agency determines that the EIS meets the standards for an adequate statement under the CEQ NEPA Regulations and its own NEPA regulations, it may adopt the EIS. 40 C.F.R. 1506.3(a). If the action covered by an original EIS prepared by another agency is substantially the same as the proposed action, a lead agency may adopt that other agency's EIS. 40 C.F.R. 1506.3(b).

b. Adoption by a Cooperating Agency

A cooperating agency may adopt an EIS prepared by a lead agency if, after independently reviewing the statement, it concludes that its comments and suggestions have been satisfied. When adopting another agency's EIS, the cooperating agency need not recirculate the statement for review. 40 C.F.R. 1506.3(c).

In some situations, the cooperating agency may not be satisfied with the EIS prepared by the lead agency. In those cases, a cooperating agency may adopt only the portion of an EIS with which it is satisfied, if it states publicly why it is rejecting the other portions. However, because a cooperating agency with jurisdiction by law has an independent obligation to comply with NEPA if it determines that the EIS is inadequate, it must prepare a supplement replacing or adding any needed information. In this situation, the cooperating agency must recirculate the supplemental EIS for public review. Forty Questions No. 30.

12. Supplement to the EIS

a. When Is a Supplement to an EIS Required?

A federal agency must prepare a supplement to a draft or final EIS if either of the following circumstances occur (Figure 3-15):

- the agency makes substantial changes in the proposed action that are relevant to the environmental effects, or

- there are significant new circumstances or information relevant to the environmental concerns that bear on the proposed action or its impacts. 40 C.F.R. 15029(c)(1).

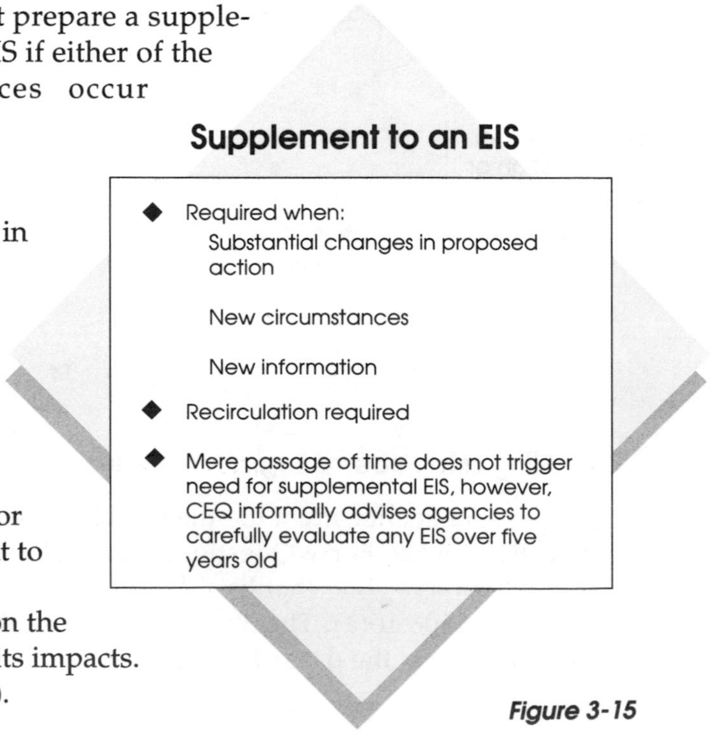

Supplement to an EIS

- ◆ Required when:
    Substantial changes in proposed action

    New circumstances

    New information

- ◆ Recirculation required

- ◆ Mere passage of time does not trigger need for supplemental EIS, however, CEQ informally advises agencies to carefully evaluate any EIS over five years old

Figure 3-15

An agency may also prepare a supplemental EIS in any other circumstances when it determines that the purposes of NEPA will be achieved. 40 C.F.R. 1502.9(c)(2).

b. Preparation Requirements

A federal agency must prepare, circulate, and file a supplemental EIS in the same fashion as the original EIS. However, the agency need not repeat the scoping process. Additionally, the agency must adopt procedures to introduce a supplement into its formal administrative record, if such record exists. 40 C.F.R. 1502.9(c)(3)(4).

CHAPTER 4   CONTENTS OF AN EIS

A. LEGAL REQUIREMENTS

CEQ's NEPA Regulations specify the following required contents and recommended format for an EIS. The requirements of the regulations are designed to bring uniformity and consistency to the NEPA process. However, some federal agencies, in their NEPA regulations and operational manuals, have deviated from these specifications, setting forth the content and format requirements to suit their particular missions and unique legal requirements. 40 C.F.R. 1502.10. See Figure 4-1.

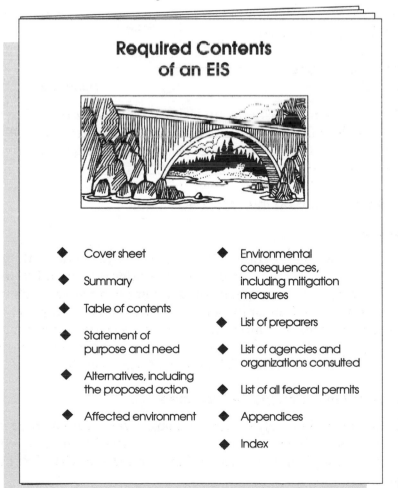

Required Contents of an EIS

- ◆ Cover sheet
- ◆ Summary
- ◆ Table of contents
- ◆ Statement of purpose and need
- ◆ Alternatives, including the proposed action
- ◆ Affected environment

- ◆ Environmental consequences, including mitigation measures
- ◆ List of preparers
- ◆ List of agencies and organizations consulted
- ◆ List of all federal permits
- ◆ Appendices
- ◆ Index

Figure 4-1

1. Cover Sheet

An EIS must contain a one-page cover sheet that includes the information listed in Figure 4-2. 40 C.F.R. 1502.11.

2. Summary

An EIS must contain a summary that adequately and accurately summarizes the statement. It must stress the major conclusions, areas of controversy, issues raised by agencies and the public, and issues to be resolved. Normally, the summary should not exceed 15 pages. 40 C.F.R. 1502.12.

3. Table of Contents

An EIS must contain a table of contents. 40 C.F.R. 1502.10(c)

4. Statement of Purpose and Need

Contents of a Draft EIS Cover Sheet

◆ Name of the lead agency and any cooperating agencies

◆ Title of the proposed action and its location

◆ Name, address, and telephone number of the lead agency contact person

◆ Designation of the EIS as a draft, final, or supplement

◆ A one-paragraph abstract of the EIS

◆ Date by which comments must be received

Figure 4-2

An EIS must briefly specify the underlying purpose and need to which the lead agency is responding in proposing the action and the alternatives. 40 C.F.R. 1502.13. The "Purpose and Need" section of an EIS is important because it drives the selection of the range of alternatives.

5. Alternatives, Including the Proposed Action

a. General

The "Alternatives" section is the heart of the EIS. The evaluation of alternatives is governed by the "rule of reason" under which an EIS must consider a reasonable range of options that could accomplish the agency's objectives (e.g., purpose and need). It must present the environmental impacts of the proposal and the alternatives in comparative form, thus sharply defining the issues and providing a clear basis for choice among options by decision-makers and the public (Figure 4-3). 40 C.F.R. 1502.14; Forty Questions No. 1.

b. Range of Alternatives to Be Evaluated

The EIS must rigorously explore and objectively evaluate the reasonable range of alternatives. If alternatives have been eliminated from detailed study, the EIS must briefly discuss the reasons for their elimination. 40 C.F.R. 1502.14(a); Forty Questions No. 1(a).

Rules Regarding Treatment of Alternatives in an EIS

◆ Alternatives are the "heart of the EIS"

◆ The evaluation of alternatives is governed by "rule of reason"

◆ An explanation of why alternatives were eliminated should be included

◆ The range of alternatives to be considered should include:

 – Alternative ways of meeting objective
 – No-action alternative
 – Alternatives outside the lead agency's Jurisdiction
 – Alternative locations

◆ Rigorous evaluation and comparison is required

◆ The preferred alternative must be identified, if one exists

◆ The environmentally preferable alternative must be identified

◆ Mitigation measures for alternatives must be described

Figure 4-3

For some proposals, a very large, or even infinite, number of possible alternatives may exist. In those situations, the EIS need only evaluate a reasonable range of alternatives. The reasonableness of the range depends on the nature of the proposal and the facts and circumstances of each project. Forty Questions No. 1(b). Reasonable alternatives are those that may be feasibly carried out based on technical and economic factors. An alternative does not become infeasible merely because the project proponent does not like it. Forty Questions No. 2(a). An approach to the screening of potential alternatives for feasibility is shown in Figure 4-4.

An alternative may be considered reasonable even if it is outside the legal jurisdiction of the lead agency. A potential conflict with local or federal law does not necessarily render an alternative unreasonable, although such conflicts must be considered. An alternative that is outside the scope of what Congress has approved or authorized may be evaluated in an EIS because the EIS may serve as the basis for modifying the Congressional approval in light of NEPA's goals and policies. 40 C.F.R. 1502.14(c); Forty Questions No. 2(b).

Screening Alternatives for Inclusion in an EIS

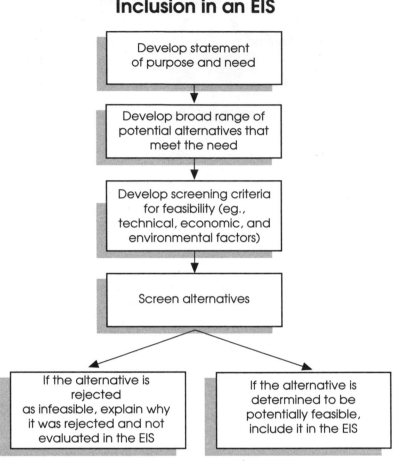

Develop statement of purpose and need

↓

Develop broad range of potential alternatives that meet the need

↓

Develop screening criteria for feasibility (eg., technical, economic, and environmental factors)

↓

Screen alternatives

If the alternative is rejected as infeasible, explain why it was rejected and not evaluated in the EIS

If the alternative is determined to be potentially feasible, include it in the EIS

Figure 4-4

The range of alternatives must include the following.

i. The "No-Action" Alternative

The definition of the "No-Action" alternative depends on the nature of the proposed action. Where the proposed action involves updating an adopted management plan or program, the "No-Action" alternative is the continuation of the current management plan or program.

Where the proposed action is a specific project, the "No-Action" alternative means the proposed project would not take place, and the resulting environmental effects from taking no action would serve as a baseline from which to compare the effects of permitting the proposed activity or an alternative to proceed.

In either case, the "No Action" alternative provides a benchmark for comparison, enabling decision-makers to compare the magnitude of the environmental effects of the various alternatives. Forty Questions No. 3.

ii. The Agency's "Preferred" Alternative

The draft EIS must identify the lead agency's "Preferred Alternative," if one exists. The final EIS must identify the preferred alternative. 40 C.F.R. 1502.14(e); Forty Questions No. 4(b).

The agency's preferred alternative is the one that it believes would fulfill its statutory mission and responsibilities, giving consideration to economic, environmental, technical, and other factors. Forty Questions No. 4(a). Even though the agency's preferred alternative is identified, the EIS must objectively evaluate all the alternatives and not be slanted to support the preferred alternative above the others. Forty Questions No. 4(b).

iii. The "Environmentally Preferable" Alternative

The EIS should identify the "Environmentally Preferable" alternative from the range considered. The "Environmentally Preferable" alternative is the alternative that best promotes the national environmental policy expressed in NEPA. Generally, this means the alternative that causes the least damage to the environment and best protects natural and cultural resources. Forty Questions No. 6(a), 6(b).

c. Relationship of Alternatives to Purpose and Need

The statement of purpose and need is important in determining the range of alternatives to be evaluated in the EIS. If the purpose and need for a proposed action are stated very narrowly, the EIS may include a narrow range of alternatives. Conversely, if the purpose and need are broad, a broader range of alternatives may be justified. See Figure 4-5. The federal agency may not define the purpose and need so narrowly that only one alternative is presented.

d. Level of Analysis

The EIS must rigorously evaluate all reasonable alternatives in comparative form to provide a clear basis for choice among options. No particular level of treatment is required; however, the degree of analysis devoted to each alternative must be substantially similar to that devoted to the proposed action. Forty Questions No. 5(b).

6. List of Federal Permits

An EIS must include a list of all federal permits, licenses, and other approvals that need to be obtained to implement the proposed action. If it is uncertain whether a permit is necessary, the EIS must so indicate. A federal agency has an obligation to ascertain whether a project applicant is, or will be, seeking other federal assistance or approval. 40 C.F.R. 1502.25(b); Forty Questions No. 9.

7. Affected Environment

An EIS must succinctly describe the environment of the area to be affected or created by the alternatives under consideration. The affected environment discussion should be no longer than necessary to understand the impacts of the proposed actions and alternatives, be commensurate in detail with the importance of the impacts, and should avoid useless information and verbose descriptions. 40 C.F.R. 1502.15.

Determining the Range of Alternatives

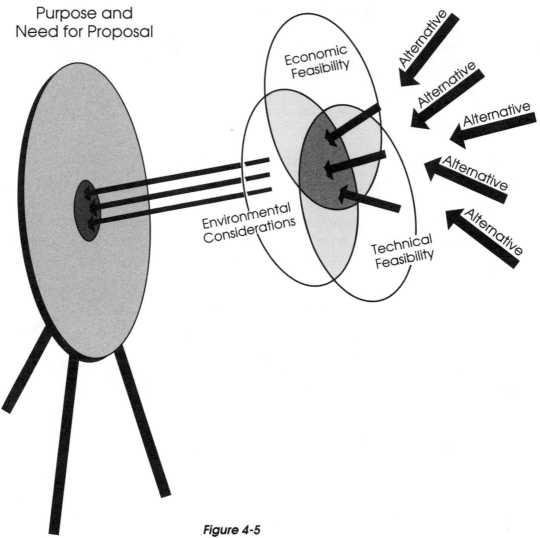

Figure 4-5

8. Environmental Consequences

The "Environmental Consequences" section of an EIS forms the scientific and analytic basis for the comparison of alternatives. The discussion of environmental consequences must include the environmental effects of the alternatives, any adverse environmental effects which cannot be avoided, the relationship between short-term uses of the environment and the maintenance and enhancement of long-term productivity, and any irreversible or irretrievable commitments of resources that would be involved if the proposal is implemented. Environmental effects include ecological, aesthetic, historical, cultural, economic, social, and health (see Figure 4-6). The types of environmental effects required to be discussed in an EIS are summarized below. 40 C.F.R. 1502.16, 1508.8.

Types of Environmental Effects

◆ Direct effects

◆ Indirect effects
 – Reasonably foreseeable consequences
 – Growth-including effects
 – Changes in land use patterns, population density, or growth rate

◆ Cumulative effects

◆ Conflicts with land use plans, policies, or controls

◆ Other types of effects
 – Unavoidable effects
 – The relationship between short-term uses of the environment versus long-term productivity
 – Irreversible or irretrievable commitments of resources
 – Energy requirements and conservation potential
 – Natural or depletable resource requirements
 – Effect on urban quality
 – Effect on historical and cultural quality
 – Socioeconomic and market effects

Figure 4-6

GLOBAL EFFECTS - THE CUTTING EDGE OF IMPACT ANALYSIS

One of the newest areas of concern in NEPA compliance is the incremental contribution that a proposed action will have on the global commons. Increasingly, the scientific community and the public are demanding that an EIS discuss whether the proposed action or the alternatives contribute cumulatively to acid precipitation, global climate change, ocean pollution, or the global loss of biodiversity. Although some might argue that any quantitative evaluation of such impacts would be remote and speculative, they should at least be described qualitatively in an EIS when relevant.

Noted landscape architect and urban planner Ian McHarg and his theories of ecological planning, have left an indelible mark on the development of NEPA and the EIS in particular. In his book *Design with Nature*, published in 1969 (the same year NEPA was signed), McHarg called for a systematic approach to planning that is based on ecological capability and suitability. His method for applying this concept was the overlay map, on which a variety of ecological factors were superimposed to determine the capability of the land to support human activity and the land's suitability for a particular type of development. McHarg's interdisciplinary approach to ecological evaluation quickly became a universal model that many federal agencies incorporated into their early NEPA practices. McHarg has served as an informal advisor to several CEQ members since the enactment of NEPA, and his theories have pervaded not only NEPA, but other federal and state environmental management programs as well.

The McHarg Concept

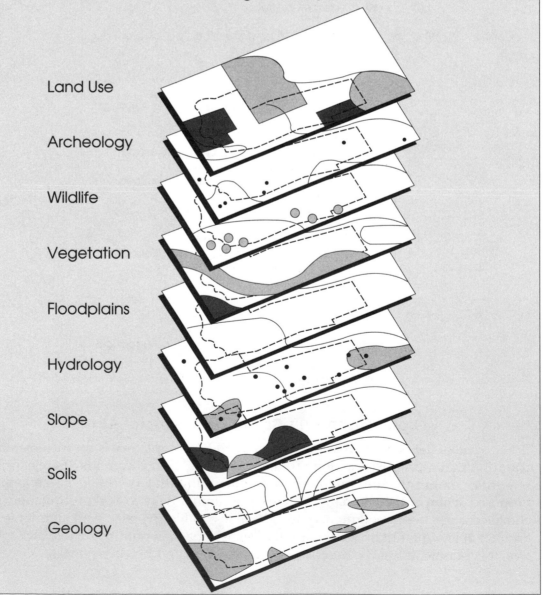

Land Use

Archeology

Wildlife

Vegetation

Floodplains

Hydrology

Slope

Soils

Geology

a. Direct Effects

Direct effects are caused by the action and occur at the same time and place. For example, the removal of vegetation from a project site to allow the construction of a facility is a direct effect. 40 C.F.R. 1508.8(a).

b. Indirect Effects

Indirect effects are caused by the action but are later in time or further removed in distance from the direct effects and yet are reasonably foreseeable. Indirect effects include those that are growth inducing or otherwise related to changes in land use patterns, population density, or growth rate. For example, future automobile pollution from employees driving to a building is a reasonably foreseeable indirect effect of constructing the building. 40 C.F.R. 1508.8(b); Forty Questions No. 18.

An EIS must identify all the indirect effects that are known and make a good-faith effort to explain the effects that are known. If there is complete uncertainty about a future landowner or land use, the agency is not required to engage in speculation but should make a judgment based on reasonably foreseeable occurrences.

c. Cumulative Effects

Cumulative effects result from the incremental impact of the proposed action when added to other past, present, and reasonably foreseeable future actions, regardless of which agency or person undertakes them. Cumulative effects can result from individually minor, but collectively significant, actions taking place over time. For example, numerous stationary sources producing small quantities of air pollution in the same air basin may result in cumulatively significant violations of ambient air quality standards. 40 C.F.R. 1508.7.

d. Conflicts with Plans

Conflicts between the proposed action and any federal, state, local, or tribal land use plans, policies, or controls for the area are considered environmental effects under NEPA and must be discussed in an EIS. The term "land use plan" includes all types of formally adopted documents for land use planning, zoning, and related regulatory requirements, including formally proposed plans. The term "policy" includes formally adopted statements of land use policy as embodied in laws or regulations, including formally proposed policies. For example, if a proposed federal building would be inconsistent with local residential zoning for the proposed site, the inconsistency must be identified and discussed in the EIS. 40 C.F.R. 1502.16 (c); Forty Questions No. 23.

e. Other Types of Effects

NEPA and CEQ's NEPA Regulations list several other categories of environmental consequences that must be considered in an EIS (see Figure 4-6):

- Adverse environmental effects that cannot be avoided (40 C.F.R. 1502.1)

- The relationship between short-term uses of the environment and the maintenance and enhancement of long-term productivity (40 C.F.R. 1502.16)

- Irreversible or irretrievable commitments of resources (40 C.F.R. 1502.16)

- Energy requirements and conservation potential (40 C.F.R. 1502.16(e))

- Natural or depletable resource requirements and conservation potential (40 C.F.R. 1502.16(f))

- Economic and social effects (40 C.F.R. 1508.8(b))

- Effects on urban quality; historical and cultural resources; and the design of the built environment, including the reuse and conservation potential (40 C.F.R. 1502.16(g))

f. Dealing with Incomplete or Unavailable Information

Prior to 1986, CEQ's regulations required agencies confronted with incomplete or unavailable information to conduct "worst-case analyses." In 1986, CEQ revoked the worst-case analysis requirement because it often resulted in expensive and unreasonable technical studies and analyses. Under the new regulation, when information is incomplete or unavailable, the information must be obtained if costs are not exorbitant. 40 C.F.R. Sec. 1502.22. The Supreme Court upheld CEQ's revised regulation in *Robertson v. Methow Valley Citizens Council*, 490 U.S. 332 (1989). Figure 4-7 summarizes what agencies must do when faced with incomplete or unavailable information.

9. Mitigation Measures for Adverse Environmental Impacts

a. Definition of Adequate Mitigation

Simply stated, a mitigation measure is a solution to an environmental problem. To be adequate and effective, mitigation measures should fit into one of five

Dealing with Incomplete or Unavailable Information

◆ If costs of obtaining information are not exorbitant, the agency must include the information in the EIS

◆ If costs of obtaining information are exorbitant, EIS must:

— State that the information is incomplete or unavailable
— State relevance of information to evaluating reasonably foreseeable significant effects
— Summarize credible scientific evidence about impacts
— Use methods generally accepted by the scientific community

Figure 4-7

categories of activities. See Figure 4-8. Mitigation measures that do not fall within one of these categories are generally ineffective. The mitigation measures discussed in an EIS must cover the entire range of impacts of the proposal. The measures may include design changes to the proposal and alternative locations. 40 C.F.R. 1508.20; Forty Questions No. 19(a).

b. Feasibility of Mitigation Measures

All relevant, reasonable mitigation measures that could improve the project must be identified in the EIS. Because an EIS is the most comprehensive environmental document available, it is an ideal place in which to lay out not only the full range of environmental impacts, but also the full spectrum of appropriate mitigation. Mitigation measures should not be eliminated from consideration in an EIS because they are outside the jurisdiction of the lead agency or because they are unlikely to be adopted or enforced by the lead agency. However, to ensure that the environmental effects of a proposed action are fairly assessed, the probability of the mitigation measures being implemented must be discussed. Forty Questions No. 19(b).

The Five Categories of Mitigation under the CEQ Regulations

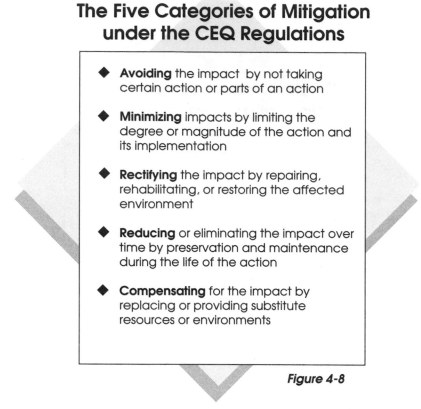

◆ **Avoiding** the impact by not taking certain action or parts of an action

◆ **Minimizing** impacts by limiting the degree or magnitude of the action and its implementation

◆ **Rectifying** the impact by repairing, rehabilitating, or restoring the affected environment

◆ **Reducing** or eliminating the impact over time by preservation and maintenance during the life of the action

◆ **Compensating** for the impact by replacing or providing substitute resources or environments

Figure 4-8

c. Commitment to Implementing Mitigation Measures

A lead agency need not present a detailed mitigation plan in the EIS or commit to implementing the mitigation measures. *Robertson v. Methow Valley Citizens Council*, 490 U.S. 332 (1989). Therefore, an agency need not adopt mitigation measures contained in an EIS unless agency-specific NEPA procedures require adoption of mitigation measures or the agency commits to implementing mitigation measures in the Record of Decision.

MITIGATION IN THEORY AND PRACTICE

The CEQ NEPA Regulations provide five seemingly straightforward ways of dealing with significant environmental effects:

"Avoiding. . ."
"Minimizing. . ."
"Rectifying. . ."
"Reducing. . ."
"Compensating. . ."

The common thread that runs through these concepts of mitigation is that the measure will result in a physical change to the proposed action that will actually reduce or eliminate impacts. In its simplest terms, a mitigation measure should be a solution to an identified environmental problem.

In practice, however, many agencies write mitigation measures that do not meet any of NEPA's definitions of mitigation. For example, some of the following measures are commonly found in NEPA documents (see Figure 4-9):

"Consult with. . ."
"Conduct further studies. . ."
"Prepare a plan to mitigate. . ."
"Strive to protect the resource. . ."
"Monitor the problem. . ."
"Submit a recommended solution for review by. . ."

The common thread running through these types of "paper mitigation" measures is that they do not solve the environmental problems disclosed in the NEPA document. Other mitigation measures, such as complying with plans and policies, or providing funding for mitigation implementation, may be effective if they are actually shown to solve a problem.

In a one-year study conducted in 1987, EPA questioned the adequacy of mitigation measures in approximately 20% of the EISs that it reviewed. Of far greater concern was that, based on a selective review of more than 1,200 EAs and FONSIs, EPA estimates that approximately 70% contained either no mitigation or measures that were ineffective or inadequate under NEPA's definition of mitigation. To ensure the effectiveness of NEPA documents, federal agencies should carefully develop their mitigation measures to fall within the definitions in the CEQ NEPA Regulations. The best test to judge the adequacy of a recommended mitigation measure is to ask: Is this measure a specific, tangible action that will reduce a physical environmental effect?

10. List of Preparers

An EIS must state the names and qualifications, including expertise, experience, and professional discipline, of the persons who were primarily responsible for preparing it. Where possible, the persons who are responsible for a particular

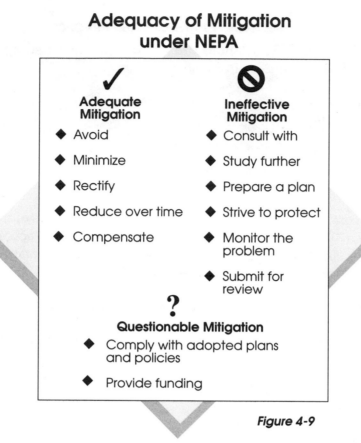

Adequacy of Mitigation under NEPA

✓ **Adequate Mitigation**
- Avoid
- Minimize
- Rectify
- Reduce over time
- Compensate

🚫 **Ineffective Mitigation**
- Consult with
- Study further
- Prepare a plan
- Strive to protect
- Monitor the problem
- Submit for review

?
Questionable Mitigation
- Comply with adopted plans and policies
- Provide funding

Figure 4-9

analysis, including analysis in background areas, should be identified. If consultants were used in its preparation, the EIS should list the members of the consulting firm in addition to the agency staff who were primarily responsible. The EIS should list the writers of basic components and the technical editors who reviewed or edited the EIS. 40 C.F.R. 1502.17; Forty Questions No. 27.

11. List of Agencies and Organizations

The EIS must list the names of all agencies and organizations to which the document has been sent for review.

12. Appendices

An EIS may include appendices that contain all background material prepared in connection with the statement. An appendix normally consists of any material that substantiates any analysis that is fundamental to the EIS. Whereas the body of the EIS should contain succinct statements about the impacts and alternatives to be used by the decision-makers, the appendix should include the more lengthy technical discussions of modeling methodology, baseline studies, or other detailed background information. However, an appendix must be analytic and relevant to the decision to be made. 40 C.F.R. 1502.18; Forty Questions No. 25(a).

An appendix must be circulated with the EIS or be readily available on request. This procedure differs from "incorporation by reference" under which the referenced documents do not have to accompany the EIS. 40 C.F.R. 1502.18(d); Forty Questions No. 25(b).

13. Index

An EIS must include an index having a level of detail to focus on areas of reasonable interest to the reader. A "key word" index may also be prepared but is not required. 40 C.F.R. 1502.10; Forty Questions No. 26.

14. Contents of a Final EIS

a. General

The final EIS must include all of the substantive comments received on the draft EIS. If, however, the comments are exceptionally voluminous, the final EIS may contain summaries of the comments. The final EIS must also include responses to the comments received during the review of the draft EIS. 40 C.F.R. 1503.4(b).

b. Responding to Comments

The final EIS must discuss any responsible opposing view that was not adequately discussed in the draft EIS and must indicate the agency's response to the issues raised. If the methodology used in preparing a section of the EIS is questioned, the lead agency must, in a substantive and meaningful manner, explain why the particular methodology was used and why the alternative methodology is not appropriate. 40 C.F.R.1503.4(a) (5) 1509.9(b); Forty Questions No. 29(a).

Generally, a final EIS consists of a rewrite of the draft EIS that incorporates the suggestions made in the comments and adds any new analysis and information to the draft EIS. If, however, the changes to the EIS in response to comments are minor, the lead agency may write them on errata sheets and attach them to the draft EIS instead of rewriting the entire draft EIS. 40 C.F.R. 1503.4(c). If changes are major, the lead agency may need to supplement the draft EIR and recirculate it.

c. Possible Ways to Respond to Comments

A lead agency must respond individually and collectively to comments received on the draft EIS. The types of possible responses to comments are shown in Figure 4-10. The agency must respond to all substantive comments; one response may be that the EIS analysis is sufficient and that no further response is necessary. If the agency draws this conclusion, it should state its reason and cite references. If the lead agency decides not to respond to a comment, it must cite the sources, authorities, or reasons that support its position. 40 C.F.R. 1503.4(a),(b).

If a commentor raises a new alternative that the lead agency feels is unreasonable, the lead agency need not evaluate it in the final EIS but must explain why the alternative is being rejected from further consideration. If a commenter raises a new variation to, or suggests additional mitigation for, one of the alternatives in the draft EIS, the lead agency should develop and evaluate the revised alternative in the final EIS. If a commenter raises an entirely new alternative that the lead agency wants to consider further, it must prepare a supplement to the draft EIS. Forty Questions No. 29(b). See the discussion of supplemental EISs in Chapter 3.

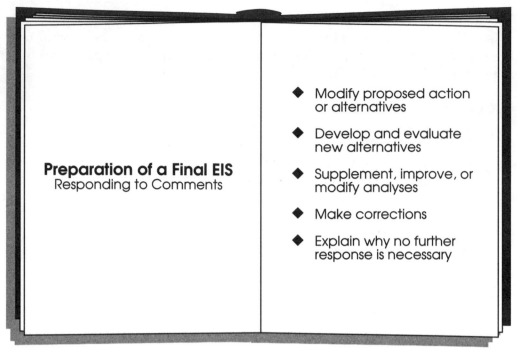

Preparation of a Final EIS
Responding to Comments

◆ Modify proposed action or alternatives

◆ Develop and evaluate new alternatives

◆ Supplement, improve, or modify analyses

◆ Make corrections

◆ Explain why no further response is necessary

Figure 4-10

B. GENERAL PRINCIPLES OF EIS PREPARATION

1. Analytic, Not Encyclopedic

An EIS should be analytic, not encyclopedic. It should emphasize the analysis of key issues that bear on the decision-making process rather than irrelevant, detailed background data. See 4-11. 40 C.F.R. 1502.2(a).

2. Focus on Significant Impacts

An EIS must focus on the significant environmental impacts. The impacts should be discussed in proportion to their significance. Impacts that are insignificant shall be discussed only briefly with an explanation of why further detailed study is not warranted. 40 C.F.R. 1502.2(b).

3. Conciseness and Page Limits

An EIS must be concise and no longer than absolutely necessary to comply with NEPA. 40 C.F.R. 1502(c). According to CEQ's NEPA Regulations, the text of a final EIS should normally be less than 150 pages and no more than 300 pages for proposals of unusual scope or complexity. In practice, however, these recommended page limits are often exceeded. 40 C.F.R. 1502.7.

4. Emphasis on Alternatives

An EIS must state how each alternative will achieve NEPA's goals. The range of alternatives in an EIS must include all those to be considered by the agency decision-makers. An agency must not commit resources that will prejudice the selection of alternatives prior to making a final decision. 40 C.F.R. 1502.2(d),(e),(f).

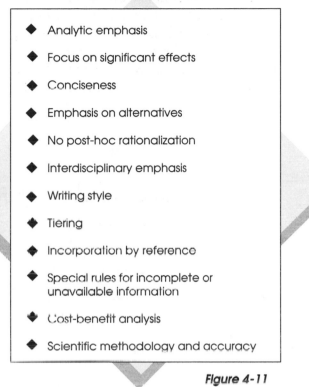

General Principles and Special Considerations in EIS Preparation

◆ Analytic emphasis

◆ Focus on significant effects

◆ Conciseness

◆ Emphasis on alternatives

◆ No post-hoc rationalization

◆ Interdisciplinary emphasis

◆ Writing style

◆ Tiering

◆ Incorporation by reference

◆ Special rules for incomplete or unavailable information

◆ Cost-benefit analysis

◆ Scientific methodology and accuracy

Figure 4-11

5. No Post-Hoc Rationalization

An EIS must serve as the means of assessing the impacts of a proposed action, rather than justifying decisions that have already been made. 40 C.F.R. 1502.2(g).

6. Interdisciplinary Emphasis

An EIS must be prepared using an interdisciplinary approach that will ensure the integrated use of the natural sciences, social sciences, and design arts. 40 C.F.R. 1502.6.

7. Writing Style

An EIS must be written in plain language and should use appropriate graphics so that decision-makers and the public can readily understand its contents. 40 C.F.R. 1502.8.

C. OTHER SPECIAL CONSIDERATIONS IN EIS PREPARATION

1. Tiering

"Tiering" refers to the concept of a "multi-tiered" approach to preparing EISs. The first-tier EIS would cover general issues in a broader program-oriented analysis. Subsequent tiers would incorporate by reference the general discussions from the broader EIS, while primarily concentrating on the issues specific to the action being evaluated. Agencies are encouraged to tier their EISs to avoid repetition of issues and to focus on the issues for decision at each level of review. Tiering is appropriate when the sequence of statements progresses from a program, plan, or policy EIS to a site-specific statement, or when the sequence evolves from an EIS on a specific action at an early stage to a subsequent EIS at a later stage. In either of these situations, the more specific EIS need only summarize and incorporate by reference the issues discussed in the broader program-oriented EIS, while focusing on the issues specific to the subsequent action. The project-specific EIS must state where the broader program-oriented EIS is available for review. 40 C.F.R. 1502.20, 1508.28; Forty Questions No. 24(c). See 4-12.

Tiering

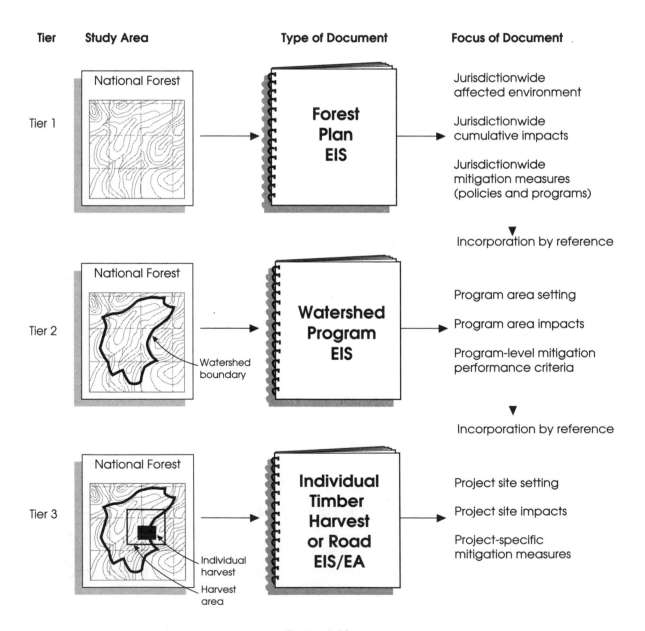

Figure 4-12

2. Incorporation by Reference

Agencies may incorporate material into an EIS by reference. The incorporated material must be cited and summarized in the EIS. Any material incorporated by reference must be available for inspection. Material based on proprietary data that is unavailable for review may not be incorporated by reference. 40 C.F.R. 1502.21.

3. Cost-Benefit Analysis

NEPA does not require that a federal agency prepare a cost-benefit analysis as a part of an EIS. However, if a cost-benefit analysis is prepared, it must be included or incorporated by reference in the EIS to aid in evaluating the proposed action. 40 C.F.R. 1502.23.

4. Methodology and Scientific Accuracy

In preparing an EIS, a federal agency must ensure the scientific and professional integrity of the discussions and analysis. An agency must identify any methodologies used in preparing the statement and include footnotes to the scientific and other sources relied on for conclusions. An agency may, however, place the discussion of methodology in an appendix. 40 C.F.R. 1502.24.

CHAPTER 5   NEPA AND FEDERAL AGENCY DECISION-MAKING

A. NEPA's ROLE IN AGENCY DECISION-MAKING

1. Promote Consideration of Environmental Consequences

NEPA's purpose is not to generate paperwork (even excellent paperwork) but to foster excellent action. The NEPA process is intended to help agencies make decisions based on an understanding of the environmental consequences and to take actions that protect, restore, and enhance the environment. 40 C.F.R. 1500.1(c). Figure 5-1 summarizes NEPA's role in agency decision-making.

Summary of Agency Decision-Making under NEPA

- ◆ Agency procedures must ensure that environmental factors are considered

- ◆ NEPA contains no substantive requirement to protect the environment

- ◆ Agency may only select alternatives that have been adequately discussed in the EIS

- ◆ No decision can be made until 30 days after *Federal Register* notice of availability of the final EIS

- ◆ Environmentally unacceptable projects may be referred to CEQ

- ◆ Record of Decision must be written to explain the agency's decision

Figure 5-1

2. No Substantive Effect

NEPA requires only that federal agencies disclose the environmental effects of their actions and identify alternatives and mitigation measures; however, it does not require that federal agencies adopt environmentally preferred alternatives or mitigation measures. See *Robertson v. Methow Valley Citizens Council*, 490 U.S. 1835 (1989).

3. Limitation on Alternatives That May Be Selected

A federal agency may not select an alternative unless it was adequately discussed and evaluated in an EIS. 40 C.F.R. 1505.5(e).

4. Agency Decision-Making Procedures

Each federal agency is required to adopt procedures to ensure that its decisions consider environmental effects. 40 C.F.R. 1505.1, 1507.3(b). See Figure 5-2. The procedures may be adopted only after public review and CEQ review for conformity with CEQ's NEPA Regulations.

Federal Agency Decision-Making Procedures: Required Contents

◆ Procedures to ensure that environmental documents accompany a proposal through the agency's decision process

◆ Procedures to ensure decisions are made in accordance with NEPA's policies

◆ Procedures to ensure that alternatives are adequately considered

Figure 5-2

B. LIMITATIONS ON ACTION DURING NEPA PROCESS

1. Limitations on Agency Decision

A federal decision on a proposed action may not be made until 90 days after publication of the notice of availability of the draft EIS or 30 days after EPA publication of the notice that the final EIS has been filed with EPA, whichever is later. An exception to these timing rules may be made for an agency decision subject to formal internal appeal. 40 C.F.R. Sec. 1505.2, 1506.10; Forty Questions No. 10(a).

2. Limitations on Agency Actions

Until a Record of Decision (ROD) is issued, a federal agency may not take an action concerning the proposal that would have an adverse environmental impact or limit the choice of reasonable alternatives. 40 C.F.R. 1506.1(a); Forty Questions 10(a).

3. Limitations on Applicant Actions

If an agency considering an application becomes aware that the applicant is about to take an action that would have an adverse impact or limit the choice of reasonable alternatives, it must notify the applicant that it will take appropriate steps to ensure NEPA compliance. 40 C.F.R. 1506.1(b); Forty Questions No. 11. An applicant is not, however, precluded from developing plans or designs needed to support applications for permits or assistance. 40 C.F.R. 1506.1(d); Forty Questions No. 10(a).

4. Interim Actions

During preparation of a program EIS, an agency may not undertake a major federal action that is covered by the program and that has significant environmental effects unless the action is independently justified, is accompanied by an EIS, and will not prejudice the ultimate decision on the program. 40 C.F.R. Sec. 1506.1(c); Forty Questions No. 10(a).

5. Applicability to State and Local Agencies

The above limitations apply to state and local agencies that have statutorily delegated responsibility for preparing NEPA documents. Forty Questions No. 10(b).

C. PREDECISION REFERRALS TO CEQ

1. Purpose of Referrals

CEQ's NEPA Regulations establish procedures for referring to CEQ interagency disagreements about proposed major federal actions that might cause unsatisfactory environmental effects. The referral process is intended to provide early resolution of these disagreements. 40 C.F.R. 1504.1(a). Although a CEQ decision on a referral does not bind the affected agencies, usually the agencies accept the CEQ recommendations.

2. Who May Initiate Referrals?

Section 309 of the Clean Air Act requires EPA to refer to CEQ those federal activities rated unsatisfactory from a health, welfare, or environmental quality standpoint. Although EPA is only required to review EISs, it may nevertheless refer issues to CEQ for which an EIS was not prepared. Other federal agencies may also make referrals regarding projects or proposals for which an EIS has been prepared. 40 C.F.R. 1504.1(b),(c).

3. Criteria for Referrals

Referrals are made by the head of a federal agency and should be made only after concerted attempts to directly resolve conflicts with the lead agency. Agencies considering referrals should weigh potential adverse impacts and consider the factors shown in Figure 5-3. 40 C.F.R. 1504.2; Forty Questions No. 33(a).

Factors to Consider in Agency Referrals to CEQ

◆ Possibility of violating national environmental standards or policies

◆ Severity of the impacts

◆ Geographic scope of the impacts

◆ Duration of the impacts

◆ Importance of the action as a precedent

◆ Availability of environmentally preferable alternatives

Figure 5-3

4. Timing of Referrals

A referring agency must deliver its referral to CEQ no later than 25 days after EPA publication of the notice of availability of the final EIS. 40 C.F.R. 1504.3(a). CEQ's responses to referrals may include mediation, fact finding, or submitting the referral and a CEQ recommendation for action to the President. 40 C.F.R. 1504.3(a); Forty Questions Nos. 33(a), 33(b). A federal agency that is referring a proposal to CEQ must notify the lead agency of its intentions at the earliest possible time.

5. Efficacy of Referral Process

As of 1992 there have been only 24 referrals to CEQ. In general, the referral process has been effective in resolving interagency disagreements. CEQ staff and Special Report: Agency Referrals to CEQ, CEQ 15th Annual Report (1984).

6. Content of Referral Request

If the issues have not been resolved between the agencies after publication of the final EIS, the head of the referring agency must send a letter and statement to CEQ and the lead agency and request that no action be taken to implement the proposal until CEQ acts on the referral. 40 C.F.R. 1504.3(b). The letter and statement to CEQ must include the information shown in Figure 5-4.

Required Contents of a Referral to CEQ

A referral letter to CEQ must:

◆ Identify the material facts in the controversy

◆ Identify environmental policies or requirements that would be violated by the proposal

◆ Present the reasons why the referring agency believes the proposal is environmentally unsatisfactory

◆ Contain a finding that the issue raised is of national importance

◆ Review the steps taken by the referring agency to resolve the matter with the lead agency prior to referral

◆ Offer the referring agency's recommendations in regard to the proposed action

Figure 5-4

7. Lead Agency Response

The lead agency for the proposal has 25 days to respond to the referring agency's letter and statement. 40 C.F.R. 1504(a). Interested parties, both in and outside of government, may deliver written views in support of the referral to CEQ no later than the time that the referral is transmitted to CEQ; parties wishing to submit written comments in support of the lead agency's position may deliver them to CEQ no later than the date of the lead agency's response. 40 C.F.R. 1504(e).

8. CEQ Action on Referrals

After the response to the referral has been received, CEQ may take one of the seven actions listed in Figure 5-5. 40 C.F.R. 1504.3(f).

Actions CEQ May Take on Referrals

- ◆ Conclude that the referral process has successfully resolved the problem

- ◆ Initiate discussions with the agencies with the objective of mediating the differences between referring and lead agencies

- ◆ Hold public meetings or hearings to obtain additional views and information

- ◆ Determine that the issue is not one of national importance and request that the referring and lead agencies pursue their decision processes

- ◆ Determine that the issue should be further negotiated by the referring and lead agencies and is not appropriate for Council consideration until one or more heads of agencies report to the CEQ that the agencies' disagreements are irreconcilable

- ◆ Publish its findings and recommendations including, where appropriate, a finding that the evidence submitted does not support the position of an agency

- ◆ Submit the referral and the response together with CEQ's recommendation to the President for action

Figure 5-5

D. RECORD OF DECISION

1. Purpose and Contents

After preparing an EIS, at the time of its decision, a federal agency must prepare a Record of Decision (ROD), a written public record explaining why it has taken a particular course of action. 40 C.F.R. 1505.2; Forty Questions Nos. 34(b), 34(c). Required contents are shown in Figure 5-6.

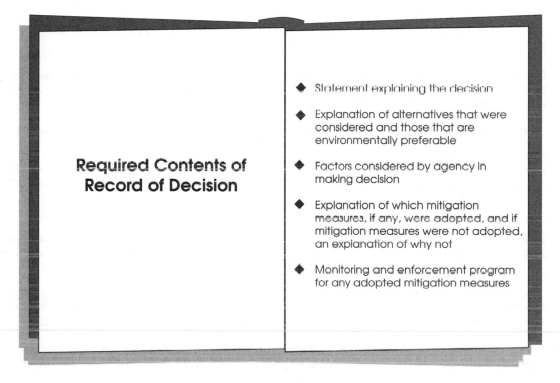

Required Contents of Record of Decision

- ◆ Statement explaining the decision

- ◆ Explanation of alternatives that were considered and those that are environmentally preferable

- ◆ Factors considered by agency in making decision

- ◆ Explanation of which mitigation measures, if any, were adopted, and if mitigation measures were not adopted, an explanation of why not

- ◆ Monitoring and enforcement program for any adopted mitigation measures

Figure 5-6

AGENCY REFERRALS TO CEQ

As of 1992 there have been only 24 referrals to CEQ. When CEQ takes a referral, it most frequently engages in discussion with the involved agencies and other interested parties with the objective of mediation and publication of CEQ's findings and recommendations. In the course of several referrals, interagency agreements were made to proceed with the project in a manner that significantly moderates adverse environmental impacts. In some cases, proposals have been withdrawn after the referral process has been concluded. In a few instances, CEQ has determined that the issue raised in the referral was not one of national importance and requested that referring and lead agencies work out their own solution.

Source: CEQ, 15th Annual Report of the Council on Environmental Quality (1984) and CEQ staff.

REFERRALS OF INTERAGENCY DISAGREEMENTS TO CEQ

(Page 1 of 2)

PROJECT	LEAD AGENCY	REFERRING AGENCY	DATE OF REFERRAL	ISSUE
1. Shearon Harris Nuclear Power Plants Units 1-4, Wake and Chatham Counties, North Carolina[a]	AEC	EPA	1/10/74	No data available from CEQ about this referral
2. Phosphate leasing on Osceola National Forest, north-central Florida	BLM	EPA	12/31/74	Adequacy of mitigation for 28,000 acres of land leased for phosphate mining
3. Oil and Gas Lease Sale no. 39, Northern Gulf of Alaska, outer continental shelf	BLM	EPA	12/18/75	On-shore impacts of a 1.8 million-acre oil and gas lease
4. Permit application by Deltona Corporation, Marco Island, Collier County, Florida	Corps	EPA	3/15/76	Dredge and fill permits affecting water quality and mangrove habitat
5. Kaiparowits Power Plant, Kaiparowits Plateau, Utah	BLM	EPA	6/4/77	Construction and operation of a 3,000-megawatt, coal-fired, electric generating station in a scenically unique area
6. Westside Highway Project, New York City, New York	FHWA	EPA	2/14/77	Consistency of air quality standards and long-range transportation goals with construction of a highway
7. Lake Alma Project, construction of water reservoir, Alma, Bacon County, Georgia	HUD	EPA	3/24/77	Water quality and the replacement of 1,400 acres of bay wetlands with an equal acreage artificial lake
8. Wando and Cooper Rivers, permit dredge, fill, construction-Marine Terminal, Charleston County, South Carolina	Corps	EPA	4/20/77	Analysis of impacts in the construction of a marine terminal in undeveloped wetland
9. County Trunk Highway "Q," Kenosha County, Wisconsin	FHWA	EPA	12/9/77	Cumulative impacts on wetlands in the construction of a highway over quality marshes and pike spawning areas
10. Barge Terminal Expansion, Packer River Terminal, Dakota County, Minnesota	Corps	EPA	1/11/78	Alternative site analysis and violation of Section 404 guidelines in the filling of 23 acres of wetlands
11. Proposed Foothills Project, Colorado	BLM	EPA	1/17/78	Water consumption, air quality, and urban sprawl impacts created by the proposed construction of a reservoir needing public land right-of-way permits
12. Fire Island to Montauk Point, beach erosion control and hurricane protection project, New York	Corps	DOI	3/7/78	Reconstruction of 83 miles of National Seashore beach to slow erosion and prevent flooding
13. Central and Southern Florida Flood Control Project, Hendry County, Florida	Corps	DOI	3/9/79	Wetland ecosystem and hydrology impacts for a drainage and flood control project

REFERRALS OF INTERAGENCY DISAGREEMENTS TO CEQ

(Page 2 of 2)

PROJECT	LEAD AGENCY	REFERRING AGENCY	DATE OF REFERRAL	ISSUE
14. I-84 and I-86, East Hartford-Manchester, Hartford County, Connecticut and Rhode Island	FHWA	EPA	12/13/79	Cumulative impacts, alternatives and mitigation measures for a series of free-ways
15. I-476, Mid-County Expressway, Delaware and Montgomery Counties, Pennsylvania	DOT	DOI	11/10/80	Elimination of open space, natural urban area amenities, and recreation values by constructing an expressway
16. Jackson Hole Airport, airport dispute, aviation noise, Jackson Hole, Wyoming	DOT	DOI and EPA	1/9/81	Noise impacts of allowing Boeing 737 service near a national park
17. Elk Creek Dam, resulting in the prolonged period of increased turbidity in the Rogue River, Elk Creek Lake, Oregon[b]	Corps	DOI	1/19/81	Biological impacts of inundating 1,290 acres of mixed conifer, oak, meadow, and riparian habitat
18. Dickey-Lincoln Schools Lake Project, proposed dam of St. John River, Maine	Corps	DOI	9/28/81	Adequacy of mitigation for the large-scale destruction of riparian resources and a wilderness recreation area
19. Palmdale International Airport, Los Angeles County, Palmdale, California	FAA	DOD	8/31/82	Air space conflicts
20. Presidential Parkway, Fulton and DeKalb Counties, Atlanta, Georgia[c]	FHWA	ACHP	6/25/84	Impacts on historic neighborhoods and consideration of alternatives
21. Tennessee-Tombigbee Wildlife Mitigation Plan, Alabama and Mississippi	Corps	DOI	12/28/84	Adequacy of mitigation and indirect impacts in the destruction of 34,000 acres of forested wetland
22. U.S. Army Corps of Engineers NEPA Procedures	Corps	EPA	2/15/85	Adequacy of the scope, purpose and needs analysis, analysis of alternatives in the EAs, and page limits on the EISs for the 404 permit process
23. Cherry Point	USMC	NPS	12/87	Adequacy of interagency coordination and cumulative impact evaluation of military agency airspace activity
24. Orange Cove and other Friant Unit Irrigation District of the Central Valley Project, California	DOI	EPA	2/3/89	Determination not to prepare an EIS on the terms of contracts for the renewal of long-term water contracts

Notes:

a) All documents regarding this case are missing from CEQ.

b) This was the only case withdrawn.

c) This was the only case that was not considered of national importance.

2.   Public Availability

Because it is an "environmental document," the ROD must be made available to the public through appropriate public notice. There is no specific requirement for publication of the ROD in the *Federal Register* or elsewhere, although some agencies do publish their RODs in the *Federal Register*. Forty Questions No. 34(a).

3.   Mitigation Measure Monitoring and Enforcement

The ROD must specifically identify which mitigation measures were selected and adopted as part of the agency's action. The agency must also include in the ROD a monitoring and enforcement program for each mitigation measure. A ROD can be used to compel compliance with or execution of the mitigation measures contained in it. Sec. 1505.2 (c). Forty Questions No. 34(d).

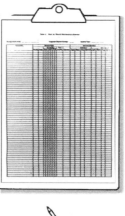

To ensure enforcement of its decision, an agency may include conditions in grants, permits, or other approvals; condition funding actions on mitigation; inform cooperating or commenting agencies on progress of mitigation measures they have proposed; and make monitoring results available to the public. 40 C.F.R. 1505.3.

NEPA SUCCESS STORY:
THE STONE LAKES NATIONAL WILDLIFE REFUGE

For many years, the U.S. Fish and Wildlife Service (USFWS), other agencies, and conservation organizations have sought to preserve and restore a portion of the vast wetland-grassland communities that once dominated California's Central Valley. To further this goal, in July 1992, USFWS approved the creation of the Stone Lakes National Wildlife Refuge. The Stone Lakes area is a mosaic of natural habitats and agricultural lands south of Sacramento. The area provides a unique opportunity to preserve, restore, and enhance wildlife habitats in a setting close to a major urban area. Various organizations and agencies made proposals to protect the area's natural values over the last 20 years.

NEPA played a vital role in determining the outcome of this unique project. The environmental impact assessment process served as a catalyst around which public opinion about the project was focused.

USFWS initiated the preparation of an EA to explore the feasibility of establishing the Stone Lakes refuge in March 1990. An interagency policy group and a steering committee consisting of representatives from various interest groups were formed to assist USFWS in planning for the proposed refuge. USFWS conducted two public workshops to identify a preliminary list of issues and concerns for consideration in the EA. The potential effects of the project on agricultural resources

(continued)

surfaced as a major issue at this stage of the EA process; concerns included loss of prime agricultural land, potential for restrictions on farming practices, and the effects of eminent domain authority of USFWS on land values and farmers' access to credit.

As a result of scoping for the EA, USFWS determined that preparation of an EIS was required. A Notice of Intent (NOI) to prepare an EIS was published in October 1990. Over the next 1.5 months, USFWS conducted two open-house scoping sessions and worked closely with agencies, interest groups, and individuals to assist the public in understanding the refuge planning and environmental review process and to provide opportunities for public input on important issues. Conservation and agricultural interest groups and individual farmers were heavily involved in the process.

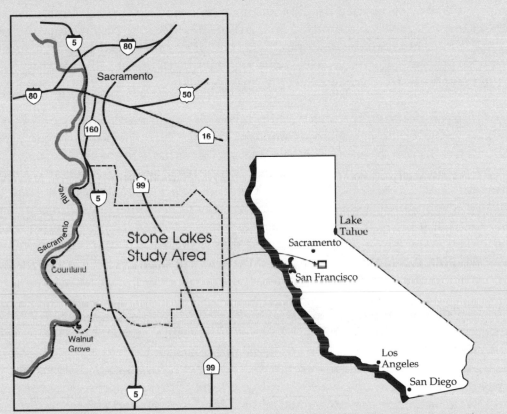

The draft EIS, released for public review and comment in May 1991, evaluated the environmental impacts of six refuge alternatives, ranging in size from 13,700 to 74,200 acres. Each of the alternatives would have accomplished the goals of USFWS but with very different degrees of environmental and socioeconomic impacts. Among the key issues evaluated in the draft EIS were land use, economic and fiscal resources, mosquitoes and public health, biological resources, agriculture, recreation, hydrology, and water quality.

Because of the intensity of public interest and controversy over the proposed project, the review period for the draft EIS was extended twice at public request to 150 days. During this period, USFWS conducted three public workshops to answer questions and disseminate information on the project. Four formal public hearings to receive verbal testimony were held.

(continued)

During the preparation of the draft EIS, USFWS also participated in several consensus-building workshops (i.e., planning charettes) with other public agencies, landowners, and non-profit conservation organizations that were interested in the possibilities for open space management and habitat restoration in the Stone Lakes region. These informal efforts helped to clarify the goals and activities of various parties engaged in parallel planning projects, solve potential conflicts or duplicative efforts, and direct USFWS refuge priorities where they were needed most. Many of these parallel restoration and open space projects have since been implemented in ways that are compatible with, and complimentary to, the federal refuge master plan that is expected to take several years to accomplish.

Over 6,000 written public comments representing diverse community opinions about the refuge were submitted on the draft EIS. Because public response was extensive, USFWS evaluated each written and verbal comment and prepared summaries of each major issue. Rather than responding to each comment individually, USFWS provided responses to major issues in the final EIS.

In response to the major issues raised during the comment period on the draft EIS, the project planning team recommended important changes to the preferred project alternative to reduce environmental and socioeconomic impacts. These recommendations resulted in the development of a Mitigated Preferred Alternative, which was presented and analyzed in detail in the final EIS. The most notable changes in the USFWS proposal were the reduction in the size of the Stone Lakes refuge and the establishment of a Cooperative Wildlife Management Area; these changes reduced the potential impacts on prime agricultural lands. This alternative also incorporated USFWS policy commitments designed to minimize the adverse impacts of the acquisition and management of the refuge.

Following the required 30-day public circulation of the final EIS, USFWS issued a Record of Decision (ROD) approving the creation of the Stone Lakes refuge and wildlife management area. The approval authorizes USFWS to acquire lands in fee title and purchase conservation easements to protect refuge lands. Ultimately, complete implementation will involve cooperative efforts to protect and restore habitats by federal, state, and local governments; private landowners; and concerned organizations and individuals. This important regional project may never have been approved without the benefit of the NEPA process and its emphasis on identification of significant issues, evaluation of alternatives, mitigation of impacts, public participation, and intergovernmental coordination.

CHAPTER 6   JUDICIAL REVIEW UNDER NEPA

A. IMPORTANCE OF THE COURTS IN NEPA ENFORCEMENT

1. General

NEPA has no enforcement mechanism specified in statute, and CEQ and EPA have no enforcement authority and limited staffing. Therefore, the primary means of enforcing NEPA has been through lawsuits brought by concerned private citizens, interest groups, and state and local agencies. The plaintiffs in NEPA cases filed in 1990 are representative of those throughout the history of NEPA litigation. See Figure 6-1.

2. Judicial Development of NEPA

The Supreme Court has sided with federal agency defendants in every NEPA case it has heard and has generally made narrow interpretations of the law. However, federal appellate and district courts have been more supportive of broad interpretations and have played a major role in expanding NEPA's applicability and interpretation. They are the major institutions responsible for much of NEPA's enforcement and interpretation.

Early NEPA cases in the lower courts:

- established liberal standing requirements for NEPA plaintiffs,

- held that NEPA's procedural requirements applied to independent regulatory agencies,

- gave deference to CEQ's NEPA guidelines, and

- required good-faith efforts to comply with NEPA's full disclosure objectives.

Plaintiffs in 1990 NEPA Lawsuits

Type of Plaintiff	Number of 1990 Cases
Environmental groups	38
Individuals or citizen groups	38
State governments	5
Local governments	9
Business groups	5
Property owners or residents	13
Native American tribes	2
Other	2
Total	112

Source: CEQ, 22nd Annual Report of the Council on Environmental Quality, 1991

Figure 6-1

3. Typical Causes of Action

The most common causes of action in recent NEPA cases are shown in Figure 6-2.

Causes of Action in NEPA Litigation

Action	Number of 1990 Cases
No environmental impact statement when one should have been prepared	24
Inadequate environmental impact statement	53
Inadequate environmental assessment	16
No environmental assessment when one should have been prepared	8
No supplemental environmental impact statement when one should have been prepared	5
Other	6
Total	112

Source: CEQ, 22nd Annual Report of the Council on Environmental Quality, 1991

Figure 6-2

4. NEPA Litigation Statistics

Thousands of lawsuits have been filed to enforce NEPA during its history. NEPA litigation statistics are reported by CEQ in its annual report. Figure 6-3 shows the number of NEPA cases filed between 1974 and 1990. Virtually every agency of the

NEPA Cases Filed from 1974 to 1990

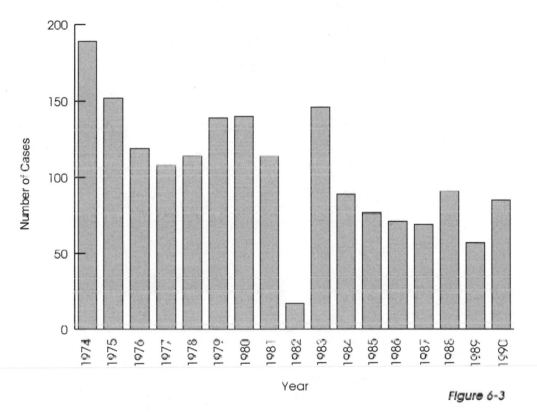

Figure 6-3

federal government has been a defendant in a NEPA case; however, some federal agencies are more commonly involved in NEPA litigation. Figure 6-4 shows the breakdown of agency defendants in litigation filed in 1990.

5. Judicial Role

The judicial role is to ensure that the agency has taken a "hard look" at environmental consequences; it is not to second-guess the correctness of the agency's decision. The courts have recognized that NEPA does not impose a substantive duty on federal agencies to protect the environment. Rather, NEPA is essentially procedural; it does not require the federal agency to adopt the environmentally preferred alternative or to mitigate significant impacts. See *Robertson v. Methow Valley Citizens Council*, 490 U.S. 332 (1989).

Federal Agency Defendants
in 1990 NEPA Litigation

Federal Agency	Number of 1990 Cases
Environmental Protection Agency	8
Federal Energy Regulatory Commission	4
Interstate Commerce Commission	1
Nuclear Regulatory Commission	1
United States Postal Service	4
Department of Army	1
Department of the Army, U.S. Army Corps of Engineers	6
Department of Commerce	10
Department of Defense	1
Department of Energy	2
Department of Housing and Urban Development	5
Department of Interior	2
Department of Navy	6
Department of State	5
Department of Transportation	27
Department of Treasury	1
Other	1
Total	85

Source: CEQ, 22nd Annual Report of the Council on Environmental Quality, 1991

Figure 6-4

B. OVERVIEW OF NEPA LITIGATION PROCESS

1. General

NEPA cases are filed in federal court. The federal court must have jurisdiction over the subject matter of the lawsuit and the parties, and there must be a case or controversy for the court to decide. Issues arising frequently in NEPA litigation are reviewed below.

2. Standing

To have standing to sue under NEPA, a plaintiff must assert an actual or threatened injury caused by an agency's action that is not in compliance with NEPA, either in fact or alleged, and that such injury can be remedied by a favorable judgment. Also, the plaintiff must not be asserting the legal interests of others, must not claim standing based on generalized grievances, and must fall within the zone of interests that NEPA protects. See *Valley Forge Christian College v. Americans United for Separation of Church and State, Inc.*, 454 U.S. 464 (1982). Because NEPA protects environmental interests, a plaintiff who files a lawsuit solely to protect economic interests does not have standing.

3. Venue

NEPA cases are typically brought in federal district court where a project is located. Many cases are also heard in the U.S. District Court for the District of Columbia, because numerous agencies are located in Washington, D.C. However, NEPA violations may be heard in courts of appeals when they arise under federal statutes requiring review exclusively in courts of appeals.

4. Introduction of Evidence Outside the Administrative Record

Generally, courts are restricted to reviewing the administrative record in determining whether a federal agency violated NEPA. Courts have limited authority to take additional evidence outside the agency's administrative record. See *Valley Citizens for a Safe Environment v. Aldridge*, 886 F.2d 4558 (CA1, 1989).

5. Remedies

a. Preliminary Injunction

Typically, plaintiffs in a NEPA case seek a preliminary injunction to enjoin the agency's activities until it has complied with NEPA. The courts decide to grant a preliminary injunction based on the plaintiff's probability of success on the merits of the claim, a balancing of the harm to the plaintiff if the injunction is denied versus the harm to the agency if it is granted, and whether the public interest would be served by granting the injunction. In most NEPA cases, courts are reluctant to grant injunctions. For example, of the 85 cases filed in 1990, preliminary injunctions were granted in only 11. CEQ, 22nd Annual Report of the Council on Environmental Quality (1991).

b. Permanent Injunction and Declaratory Relief

In addition to a preliminary injunction, plaintiffs in NEPA cases often seek a permanent injunction, which is granted based on the balancing and public interest tests discussed above. Plaintiffs often seek declaratory relief to establish the agency's legal obligations under NEPA. Courts do not award monetary damages in NEPA cases.

c. Attorney's Fees and Expenses

Prevailing NEPA plaintiffs may be entitled to attorney's fees and litigation expenses against the United States, unless the agency's position is "substantially justified" under the Equal Access to Justice Act. 28 U.S.C. Sec. 2412(b),(d).

6. Defenses

A number of defenses are generally available to federal agencies in NEPA litigation. See Figure 6-5.

Common Defenses in NEPA Cases

◆ Lack of standing

◆ Laches (excessive delay in filing a claim)

◆ Ripeness

◆ Failure to exhaust administrative remedies

◆ Mootness

◆ Trivial violations

◆ Functional equivalence (only available to EPA)

Figure 6-5

C. STANDARDS OF REVIEW

1. Failure to Prepare an EIS

For many years, federal courts reviewing agency decisions not to prepare an EIS were split over whether to apply an "arbitrary and capricious" standard of review, which is highly deferential to the agency decision, or a less deferential "reasonableness" standard of review. The Supreme Court in *Marsh v. Oregon Natural Resources Council*, 490 U.S. 332 (1989), resolved this split in 1989, holding that the "arbitrary and capricious" standard applies to agency decisions not to prepare an EIS because impacts were not significant.

2. Inadequate EIS

Courts use a "rule of reason" when reviewing the adequacy of an EIS. Under the rule of reason, the EIS must set forth sufficient information for the public to make an informed evaluation and for the decision-maker to fully consider the environmental factors involved and make a reasonable decision. *Sierra Club v. Corps of Engineers*, 701 F.2d 1011 (CA2, 1983).

3. Failure to Prepare Supplemental EIS

The Supreme Court in *Marsh v. Oregon Natural Resources Council,* 109 S.Ct. 1851 (1989), held that the deferential "arbitrary and capricious" standard of review applies to agency decisions not to prepare a supplemental EIS.

4. Review of Agency Decision on the Merits

The Supreme Court has characterized NEPA as "essentially procedural" and consistently ruled that a federal court may not set aside an agency decision because of insufficient protection of environmental values. *Strycker's Bay Neighborhood Council, Inc. v. Karlen,* 100 S.Ct. 497 (1980).

U.S. SUPREME COURT CONSISTENTLY SUPPORTS FEDERAL AGENCIES IN NEPA CASES

The U.S. Supreme Court has supported the federal agency in each NEPA case that it has heard. The court has also been consistent in holding that NEPA is "essentially procedural" and that agencies have no substantive duty under NEPA to protect the environment.

Following are brief summaries of the Supreme Court's NEPA decisions:

Aberdeen & Rockfish R. Co. v. Students Challenging Regulatory Agency Procedures, 422 U.S. 289, 95 S.Ct. 2336, 45 L.Ed.2d 191 (1975).

NEPA was satisfied by the Interstate Commerce Commission's EIS, which considered the environmental consequences of proposed freight rate increases and the possibility that increases could deter the use of recycled materials.

Flint Ridge Development Co. v. Scenic Rivers Assn., 426 U.S. 776, 96 S.Ct. 2430, 49 L.Ed.2d 205 (1976).

The Department of Housing and Urban Development (HUD) was not required to prepare an EIS before a disclosure statement was filed because NEPA requires compliance only to the fullest extent possible, and NEPA must yield when there is a "clear and unavoidable conflict" with another statute.

Kleppe v. Sierra Club, 427 U.S. 390, 96 S.Ct. 2718, 49 L.Ed.2d 576 (1976).

The Department of Interior was not required to prepare a "regional" EIS when the project did not propose the development of region-wide coal leasing. A lead agency has broad discretion to determine when a proposal for action exists.

(continued)

Vermont Yankee Nuclear Power Corp. v. Natural Resources Defense Council, 435 U.S. 519, 98 S.Ct. 1197, 55 L.Ed.2d 460 (1978).

The Nuclear Regulatory Commission correctly followed administrative procedures, thereby complying with NEPA in the licensing of two nuclear power plants.

Andrus v. Sierra Club, 442. U.S. 347, 99 S.Ct. 2335, 60 L.Ed.2d 943 (1979).

Although NEPA requires EISs on "proposals for legislation and other major actions," EISs are not required for federal agencies' appropriation requests.

Strycker's Bay Neighborhood Council, Inc. v. Karlen, 444 U.S. 223, 100 S.Ct. 497, 62 L.Ed.2d 433 (1980).

HUD was not required to make environmental factors the determining element in its decision to site a low-income housing project.

Weinberger v. Catholic Action of Hawaii/Peace Education Project, 454 U.S. 139, 102 S.Ct. 1917, 70 L.Ed.2d 298 (1981).

The Navy was not required to prepare a "hypothetical environmental impact statement" addressing the possible storage of nuclear weapons; NEPA's public disclosure provisions are governed by the Freedom of Information Act.

Metropolitan Edison Co. v. People Against Nuclear Energy, 460 U.S. 766, 103 S.Ct. 1556, 75 L.Ed.2d 534 (1983).

Psychological health did not have to be considered in an EIS and did not provide grounds to prevent the restart of Three Mile Island's undamaged reactor.

Baltimore Gas and Electric Co. v. Natural Resources Defense Council, Inc., 462 U.S. 87, 103 S.Ct. 2246, 76 L.Ed.2d 437.

The Nuclear Regulatory Commission did not make an "arbitrary and capricious" decision in determining generic rules for considering environmental impacts of the nuclear fuel cycle in nuclear reactor licensing decisions.

Marsh v. Oregon Natural Resources Council, 490 U.S. 360, 109 S.Ct. 1851, 104 L.Ed.2d 377 (1989).

Federal agency decisions on whether to prepare a supplemental EIS are reviewed under the "arbitrary and capricious" standard. The U.S. Army Corps of Engineers made a reasonable decision not to prepare a supplemental EIS for a proposed dam.

(continued)

Robertson v. Methow Valley Citizens Council, 490 U.S. 332, 109 S.Ct. 1851, 104 L.Ed.2d 377 (1989).

The U.S. Forest Service was not required to include adopted detailed mitigation measures because NEPA imposes procedural requirements. CEQ properly removed the worst-case analysis requirement from CEQ's NEPA Regulations.

Lujan v. National Wildlife Federation, 497 U.S. 871. 110 S.Ct. 3177, 111 L.Ed.2d 695 (1990).

Individuals challenging proposed BLM mining orders did not have standing because neither NEPA nor FLPMA provides for a private right of action. An injured party must be within the statute's "zone of interests."

APPENDIX 1   THE NATIONAL ENVIRONMENTAL POLICY ACT

The National Environmental Policy Act of 1969, as amended (Pub. L. 91-190, 42 U.S.C. 4321-4347, January 1, 1970, as amended by Pub. L. 94-52, July 3, 1975, Pub. L. 94-83, August 9, 1975, and Pub. L. 97-258, § 4(b), Sept. 13, 1982)

An Act to establish a national policy for the environment, to provide for the establishment of a Council on Environmental Quality, and for other purposes.

Be it enacted by the Senate and House of Representatives of the United States of America in Congress assembled, That this Act may be cited as the "National Environmental Policy Act of 1969."

CONGRESSIONAL DECLARATION OF PURPOSE

Sec. 2 [42 USC § 4321]. The purposes of this Act are: To declare a national policy which will encourage productive and enjoyable harmony between man and his environment; to promote efforts which will prevent or eliminate damage to the environment and biosphere and stimulate the health and welfare of man; to enrich the understanding of the ecological systems and natural resources important to the Nation; and to establish a Council on Environmental Quality.

TITLE I

CONGRESSIONAL DECLARATION OF NATIONAL ENVIRONMENTAL POLICY

Sec. 101 [42 USC § 4331].

(a)   The Congress, recognizing the profound impact of man's activity on the interrelations of all components of the natural environment, particularly the profound influences of population growth, high-density urbanization, industrial expansion, resource exploitation, and new and expanding technological advances and recognizing further the critical importance of restoring and maintaining environmental quality to the overall welfare and development of man, declares that it is the continuing policy of the Federal Government, in cooperation with State and local governments, and other concerned public and private organizations, to use all practicable means and measures, including financial and technical assistance, in a manner calculated to foster and promote the general welfare, to create and maintain conditions under which man and nature can exist in productive harmony, and fulfill the social, economic, and other requirements of present and future generations of Americans.

(b) In order to carry out the policy set forth in this Act, it is the continuing responsibility of the Federal Government to use all practicable means, consist with other essential considerations of national policy, to improve and coordinate Federal plans, functions, programs, and resources to the end that the Nation may --

   (1) fulfill the responsibilities of each generation as trustee of the environment for succeeding generations;

   (2) assure for all Americans safe, healthful, productive, and aesthetically and culturally pleasing surroundings;

   (3) attain the widest range of beneficial uses of the environment without degradation, risk to health or safety, or other undesirable and unintended consequences;

   (4) preserve important historic, cultural, and natural aspects of our national heritage, and maintain, wherever possible, an environment which supports diversity, and variety of individual choice;

   (5) achieve a balance between population and resource use which will permit high standards of living and a wide sharing of life's amenities; and

   (6) enhance the quality of renewable resources and approach the maximum attainable recycling of depletable resources.

(c) The Congress recognizes that each person should enjoy a healthful environment and that each person has a responsibility to contribute to the preservation and enhancement of the environment.

Sec. 102 [42 USC § 4332]. The Congress authorizes and directs that, to the fullest extent possible: (1) the policies, regulations, and public laws of the United States shall be interpreted and administered in accordance with the policies set forth in this Act, and (2) all agencies of the Federal Government shall --

   (A) utilize a systematic, interdisciplinary approach which will insure the integrated use of the natural and social sciences and the environmental design arts in planning and in decisionmaking which may have an impact on man's environment;

   (B) identify and develop methods and procedures, in consultation with the Council on Environmental Quality established by title II of this Act, which will insure that presently unquantified environmental amenities and values may be given appropriate consideration in decisionmaking along with economic and technical considerations;

   (C) include in every recommendation or report on proposals for legislation and other major Federal actions significantly affecting the quality of the human environment, a detailed statement by the responsible official on --

      (i) the environmental impact of the proposed action,

      (ii) any adverse environmental effects which cannot be avoided should the proposal be implemented,

      (iii) alternatives to the proposed action,

(iv) the relationship between local short-term uses of man's environment and the maintenance and enhancement of long-term productivity, and

(v) any irreversible and irretrievable commitments of resources which would be involved in the proposed action should it be implemented.

Prior to making any detailed statement, the responsible Federal official shall consult with and obtain the comments of any Federal agency which has jurisdiction by law or special expertise with respect to any environmental impact involved. Copies of such statement and the comments and views of the appropriate Federal, State, and local agencies, which are authorized to develop and enforce environmental standards, shall be made available to the President, the Council on Environmental Quality and to the public as provided by section 552 of title 5, United States Code, and shall accompany the proposal through the existing agency review processes;

(D) Any detailed statement required under subparagraph (C) after January 1, 1970, for any major Federal action funded under a program of grants to States shall not be deemed to be legally insufficient solely by reason of having been prepared by a State agency or official, if:

(i) the State agency or official has statewide jurisdiction and has the responsibility for such action,

(ii) the responsible Federal official furnishes guidance and participates in such preparation,

(iii) the responsible Federal official independently evaluates such statement prior to its approval and adoption, and

(iv) after January 1, 1976, the responsible Federal official provides early notification to, and solicits the views of, any other State or any Federal land management entity of any action or any alternative thereto which may have significant impacts upon such State or affected Federal land management entity and, if there is any disagreement on such impacts, prepares a written assessment of such impacts and views for incorporation into such detailed statement.

The procedures in this subparagraph shall not relieve the Federal official of his responsibilities for the scope, objectivity, and content of the entire statement or of any other responsibility under this Act; and further, this subparagraph does not affect the legal sufficiency of statements prepared by State agencies with less than statewide jurisdiction.

(E) study, develop, and describe appropriate alternatives to recommended courses of action in any proposal which involves unresolved conflicts concerning alternative uses of available resources;

(F) recognize the worldwide and long-range character of environmental problems and, where consistent with the foreign policy of the United States, lend appropriate support to initiatives, resolutions, and programs designed to maximize international cooperation in anticipating and preventing a decline in the quality of mankind's world environment;

(G) make available to States, counties, municipalities, institutions, and individuals, advice and information useful in restoring, maintaining, and enhancing the quality of the environment;

(H) initiate and utilize ecological information in the planning and development of resource-oriented projects; and

(I) assist the Council on Environmental Quality established by title II of this Act.

Sec. 103 [42 USC § 4333]. All agencies of the Federal Government shall review their present statutory authority, administrative regulations, and current policies and procedures for the purpose of determining whether there are any deficiencies or inconsistencies therein which prohibit full compliance with the purposes and provisions of this Act and shall propose to the President not later than July 1, 1971, such measures as may be necessary to bring their authority and policies into conformity with the intent, purposes, and procedures set forth in this Act.

Sec. 104 [42 USC § 4334]. Nothing in section 102 [42 USC § 4332] or 103 [42 USC § 4333] shall in any way affect the specific statutory obligations of any Federal agency (1) to comply with criteria or standards of environmental quality, (2) to coordinate or consult with any other Federal or State agency, or (3) to act, or refrain from acting contingent upon the recommendations or certification of any other Federal or State agency.

Sec. 105 [42 USC § 4335]. The policies and goals set forth in this Act are supplementary to those set forth in existing authorizations of Federal agencies.

TITLE II

COUNCIL ON ENVIRONMENTAL QUALITY

Sec. 201 [42 USC § 4341]. The President shall transmit to the Congress annually beginning July 1, 1970, an Environmental Quality Report (hereinafter referred to as the "report") which shall set forth (1) the status and condition of the major natural, manmade, or altered environmental classes of the Nation, including, but not limited to, the air, the aquatic, including marine, estuarine, and fresh water, and the terrestrial environment, including, but not limited to, the forest, dryland, wetland, range, urban, suburban an rural environment; (2) current and foreseeable trends in the quality, management and utilization of such environments and the effects of those trends on the social, economic, and other requirements of the Nation; (3) the adequacy of available natural resources for fulfilling human and economic requirements of the Nation in the light of expected population pressures; (4) a review of the programs and activities (including regulatory activities) of the Federal Government, the State and local governments, and nongovernmental entities or individuals with particular reference to their effect on the environment and on the conservation, development and utilization of natural resources; and (5) a program for remedying the deficiencies of existing programs and activities, together with recommendations for legislation.

Sec. 202 [42 USC § 4342]. There is created in the Executive Office of the President a Council on Environmental Quality (hereinafter referred to as the "Council"). The Council shall be composed of three members who shall be appointed by the President to serve at his pleasure, by and with the advice and consent of the Senate. The President shall designate one of the members of the Council to serve as Chairman. Each member shall be a person who, as a result of his training, experience, and attainments, is exceptionally well qualified to analyze and interpret environmental trends and information of all kinds; to appraise programs and activities of the Federal Government in the light of the policy set forth in title I of this Act; to be conscious of and responsive to the scientific, economic, social, aesthetic, and cultural needs and interests of the Nation; and to formulate and recommend national policies to promote the improvement of the quality of the environment.

Sec. 203 [42 USC § 4343].

(a)   The Council may employ such officers and employees as may be necessary to carry out its functions under this Act. In addition, the Council may employ and fix the compensation of such experts and consultants as may be necessary for the carrying out of its functions under this Act, in accordance with section 3109 of title 5, United States Code (but without regard to the last sentence thereof).

(b)   Notwithstanding section 1342 of Title 31, the Council may accept and employ voluntary and uncompensated services in furtherance of the purposes of the Council.

Sec. 204 [42 USC § 4344]. It shall be the duty and function of the Council --

(1)   to assist and advise the President in the preparation of the Environmental Quality Report required by section 201 [42 USC § 4341] of this title;

(2)   to gather timely and authoritative information concerning the conditions and trends in the quality of the environment both current and prospective, to analyze and interpret such information for the purpose of determining whether such conditions and trends are interfering, or are likely to interfere, with the achievement of the policy set forth in title I of this Act, and to compile and submit to the President studies relating to such conditions and trends;

(3)   to review and appraise the various programs and activities of the Federal Government in the light of the policy set forth in title I of this Act for the purpose of determining the extent to which such programs and activities are contributing to the achievement of such policy, and to make recommendations to the President with respect thereto;

(4)   to develop and recommend to the President national policies to foster and promote the improvement of environmental quality to meet the conservation, social, economic, health, and other requirements and goals of the Nation;

(5)   to conduct investigations, studies, surveys, research, and analyses relating to ecological systems and environmental quality;

(6)   to document and define changes in the natural environment, including the plant and animal systems, and to accumulate necessary data and other information for a continuing analysis of these changes or trends and an interpretation of their underlying causes;

(7)   to report at least once each year to the President on the state and condition of the environment; and

(8)   to make and furnish such studies, reports thereon, and recommendations with respect to matters of policy and legislation as the President may request.

Sec. 205 [42 USC § 4345]. In exercising its powers, functions, and duties under this Act, the Council shall --

(1)   consult with the Citizens' Advisory Committee on Environmental Quality established by Executive Order No. 11472, dated May 29, 1969, and with such representatives of science, industry, agriculture, labor, conservation organizations, State and local governments and other groups, as it deems advisable; and

(2)   utilize, to the fullest extent possible, the services, facilities and information (including statistical information) of public and private agencies and organizations, and individuals, in order that duplication of effort and expense may be avoided, thus assuring that the Council's activities will not unnecessarily overlap or conflict with similar activities authorized by law and performed by established agencies.

Sec. 206 [42 USC § 4346]. Members of the Council shall serve full time and the Chairman of the Council shall be compensated at the rate provided for Level II of the Executive Schedule Pay Rates [5 USC § 5313]. The other members of the Council shall be compensated at the rate provided for Level IV of the Executive Schedule Pay Rates [5 USC § 5315].

Sec. 207 [42 USC § 4346a]. The Council may accept reimbursements from any private non-profit organization or from any department, agency, or instrumentality of the Federal Government, any State, or local government, for the reasonable travel expenses incurred by an officer or employee of the Council in connection with his attendance at any conference, seminar, or similar meeting conducted for the benefit of the Council.

Sec. 208 [42 USC § 4346b]. The Council may make expenditures in support of its international activities, including expenditures for: (1) international travel; (2) activities in implementation of international agreements; and (3)   the support of international exchange programs in the United States and in foreign countries.

Sec. 209 [42 USC § 4347]. There are authorized to be appropriated to carry out the provisions of this chapter not to exceed $300,000 for fiscal year 1970, $700,000 for fiscal year 1971, and $1,000,000 for each fiscal year thereafter.

The Environmental Quality Improvement Act, as amended (Pub. L. No. 91-224, Title II, April 3, 1970; Pub. L. No. 97-258, September 13, 1982; and Pub. L. No. 98-581, October 30, 1984.

42 USC § 4372.

(a)   There is established in the Executive Office of the President an office to be known as the Office of Environmental Quality (hereafter in this chapter referred to as the "Office"). The Chairman of the Council on Environmental Quality established by Public Law 91-190 shall be the Director of the Office. There shall be in the Office a Deputy Director who shall be appointed by the President, by and with the advice and consent of the Senate.

(b)   The compensation of the Deputy Director shall be fixed by the President at a rate not in excess of the annual rate of compensation payable to the Deputy Director of the Office of Management and Budget.

(c)   The Director is authorized to employ such officers and employees (including experts and consultants) as may be necessary to enable the Office to carry out its functions ;under this chapter and Public Law 91-190, except that he may employ no more than ten specialists and other experts without regard to the provisions of Title 5, governing appointments in the competitive service, and pay such specialists and experts without regard to the provisions of chapter 51 and subchapter III of chapter 53 of such title relating to classification and General Schedule pay rates, but no such specialist or expert shall be paid at a rate in excess of the maximum rate for GS-18 of the General Schedule under section 5332 of Title 5.

(d)   In carrying out his functions the Director shall assist and advise the President on policies and programs of the Federal Government affecting environmental quality by --

    (1)   providing the professional and administrative staff and support for the Council on Environmental Quality established by Public Law 91-190;

    (2)   assisting the Federal agencies and departments in appraising the effectiveness of existing and proposed facilities, programs, policies, and activities of the Federal Government, and those specific major projects designated by the President which do not require individual project authorization by Congress, which affect environmental quality;

    (3)   reviewing the adequacy of existing systems for monitoring and predicting environmental changes in order to achieve effective coverage and efficient use of research facilities and other resources;

    (4)   promoting the advancement of scientific knowledge of the effects of actions and technology on the environment and encouraging the development of the means to prevent or reduce adverse effects that endanger the health and well-being of man;

    (5)   assisting in coordinating among the Federal departments and agencies those programs and activities which affect, protect, and improve environmental quality;

    (6)   assisting the Federal departments and agencies in the development and interrelationship of environmental quality criteria and standards established throughout the Federal Government;

    (7)   collecting, collating, analyzing, and interpreting data and information on environmental quality, ecological research, and evaluation.

(e)   The Director is authorized to contract with public or private agencies, institutions, and organizations and with individuals without regard to section 3324(a) and (b) of Title 31 and section 5 of Title 41 in carrying out his functions.

42 USC § 4373. Each Environmental Quality Report required by Public Law 91-190 shall, upon transmittal to Congress, be referred to each standing committee having jurisdiction over any part of the subject matter of the Report.

42 USC § 4374. There are hereby authorized to be appropriated for the operations of the Office of Environmental Quality and the Council on Environmental Quality not to exceed the following sums for the following fiscal years which sums are in addition to those contained in Public Law 91-190:

(a) $2,126,000 for the fiscal year ending September 30, 1979.

(b) $3,000,000 for the fiscal years ending September 30, 1980, and September 30, 1981.

(c) $44,000 for the fiscal years ending September 30, 1982, 1983, and 1984.

(d) $480,000 for each of the fiscal years ending September 30, 1985 and 1986.

42 USC § 4375.

(a)   There is established an Office of Environmental Quality Management Fund (hereinafter referred to as the "Fund") to receive advance payments from other agencies or accounts that may be used solely to finance --

  (1)   study contracts that are jointly sponsored by the Office and one or more other Federal agencies; and

  (2)   Federal interagency environmental projects (including task forces) in which the Office participates.

(b)   Any study contract or project that is to be financed under subsection (a) of this section may be initiated only with the approval of the Director.

(c)   The Director shall promulgate regulations setting forth policies and procedures for operation of the Fund.

Appendix 2 Council on Environmental Quality NEPA Regulations

40 CFR PART 1500 -- PURPOSE, POLICY, AND MANDATE

Sec.
1500.1 Purpose.
1500.2 Policy.
1500.3 Mandate.
1500.4 Reducing Paperwork.
1500.5 Reducing delay.
1500.6 Agency authority.

Authority: NEPA, the Environmental Quality Improvement Act of 1970, as amended (42 U.S.C. 4371 et seq.), sec 309 of the Clean Air Act, as amended (42 U.S.C. 7609) and E.O. 11514, Mar. 5, 1970, as amended by E.O. 11991, May 24, 1977).

Source: 43 FR 55994, Nov. 29, 1978, unless otherwise noted.

40 CFR 1500.1 Purpose.

(a) The National Environmental Policy Act (NEPA) is our basic national charter for protection of the environment. It establishes policy, sets goals (section 101), and provides means (section 102) for carrying out the policy. Section 102(2) contains "action-forcing" provisions to make sure that federal agencies act according to the letter and spirit of the Act. The regulations that follow implement section 102(2). Their purpose is to tell federal agencies what they must do to comply with the procedures and achieve the goals of the Act. The President, the federal agencies, and the courts share responsibility for enforcing the Act so as to achieve the substantive requirements of section 101.

(b) NEPA procedures must insure that environmental information is available to public officials and citizens before decisions are made and before actions are taken. The information must be of high quality. Accurate scientific analysis, expert agency comments, and public scrutiny are essential to implementing NEPA. Most important, NEPA documents must concentrate on the issues that are truly significant to the action in question, rather than amassing needless detail.

(c) Ultimately, of course, it is not better documents but better decisions that count. NEPA's purpose is not to generate paperwork -- even excellent paperwork -- but to foster excellent action. The NEPA process is intended to help public officials make decisions that are based on understanding of environmental consequences, and take actions that protect, restore, and enhance the environment. These regulations provide the direction to achieve this purpose.

40 CFR 1500.2 Policy.

Federal agencies shall to the fullest extent possible:

(a) Interpret and administer the policies, regulations, and public laws of the United States in accordance with the policies set forth in the Act and in these regulations.

(b) Implement procedures to make the NEPA process more useful to decisionmakers and the public; to reduce paperwork and the accumulation of extraneous background data; and to emphasize real environmental issues and alternatives. Environmental impact statements shall be concise, clear, and to the point, and shall be supported by evidence that agencies have made the necessary environmental analyses.

(c) Integrate the requirements of NEPA with other planning and environmental review procedures required by law or by agency practice so that all such procedures run concurrently rather than consecutively.

(d) Encourage and facilitate public involvement in decisions which affect the quality of the human environment.

(e) Use the NEPA process to identify and assess the reasonable alternatives to proposed actions that will avoid or minimize adverse effects of these actions upon the quality of the human environment.

(f) Use all practicable means, consistent with the requirements of the Act and other essential considerations of national policy, to restore and enhance the quality of the human environment and avoid or minimize any possible adverse effects of their actions upon the quality of the human environment.

40 CFR 1500.3 Mandate.

Parts 1500 through 1508 of this title provide regulations applicable to and binding on all Federal agencies for implementing the procedural provisions of the National Environmental Policy Act of 1969, as amended (Pub. L. 91-190, 42 U.S.C. 4321 et seq.) (NEPA or the Act) except where compliance would be inconsistent with other statutory requirements. These regulations are issued pursuant to NEPA, the Environmental Quality Improvement Act of 1970, as amended (42 U.S.C. 4371 et seq.) section 309 of the Clean Air Act, as amended (42 U.S.C. 7609) and Executive Order 11514, Protection and Enhancement of Environmental Quality (March 5, 1970, as amended by Executive Order 11991, May 24, 1977). These regulations, unlike the predecessor guidelines, are not confined to section 102(2)(C) (environmental impact statements). The regulations apply to the whole of section 102(2). The provisions of the Act and of these regulations must be read together as a whole in order to comply with the spirit and letter of the law. It is the Council's intention that judicial review of agency compliance with these regulations not occur before an agency has filed the final environmental impact statement, or has made a final finding of no significant impact (when such a finding will result in action affecting the environment), or takes action that will result in irreparable injury. Furthermore, it is the Council's intention that any trivial violation of these regulations not give rise to any independent cause of action.

40 CFR 1500.4 Reducing paperwork.

Agencies shall reduce excessive paperwork by:

(a) Reducing the length of environmental impact statements (Section 1502.2(c)), by means such as setting appropriate page limits (Section 1501.7(b)(1) and Section 1502.7).

(b) Preparing analytic rather than encyclopedic environmental impact statements (Section 1502.2(a)).

(c) Discussing only briefly issues other than significant ones (Section 1502.2(b)).

(d) Writing environmental impact statements in plain language (Section 1502.8).

(e) Following a clear format for environmental impact statements (Section 1502.10).

(f) Emphasizing the portions of the environmental impact statement that are useful to decision-makers and the public (Section 1502.14 and Section 1502.15) and reducing emphasis on background material (Section 1502.16).

(g) Using the scoping process, not only to identify significant environmental issues deserving of study, but also to deemphasize insignificant issues, narrowing the scope of the environmental impact statement process accordingly (Section 1501.7).

(h) Summarizing the environmental impact statement (Section 1502.12) and circulating the summary instead of the entire environmental impact statement if the latter is unusually long (Section 1502.19).

(i) Using program, policy, or plan environmental impact statements and tiering from statements of broad scope to those of narrower scope, to eliminate repetitive discussions of the same issues (Sections 1502.4 and 1502.20).

(j) Incorporating by reference (Section 1502.21).

(k) Integrating NEPA requirements with other environmental review and consultation requirements (Section 1502.25).

(l) Requiring comments to be as specific as possible (Section 1503.3).

(m) Attaching and circulating only changes to the draft environmental impact statement, rather than rewriting and circulating the entire statement when changes are minor (Section 1503.4(c)).

(n) Eliminating duplication with State and local procedures, by providing for joint preparation (Section 1506.2), and with other Federal procedures, by providing that an agency may adopt appropriate environmental documents prepared by another agency (Section 1506.3).

(o) Combining environmental documents with other documents (Section 1506.4).

(p) Using categorical exclusions to define categories of actions which do not individually or cumulatively have a significant effect on the human environment and which are therefore exempt from requirements to prepare an environmental impact statement (Section 1508.4).

(q) Using a finding of no significant impact when an action not otherwise excluded will not have a significant effect on the human environment and is therefore exempt from requirements to prepare an environmental impact statement (Section 1508.13).

(43 FR 55990, Nov. 29, 1978; 44 FR 873, Jan. 3, 1979)

40 CFR 1500.5 Reducing delay.

Agencies shall reduce delay by:

(a) Integrating the NEPA process into early planning (Section 1501.2).

(b) Emphasizing interagency cooperation before the environmental impact statement is prepared, rather than submission of adversary comments on a completed document (Section 1501.6).

(c) Insuring the swift and fair resolution of lead agency disputes (Section 1501.5).

(d) Using the scoping process for an early identification of what are and what are not the real issues (Section 1501.7).

(e) Establishing appropriate time limits for the environmental impact statement process (Sections 1501.7(b)(2) and 1501.8).

(f) Preparing environmental impact statements early in the process (Section 1502.5).

(g) Integrating NEPA requirements with other environmental review and consultation requirements (Section 1502.25).

(h) Eliminating duplication with State and local procedures by providing for joint preparation (Section 1506.2) and with other Federal procedures by providing that an agency may adopt appropriate environmental documents prepared by another agency (Section 1506.3).

(i) Combining environmental documents with other documents (Section 1506.4).

(j) Using accelerated procedures for proposals for legislation (Section 1506.8).

(k) Using categorical exclusions to define categories of actions which do not individually or cumulatively have a significant effect on the human environment (Section 1508.4) and which are therefore exempt from requirements to prepare an environmental impact statement.

(l) Using a finding of no significant impact when an action not otherwise excluded will not have a significant effect on the human environment (Section 1508.13) and is therefore exempt from requirements to prepare an environmental impact statement.

40 CFR 1500.6 Agency authority.

Each agency shall interpret the provisions of the Act as a supplement to its existing authority and as a mandate to view traditional policies and missions in the light of the Act's national environmental objectives. Agencies shall review their policies, procedures, and regulations accordingly and revise them as necessary to insure full compliance with the purposes and provisions of the Act. The phrase ''to the fullest extent possible'' in section 102 means that each agency of the Federal Government shall comply with that section unless existing law applicable to the agency's operations expressly prohibits or makes compliance impossible.

40 CFR PART 1501 -- NEPA AND AGENCY PLANNING

Sec.
1501.1 Purpose.
1501.2 Apply NEPA early in the process.
1501.3 When to prepare an environmental assessment.
1501.4 Whether to prepare an environmental impact statement.
1501.5 Lead agencies.
1501.6 Cooperating agencies.
1501.7 Scoping.
1501.8 Time limits.

Authority: NEPA, the Environmental Quality Improvement Act of 1970, as amended (42 U.S.C. 4371 et seq.), sec. 309 of the Clean Air Act, as amended (42 U.S.C. 7609, and E.O. 11514 (Mar. 5, 1970, as amended by E.O. 11991, May 24, 1977).

Source: 43 FR 55992, Nov. 29, 1978, unless otherwise noted.

40 CFR 1501.1 Purpose.

The purposes of this part include:

(a) Integrating the NEPA process into early planning to insure appropriate consideration of NEPA's policies and to eliminate delay.

(b) Emphasizing cooperative consultation among agencies before the environmental impact statement is prepared rather than submission of adversary comments on a completed document.

(c) Providing for the swift and fair resolution of lead agency disputes.

(d) Identifying at an early stage the significant environmental issues deserving of study and deemphasizing insignificant issues, narrowing the scope of the environmental impact statement accordingly.

(e) Providing a mechanism for putting appropriate time limits on the environmental impact statement process.

40 CFR 1501.2 Apply NEPA early in the process.

Agencies shall integrate the NEPA process with other planning at the earliest possible time to insure that planning and decisions reflect environmental values, to avoid delays later in the process, and to head off potential conflicts. Each agency shall:

(a) Comply with the mandate of section 102(2)(A) to "utilize a systematic, interdisciplinary approach which will insure the integrated use of the natural and social sciences and the environmental design arts in planning and in decisionmaking which may have an impact on man's environment," as specified by Section 1507.2.

(b) Identify environmental effects and values in adequate detail so they can be compared to economic and technical analyses. Environmental documents and appropriate analyses shall be circulated and reviewed at the same time as other planning documents.

(c) Study, develop, and describe appropriate alternatives to recommended courses of action in any proposal which involves unresolved conflicts concerning alternative uses of available resources as provided by section 102(2)(E) of the Act.

(d) Provide for cases where actions are planned by private applicants or other non-Federal entities before Federal involvement so that:

  (1) Policies or designated staff are available to advise potential applicants of studies or other information foreseeably required for later Federal action.

  (2) The Federal agency consults early with appropriate State and local agencies and Indian tribes and with interested private persons and organizations when its own involvement is reasonably foreseeable.

  (3) The Federal agency commences its NEPA process at the earliest possible time.

40 CFR 1501.3 When to prepare an environmental assessment.

(a) Agencies shall prepare an environmental assessment (Section 1508.9) when necessary under the procedures adopted by individual agencies to supplement these regulations as described in Section 1507.3. An assessment is not necessary if the agency has decided to prepare an environmental impact statement.

(b) Agencies may prepare an environmental assessment on any action at any time in order to assist agency planning and decisionmaking.

40 CFR 1501.4 Whether to prepare an environmental impact statement.

In determining whether to prepare an environmental impact statement the Federal agency shall:

(a) Determine under its procedures supplementing these regulations (described in Section 1507.3) whether the proposal is one which:

(1) Normally requires an environmental impact statement, or

(2) Normally does not require either an environmental impact statement or an environmental assessment (categorical exclusion).

(b) If the proposed action is not covered by paragraph (a) of this section, prepare an environmental assessment (Section 1508.9). The agency shall involve environmental agencies, applicants, and the public, to the extent practicable, in preparing assessments required by Section 1508.9(a)(1).

(c) Based on the environmental assessment make its determination whether to prepare an environmental impact statement.

(d) Commence the scoping process (Section 1501.7), if the agency will prepare an environmental impact statement.

(e) Prepare a finding of no significant impact (Section 1508.13), if the agency determines on the basis of the environmental assessment not to prepare a statement.

(1) The agency shall make the finding of no significant impact available to the affected public as specified in Section 1506.6.

(2) In certain limited circumstances, which the agency may cover in its procedures under Section 1507.3, the agency shall make the finding of no significant impact available for public review (including State and areawide clearinghouses) for 30 days before the agency makes its final determination whether to prepare an environmental impact statement and before the action may begin. The circumstances are:

(i) The proposed action is, or is closely similar to, one which normally requires the preparation of an environmental impact statement under the procedures adopted by the agency pursuant to Section 1507.3, or

(ii) The nature of the proposed action is one without precedent.

40 CFR 1501.5 Lead agencies.

(a) A lead agency shall supervise the preparation of an environmental impact statement if more than one Federal agency either:

(1) Proposes or is involved in the same action; or

(2) Is involved in a group of actions directly related to each other because of their functional interdependence or geographical proximity.

(b) Federal, State, or local agencies, including at least one Federal agency, may act as joint lead agencies to prepare an environmental impact statement (Section 1506.2).

(c) If an action falls within the provisions of paragraph (a) of this section the potential lead agencies shall determine by letter or memorandum which agency shall be the lead agency and which shall be cooperating agencies. The agencies shall resolve the lead agency question so as not to cause delay. If there is disagreement among the agencies, the following factors (which are listed in order of descending importance) shall determine lead agency designation:

(1) Magnitude of agency's involvement.

(2) Project approval/disapproval authority.

(3) Expertise concerning the action's environmental effects.

(4) Duration of agency's involvement.

(5) Sequence of agency's involvement.

(d) Any Federal agency, or any State or local agency or private person substantially affected by the absence of lead agency designation, may make a written request to the potential lead agencies that a lead agency be designated.

(e) If Federal agencies are unable to agree on which agency will be the lead agency or if the procedure described in paragraph (c) of this section has not resulted within 45 days in a lead agency designation, any of the agencies or persons concerned may file a request with the Council asking it to determine which Federal agency shall be the lead agency. A copy of the request shall be transmitted to each potential lead agency. The request shall consist of:

(1) A precise description of the nature and extent of the proposed action.

(2) A detailed statement of why each potential lead agency should or should not be the lead agency under the criteria specified in paragraph (c) of this section.

(f) A response may be filed by any potential lead agency concerned within 20 days after a request is filed with the Council. The Council shall determine as soon as possible but not later than 20 days after receiving the request and all responses to it which Federal agency shall be the lead agency and which other Federal agencies shall be cooperating agencies.

(43 FR 55992, Nov. 29, 1978; 44 FR 873, Jan. 3, 1979)

40 CFR 1501.6 Cooperating agencies.

The purpose of this section is to emphasize agency cooperation early in the NEPA process. Upon request of the lead agency, any other Federal agency which has jurisdiction by law shall be a cooperating agency. In addition any other Federal agency which has special expertise with respect to any environmental issue, which should be addressed in the statement may be a cooperating agency upon request of the lead agency. An agency may request the lead agency to designate it a cooperating agency.

(a) The lead agency shall:

(1) Request the participation of each cooperating agency in the NEPA process at the earliest possible time.

(2) Use the environmental analysis and proposals of cooperating agencies with jurisdiction by law or special expertise, to the maximum extent possible consistent with its responsibility as lead agency.

(3) Meet with a cooperating agency at the latter's request.

(b) Each cooperating agency shall:

(1) Participate in the NEPA process at the earliest possible time.

(2) Participate in the scoping process (described below in Section 1501.7).

(3) Assume on request of the lead agency responsibility for developing information and preparing environmental analyses including portions of the environmental impact statement concerning which the cooperating agency has special expertise.

(4) Make available staff support at the lead agency's request to enhance the latter's interdisciplinary capability.

(5) Normally use its own funds. The lead agency shall, to the extent available funds permit, fund those major activities or analyses it requests from cooperating agencies. Potential lead agencies shall include such funding requirements in their budget requests.

(c) A cooperating agency may in response to a lead agency's request for assistance in preparing the environmental impact statement (described in paragraph (b)(3), (4), or (5) of this section) reply that other program commitments preclude any involvement or the degree of involvement requested in the action that is the subject of the environmental impact statement. A copy of this reply shall be submitted to the Council.

40 CFR 1501.7 Scoping.

There shall be an early and open process for determining the scope of issues to be addressed and for identifying the significant issues related to a proposed action. This process shall be termed scoping. As soon as practicable after its decision to prepare an environmental impact statement and before the scoping process the lead agency shall publish a notice of intent (Section 1508.22) in the Federal Register except as provided in Section 1507.3(e).

(a) As part of the scoping process the lead agency shall:

(1) Invite the participation of affected Federal, State, and local agencies, any affected Indian tribe, the proponent of the action, and other interested persons (including those who might not be in accord with the action on environmental grounds), unless there is a limited exception under Section 1507.3(c). An agency may give notice in accordance with Section 1506.6.

(2) Determine the scope (Section 1508.25) and the significant issues to be analyzed in depth in the environmental impact statement.

(3) Identify and eliminate from detailed study the issues which are not significant or which have been covered by prior environmental review (Section 1506.3), narrowing the discussion of these issues in the statement to a brief presentation of why they will not have a significant effect on the human environment or providing a reference to their coverage elsewhere.

(4) Allocate assignments for preparation of the environmental impact statement among the lead and cooperating agencies, with the lead agency retaining responsibility for the statement.

(5) Indicate any public environmental assessments and other environmental impact statements which are being or will be prepared that are related to but are not part of the scope of the impact statement under consideration.

(6) Identify other environmental review and consultation requirements so the lead and cooperating agencies may prepare other required analyses and studies concurrently with, and integrated with, the environmental impact statement as provided in Section 1502.25.

(7) Indicate the relationship between the timing of the preparation of environmental analyses and the agency's tentative planning and decisionmaking schedule.

(b) As part of the scoping process the lead agency may:

(1) Set page limits on environmental documents (Section 1502.7).

(2) Set time limits (Section 1501.8).

(3) Adopt procedures under Section 1507.3 to combine its environmental assessment process with its scoping process.

(4) Hold an early scoping meeting or meetings which may be integrated with any other early planning meeting the agency has. Such a scoping meeting will often be appropriate when the impacts of a particular action are confined to specific sites.

(c) An agency shall revise the determinations made under paragraphs (a) and (b) of this section if substantial changes are made later in the proposed action, or if significant new circumstances or information arise which bear on the proposal or its impacts.

40 CFR 1501.8 Time limits.

Although the Council has decided that prescribed universal time limits for the entire NEPA process are too inflexible, Federal agencies are encouraged to set time limits appropriate to individual actions (consistent with the time intervals required by Section 1506.10). When multiple agencies are involved the reference to agency below means lead agency.

(a) The agency shall set time limits if an applicant for the proposed action requests them: Provided, That the limits are consistent with the purposes of NEPA and other essential considerations of national policy.

(b) The agency may:

(1) Consider the following factors in determining time limits:

(i) Potential for environmental harm.

(ii) Size of the proposed action.

(iii) State of the art of analytic techniques.

(iv) Degree of public need for the proposed action, including the consequences of delay.

(v) Number of persons and agencies affected.

(vi) Degree to which relevant information is known and if not known the time required for obtaining it.

(vii) Degree to which the action is controversial.

(viii) Other time limits imposed on the agency by law, regulations, or executive order.

(2) Set overall time limits or limits for each constituent part of the NEPA process, which may include:

(i) Decision on whether to prepare an environmental impact statement (if not already decided).

(ii) Determination of the scope of the environmental impact statement.

(iii) Preparation of the draft environmental impact statement.

(iv) Review of any comments on the draft environmental impact statement from the public and agencies.

(v) Preparation of the final environmental impact statement.

(vi) Review of any comments on the final environmental impact statement.

(vii) Decision on the action based in part on the environmental impact statement.

(3) Designate a person (such as the project manager or a person in the agency's office with NEPA responsibilities) to expedite the NEPA process.

(c) State or local agencies or members of the public may request a Federal Agency to set time limits.

40 CFR PART 1502 -- ENVIRONMENTAL IMPACT STATEMENT

Sec.
1502.1 Purpose.
1502.2 Implementation.
1502.3 Statutory requirements for statements.
1502.4 Major Federal actions requiring the preparation of environmental impact statements.
1502.5 Timing.
1502.6 Interdisciplinary preparation.
1502.7 Page limits.
1502.8 Writing.
1502.9 Draft, final, and supplemental statements.
1502.10 Recommended format.
1502.11 Cover sheet.
1502.12 Summary.
1502.13 Purpose and need.
1502.14 Alternatives including the proposed action.
1502.15 Affected environment.
1502.16 Environmental consequences.
1502.17 List of preparers.
1502.18 Appendix.
1502.19 Circulation of the environmental impact statement.
1502.20 Tiering.
1502.21 Incorporation by reference.
1502.22 Incomplete or unavailable information.
1502.23 Cost-benefit analysis.
1502.24 Methodology and scientific accuracy.
1502.25 Environmental review and consultation requirements.

Authority: NEPA, the Environmental Quality Improvement Act of 1970, as amended (42 U.S.C. 4371 et seq.), sec. 309 of the Clean Air Act, as amended (42 U.S.C. 7609), and E.O. 11514 (Mar. 5, 1970, as amended by E.O. 11991, May 24, 1977).

Source: 43 FR 55994, Nov. 29, 1978, unless otherwise noted.

40 CFR 1502.1 Purpose.

The primary purpose of an environmental impact statement is to serve as an action-forcing device to insure that the policies and goals defined in the Act are infused into the ongoing programs and actions of the Federal Government. It shall provide full and fair discussion of significant environmental impacts and shall inform decisionmakers and the public of the reasonable alternatives which would avoid or minimize adverse impacts or enhance the quality of the human environment. Agencies shall focus on significant environmental issues and alternatives and shall reduce paperwork and the accumulation of extraneous background data. Statements shall be concise, clear, and to the point, and shall be supported by evidence that the agency has made the necessary environmental analyses. An environmental impact statement is more than a disclosure document. It shall be used by Federal officials in conjunction with other relevant material to plan actions and make decisions.

40 CFR 1502.2 Implementation.

To achieve the purposes set forth in Section 1502.1 agencies shall prepare environmental impact statements in the following manner:

(a) Environmental impact statements shall be analytic rather than encyclopedic.

(b) Impacts shall be discussed in proportion to their significance. There shall be only brief discussion of other than significant issues. As in a finding of no significant impact, there should be only enough discussion to show why more study is not warranted.

(c) Environmental impact statements shall be kept concise and shall be no longer than absolutely necessary to comply with NEPA and with these regulations. Length should vary first with potential environmental problems and then with project size.

(d) Environmental impact statements shall state how alternatives considered in it and decisions based on it will or will not achieve the requirements of sections 101 and 102(1) of the Act and other environmental laws and policies.

(e) The range of alternatives discussed in environmental impact statements shall encompass those to be considered by the ultimate agency decisionmaker.

(f) Agencies shall not commit resources prejudicing selection of alternatives before making a final decision (Section 1506.1).

(g) Environmental impact statements shall serve as the means of assessing the environmental impact of proposed agency actions, rather than justifying decisions already made.

40 CFR 1502.3 Statutory requirements for statements.

As required by sec. 102(2)(C) of NEPA environmental impact statements (Section 1508.11) are to be included in every recommendation or report:

• On proposals (Section 1508.23).

• For legislation and (Section 1508.17).

• Other major Federal actions (Section 1508.18).

• Significantly (Section 1508.27).

• Affecting (Section 1508.3, Section 1508.8).

• The quality of the human environment (Section 1508.14).

40 CFR 1502.4 Major Federal actions requiring the preparation of environmental impact statements.

(a) Agencies shall make sure the proposal which is the subject of an environmental impact statement is properly defined. Agencies shall use the criteria for scope (Section 1508.25) to determine which proposal(s) shall be the subject of a particular statement. Proposals or parts of proposals which are related to each other closely enough to be, in effect, a single course of action shall be evaluated in a single impact statement.

(b) Environmental impact statements may be prepared, and are sometimes required, for broad Federal actions such as the adoption of new agency programs or regulations (Section 1508.18). Agencies shall prepare statements on broad actions so that they are relevant to policy and are timed to coincide with meaningful points in agency planning and decisionmaking.

(c) When preparing statements on broad actions (including proposals by more than one agency), agencies may find it useful to evaluate the proposal(s) in one of the following ways:

(1) Geographically, including actions occurring in the same general location, such as body of water, region, or metropolitan area.

(2) Generically, including actions which have relevant similarities, such as common timing, impacts, alternatives, methods of implementation, media, or subject matter.

(3) By stage of technological development including federal or federally assisted research, development or demonstration programs for new technologies which, if applied, could significantly affect the quality of the human environment. Statements shall be prepared on such programs and shall be available before the program has reached a stage of investment or commitment to implementation likely to determine subsequent development or restrict later alternatives.

(d) Agencies shall as appropriate employ scoping (Section 1501.7), tiering (Section 1502.20), and other methods listed in Section 1500.4 and Section 1500.5 to relate broad and narrow actions and to avoid duplication and delay.

40 CFR 1502.5 Timing.

An agency shall commence preparation of an environmental impact statement as close as possible to the time the agency is developing or is presented with a proposal (Section 1508.23) so that preparation can be completed in time for the final statement to be included in any recommendation or report on the proposal. The statement shall be prepared early enough so that it can serve practically as an important contribution to the decisionmaking process and will not be used to rationalize or justify decisions already made (Section 1500.2(c), Section 1501.2, and Section 1502.2). For instance:

(a) For projects directly undertaken by Federal agencies the environmental impact statement shall be prepared at the feasibility analysis (go-no go) stage and may be supplemented at a later stage if necessary.

(b) For applications to the agency appropriate environmental assessments or statements shall be commenced no later than immediately after the application is received. Federal agencies are encouraged to begin preparation of such assessments or statements earlier, preferably jointly with applicable State or local agencies.

(c) For adjudication, the final environmental impact statement shall normally precede the final staff recommendation and that portion of the public hearing related to the impact study. In appropriate circumstances the statement may follow preliminary hearings designed to gather information for use in the statements.

(d) For informal rulemaking the draft environmental impact statement shall normally accompany the proposed rule.

40 CFR 1502.6 Interdisciplinary preparation.

Environmental impact statements shall be prepared using an inter-disciplinary approach which will insure the integrated use of the natural and social sciences and the environmental design arts (section 102(2)(A) of the Act). The disciplines of the preparers shall be appropriate to the scope and issues identified in the scoping process (Section 1501.7).

40 CFR 1502.7 Page limits.

The text of final environmental impact statements (e.g., paragraphs (d) through (g) of Section 1502.10) shall normally be less than 150 pages and for proposals of unusual scope or complexity shall normally be less than 300 pages.

40 CFR 1502.8 Writing.

Environmental impact statements shall be written in plain language and may use appropriate graphics so that decisionmakers and the public can readily understand them. Agencies should employ writers of clear prose or editors to write, review, or edit statements, which will be based upon the analysis and supporting data from the natural and social sciences and the environmental design arts.

40 CFR 1502.9 Draft, final, and supplemental statements.

Except for proposals for legislation as provided in Section 1506.8 environmental impact statements shall be prepared in two stages and may be supplemented.

(a) Draft environmental impact statements shall be prepared in accordance with the scope decided upon in the scoping process. The lead agency shall work with the cooperating agencies and shall obtain comments as required in Part 1503 of this chapter. The draft statement must fulfill and satisfy to the fullest extent possible the requirements established for final statements in section 102(2)(C) of the Act. If a draft statement is so inadequate as to preclude meaningful analysis, the agency shall prepare and circulate a revised draft of the appropriate portion. The agency shall make every effort to disclose and discuss at appropriate points in the draft statement all major points of view on the environmental impacts of the alternatives including the proposed action.

(b) Final environmental impact statements shall respond to comments as required in Part 1503 of this chapter. The agency shall discuss at appropriate points in the final statement any responsible opposing view which was not adequately discussed in the draft statement and shall indicate the agency's response to the issues raised.

(c) Agencies:

   (1) Shall prepare supplements to either draft or final environmental impact statements if:

      (i)   The agency makes substantial changes in the proposed action that are relevant to environmental concerns; or

      (ii) There are significant new circumstances or information relevant to environmental concerns and bearing on the proposed action or its impacts.

   (2) May also prepare supplements when the agency determines that the purposes of the Act will be furthered by doing so.

   (3) Shall adopt procedures for introducing a supplement into its formal administrative record, if such a record exists.

   (4) Shall prepare, circulate, and file a supplement to a statement in the same fashion (exclusive of scoping) as a draft and final statement unless alternative procedures are approved by the Council.

40 CFR 1502.10 Recommended format.

Agencies shall use a format for environmental impact statements which will encourage good analysis and clear presentation of the alternatives including the proposed action. The following standard format for environmental impact statements should be followed unless the agency determines that there is a compelling reason to do otherwise:

(a) Cover sheet.

(b) Summary.

(c) Table of contents.

(d) Purpose of and need for action.

(e) Alternatives including proposed action (sections 102(2)(C)(iii) and 102(2)(E) of the Act).

(f) Affected environment.

(g) Environmental consequences (especially sections 102(2)(C)(i), (ii), (iv), and (v) of the Act).

(h) List of preparers.

(i) List of Agencies, Organizations, and persons to whom copies of the statement are sent.

(j) Index.

(k) Appendices (if any).

If a different format is used, it shall include paragraphs (a), (b), (c), (h), (i), and (j), of this section and shall include the substance of paragraphs (d), (e), (f), (g), and (k) of this section, as further described in Section 1502.11 through Section 1502.18, in any appropriate format.

40 CFR 1502.11 Cover sheet.

The cover sheet shall not exceed one page. It shall include:

(a) A list of the responsible agencies including the lead agency and any cooperating agencies.

(b) The title of the proposed action that is the subject of the statement (and if appropriate the titles of related cooperating agency actions), together with the State(s) and county(ies) (or other jurisdiction if applicable) where the action is located.

(c) The name, address, and telephone number of the person at the agency who can supply further information.

(d) A designation of the statement as a draft, final, or draft or final supplement.

(e) A one paragraph abstract of the statement.

(f) The date by which comments must be received (computed in cooperation with EPA under Section 1506.10).

The information required by this section may be entered on Standard Form 424 (in items 4, 6, 7, 10, and 18).

40 CFR 1502.12 Summary.

Each environmental impact statement shall contain a summary which adequately and accurately summarizes the statement. The summary shall stress the major conclusions, areas of controversy (including issues raised by agencies and the public), and the issues to be resolved (including the choice among alternatives). The summary will normally not exceed 15 pages.

40 CFR 1502.13 Purpose and need.

The statement shall briefly specify the underlying purpose and need to which the agency is responding in proposing the alternatives including the proposed action.

40 CFR 1502.14 Alternatives including the proposed action.

This section is the heart of the environmental impact statement. Based on the information and analysis presented in the sections on the Affected Environment (Section 1502.15) and the Environmental Consequences (Section 1502.16), it should present the environmental impacts of the proposal and the alternatives in comparative form, thus sharply defining the issues and providing a clear basis for choice among options by the decisionmaker and the public. In this section agencies shall:

(a) Rigorously explore and objectively evaluate all reasonable alternatives, and for alternatives which were eliminated from detailed study, briefly discuss the reasons for their having been eliminated.

(b) Devote substantial treatment to each alternative considered in detail including the proposed action so that reviewers may evaluate their comparative merits.

(c) Include reasonable alternatives not within the jurisdiction of the lead agency.

(d) Include the alternative of no action.

(e) Identify the agency's preferred alternative or alternatives, if one or more exists, in the draft statement and identify such alternative in the final statement unless another law prohibits the expression of such a preference.

(f) Include appropriate mitigation measures not already included in the proposed action or alternatives.

40 CFR 1502.15 Affected environment.

The environmental impact statement shall succinctly describe the environment of the area(s) to be affected or created by the alternatives under consideration. The descriptions shall be no longer than is necessary to understand the effects of the alternatives. Data and analyses in a statement shall be commensurate with the importance of the impact, with less important material summarized, consolidated, or simply referenced. Agencies shall avoid useless bulk in statements and shall concentrate effort and attention on important issues. Verbose descriptions of the affected environment are themselves no measure of the adequacy of an environmental impact statement.

40 CFR 1502.16 Environmental consequences.

This section forms the scientific and analytic basis for the comparisons under Section 1502.14. It shall consolidate the discussions of those elements required by sections 102(2)(C)(i), (ii), (iv), and (v) of NEPA which are within the scope of the statement and as much of section 102(2)(C)(iii) as is necessary to support the comparisons. The discussion will include the environmental impacts of the alternatives including the proposed action, any adverse environmental effects which cannot be avoided should the proposal be implemented, the relationship between short-term uses of man's environment and the maintenance and enhancement of long-term productivity, and any irreversible or irretrievable commitments of resources which would be involved in the proposal should it be implemented. This section should not duplicate discussions in Section 1502.14. It shall include discussions of:

(a) Direct effects and their significance (Section 1508.8).

(b) Indirect effects and their significance (Section 1508.8).

(c) Possible conflicts between the proposed action and the objectives of Federal, regional, State, and local (and in the case of a reservation, Indian tribe) land use plans, policies and controls for the area concerned. (See Section 1506.2(d).)

(d) The environmental effects of alternatives including the proposed action. The comparisons under Section 1502.14 will be based on this discussion.

(e) Energy requirements and conservation potential of various alternatives and mitigation measures.

(f) Natural or depletable resource requirements and conservation potential of various alternatives and mitigation measures.

(g) Urban quality, historic and cultural resources, and the design of the built environment, including the reuse and conservation potential of various alternatives and mitigation measures.

(h) Means to mitigate adverse environmental impacts (if not fully covered under Section 1502.14(f)).

(43 FR 55994, Nov. 29, 1978; 44 FR 873, Jan. 3, 1979)

40 CFR 1502.17 List of preparers.

The environmental impact statement shall list the names, together with their qualifications (expertise, experience, professional disciplines), of the persons who were primarily responsible for preparing the environmental impact statement or significant background papers, including basic components of the statement (Section 1502.6 and Section 1502.8). Where possible the persons who are responsible for a particular analysis, including analyses in background papers, shall be identified. Normally the list will not exceed two pages.

40 CFR 1502.18 Appendix.

If an agency prepares an appendix to an environmental impact statement the appendix shall:

(a) Consist of material prepared in connection with an environmental impact statement (as distinct from material which is not so prepared and which is incorporated by reference (Section 1502.21)).

(b) Normally consist of material which substantiates any analysis fundamental to the impact statement.

(c) Normally be analytic and relevant to the decision to be made.

(d) Be circulated with the environmental impact statement or be readily available on request.

40 CFR 1502.19 Circulation of the environmental impact statement.

Agencies shall circulate the entire draft and final environmental impact statements except for certain appendices as provided in Section 1502.18(d) and unchanged statements as provided in Section 1503.4(c). However, if the statement is unusually long, the agency may circulate the summary instead, except that the entire statement shall be furnished to:

(a) Any Federal agency which has jurisdiction by law or special expertise with respect to any environmental impact involved and any appropriate Federal, State or local agency authorized to develop and enforce environmental standards.

(b) The applicant, if any.

(c) Any person, organization, or agency requesting the entire environmental impact statement.

(d) In the case of a final environmental impact statement any person, organization, or agency which submitted substantive comments on the draft.

If the agency circulates the summary and thereafter receives a timely request for the entire statement and for additional time to comment, the time for that requestor only shall be extended by at least 15 days beyond the minimum period.

40 CFR 1502.20 Tiering.

Agencies are encouraged to tier their environmental impact statements to eliminate repetitive discussions of the same issues and to focus on the actual issues ripe for decision at each level of environmental review (Section 1508.28). Whenever a broad environmental impact statement has been prepared (such as a program or policy statement) and a subsequent statement or environmental assessment is then prepared on an action included within the entire program or policy (such as a site specific action) the subsequent statement or environmental assessment need only summarize the issues discussed in the broader statement and incorporate discussions from the broader statement by reference and shall concentrate on the issues specific to the subsequent action. The subsequent document shall state where the earlier document is available. Tiering may also be appropriate for different stages of actions. (Section 1508.28).

40 CFR 1502.21 Incorporation by reference.

Agencies shall incorporate material into an environmental impact statement by reference when the effect will be to cut down on bulk without impeding agency and public review of the action. The incorporated material shall be cited in the statement and its content briefly described. No material may be incorporated by reference unless it is reasonably available for inspection by potentially interested persons within the time allowed for comment. Material based on proprietary data which is itself not available for review and comment shall not be incorporated by reference.

40 CFR 1502.22 Incomplete or unavailable information.

When an agency is evaluating reasonably foreseeable significant adverse effects on the human environment in an environmental impact statement and there is incomplete or unavailable information, the agency shall always make clear that such information is lacking.

(a) If the incomplete information relevant to reasonably foreseeable significant adverse impacts is essential to a reasoned choice among alternatives and the overall costs of obtaining it are not exorbitant, the agency shall include the information in the environmental impact statement.

(b) If the information relevant to reasonably foreseeable significant adverse impacts cannot be obtained because the overall costs of obtaining it are exorbitant or the means to obtain it are not known, the agency shall include within the environmental impact statement:

   (1) A statement that such information is incomplete or unavailable;

   (2) a statement of the relevance of the incomplete or unavailable information to evaluating reasonably foreseeable significant adverse impacts on the human environment;

   (3) a summary of existing credible scientific evidence which is relevant to evaluating the reasonably foreseeable significant adverse impacts on the human environment, and (4) the agency's evaluation of such impacts based upon theoretical approaches or research

methods generally accepted in the scientific community. For the purposes of this section, "reasonably foreseeable" includes impacts which have catastrophic consequences, even if their probability of occurrence is low, provided that the analysis of the impacts is supported by credible scientific evidence, is not based on pure conjecture, and is within the rule of reason.

(c) The amended regulation will be applicable to all environmental impact statements for which a Notice of Intent (40 CFR 1508.22) is published in the Federal Register on or after May 27, 1986. For environmental impact statements in progress, agencies may choose to comply with the requirements of either the original or amended regulation.

(51 FR 15625, Apr. 25, 1986)

40 CFR 1502.23 Cost-benefit analysis.

If a cost-benefit analysis relevant to the choice among environmentally different alternatives is being considered for the proposed action, it shall be incorporated by reference or appended to the statement as an aid in evaluating the environmental consequences. To assess the adequacy of compliance with section 102(2)(B) of the Act the statement shall, when a cost-benefit analysis is prepared, discuss the relationship between that analysis and any analyses of unquantified environmental impacts, values, and amenities. For purposes of complying with the Act, the weighing of the merits and drawbacks of the various alternatives need not be displayed in a monetary cost-benefit analysis and should not be when there are important qualitative considerations. In any event, an environmental impact statement should at least indicate those considerations, including factors not related to environmental quality, which are likely to be relevant and important to a decision.

40 CFR 1502.24 Methodology and scientific accuracy.

Agencies shall insure the professional integrity, including scientific integrity, of the discussions and analyses in environmental impact statements. They shall identify any methodologies used and shall make explicit reference by footnote to the scientific and other sources relied upon for conclusions in the statement. An agency may place discussion of methodology in an appendix.

40 CFR 1502.25 Environmental review and consultation requirements.

(a) To the fullest extent possible, agencies shall prepare draft environmental impact statements concurrently with and integrated with environmental impact analyses and related surveys and studies required by the Fish and Wildlife Coordination Act (16 U.S.C. 661 et seq.), the National Historic Preservation Act of 1966 (16 U.S.C. 470 et seq.), the Endangered Species Act of 1973 (16 U.S.C. 1531 et seq.), and other environmental review laws and executive orders.

(b) The draft environmental impact statement shall list all Federal permits, licenses, and other entitlements which must be obtained in implementing the proposal. If it is uncertain whether a Federal permit, license, or other entitlement is necessary, the draft environmental impact statement shall so indicate.

40 CFR PART 1503 -- COMMENTING

Sec.
1503.1 Inviting comments.
1503.2 Duty to comment.
1503.3 Specificity of comments.
1503.4 Response to comments.

Authority: NEPA, the Environmental Quality Improvement Act of 1970, as amended (42 U.S.C. 4371 et seq.), sec. 309 of the Clean Air Act, as amended (42 U.S.C. 7609), and E.O. 11514 (Mar. 5, 1970, as amended by E.O. 11991, May 24, 1977).

Source: 43 FR 55997, Nov. 29, 1978, unless otherwise noted.

40 CFR 1503.1 Inviting comments.

(a) After preparing a draft environmental impact statement and before preparing a final environmental impact statement the agency shall:

    (1) Obtain the comments of any Federal agency which has jurisdiction by law or special expertise with respect to any environmental impact involved or which is authorized to develop and enforce environmental standards.

    (2) Request the comments of:

        (i) Appropriate State and local agencies which are authorized to develop and enforce environmental standards;

        (ii) Indian tribes, when the effects may be on a reservation; and

        (iii) Any agency which has requested that it receive statements on actions of the kind proposed.

    Office of Management and Budget Circular A-95 (Revised), through its system of clearinghouses, provides a means of securing the views of State and local environmental agencies. The clearinghouses may be used, by mutual agreement of the lead agency and the clearinghouse, for securing State and local reviews of the draft environmental impact statements.

    (3) Request comments from the applicant, if any.

    (4) Request comments from the public, affirmatively soliciting comments from those persons or organizations who may be interested or affected.

(b) An agency may request comments on a final environmental impact statement before the decision is finally made. In any case other agencies or persons may make comments before the final decision unless a different time is provided under Section 1506.10.

40 CFR 1503.2 Duty to comment.

Federal agencies with jurisdiction by law or special expertise with respect to any environmental impact involved and agencies which are authorized to develop and enforce environmental standards shall comment on statements within their jurisdiction, expertise, or authority. Agencies shall comment within the time period specified for comment in Section 1506.10. A Federal agency may reply that it has no comment. If a cooperating agency is satisfied that its views are adequately reflected in the environmental impact statement, it should reply that it has no comment.

40 CFR 1503.3 Specificity of comments.

(a) Comments on an environmental impact statement or on a proposed action shall be as specific as possible and may address either the adequacy of the statement or the merits of the alternatives discussed or both.

(b) When a commenting agency criticizes a lead agency's predictive methodology, the commenting agency should describe the alternative methodology which it prefers and why.

(c)   A cooperating agency shall specify in its comments whether it needs additional information to fulfill other applicable environmental reviews or consultation requirements and what information it needs. In particular, it shall specify any additional information it needs to comment adequately on the draft statement's analysis of significant site-specific effects associated with the granting or approving by that cooperating agency of necessary Federal permits, licenses, or entitlements.

(d)   When a cooperating agency with jurisdiction by law objects to or expresses reservations about the proposal on grounds of environmental impacts, the agency expressing the objection or reservation shall specify the mitigation measures it considers necessary to allow the agency to grant or approve applicable permit, license, or related requirements or concurrences.

40 CFR 1503.4 Response to comments.

(a)   An agency preparing a final environmental impact statement shall assess and consider comments both individually and collectively, and shall respond by one or more of the means listed below, stating its response in the final statement. Possible responses are to:

(1)   Modify alternatives including the proposed action.

(2)   Develop and evaluate alternatives not previously given serious consideration by the agency.

(3)   Supplement, improve, or modify its analyses.

(4)   Make factual corrections.

(5)   Explain why the comments do not warrant further agency response, citing the sources, authorities, or reasons which support the agency's position and, if appropriate, indicate those circumstances which would trigger agency reappraisal or further response.

(b)   All substantive comments received on the draft statement (or summaries thereof where the response has been exceptionally voluminous), should be attached to the final statement whether or not the comment is thought to merit individual discussion by the agency in the text of the statement.

(c)   If changes in response to comments are minor and are confined to the responses described in paragraphs (a)(4) and (5) of this section, agencies may write them on errata sheets and attach them to the statement instead of rewriting the draft statement. In such cases only the comments, the responses, and the changes and not the final statement need be circulated (Section 1502.19). The entire document with a new cover sheet shall be filed as the final statement (Section 1506.9).

40 CFR PART 1504 -- PREDECISION REFERRALS TO THE COUNCIL OF PROPOSED FEDERAL ACTIONS DETERMINED TO BE ENVIRONMENTALLY UNSATISFACTORY

Sec.
1504.1 Purpose.
1504.2 Criteria for referral.
1504.3 Procedure for referrals and response.

Authority: NEPA, the Environmental Quality Improvement Act of 1970, as amended (42 U.S.C. 4371 et seq.), sec. 309 of the Clean Air Act, as amended (42 U.S.C. 7609), and E.O. 11514 (Mar. 5, 1970, as amended by E.O. 11991, May 24, 1977).

Source: 43 FR 55998, Nov. 29, 1978, unless otherwise noted.

40 CFR 1504.1 Purpose.

(a) This part establishes procedures for referring to the Council Federal interagency disagreements concerning proposed major Federal actions that might cause unsatisfactory environmental effects. It provides means for early resolution of such disagreements.

(b) Under section 309 of the Clean Air Act (42 U.S.C. 7609), the Administrator of the Environmental Protection Agency is directed to review and comment publicly on the environmental impacts of Federal activities, including actions for which environmental impact statements are prepared. If after this review the Administrator determines that the matter is "unsatisfactory from the standpoint of public health or welfare or environmental quality," section 309 directs that the matter be referred to the Council (hereafter "environmental referrals").

(c) Under section 102(2)(C) of the Act other Federal agencies may make similar reviews of environmental impact statements, including judgments on the acceptability of anticipated environmental impacts. These reviews must be made available to the President, the Council and the public.

40 CFR 1504.2 Criteria for referral.

Environmental referrals should be made to the Council only after concerted, timely (as early as possible in the process), but unsuccessful attempts to resolve differences with the lead agency. In determining what environmental objections to the matter are appropriate to refer to the Council, an agency should weigh potential adverse environmental impacts, considering:

(a) Possible violation of national environmental standards or policies.

(b) Severity.

(c) Geographical scope.

(d) Duration.

(e) Importance as precedents.

(f) Availability of environmentally preferable alternatives.

40 CFR 1504.3 Procedure for referrals and response.

(a) A Federal agency making the referral to the Council shall:

(1) Advise the lead agency at the earliest possible time that it intends to refer a matter to the Council unless a satisfactory agreement is reached.

(2) Include such advice in the referring agency's comments on the draft environmental impact statement, except when the statement does not contain adequate information to permit an assessment of the matter's environmental acceptability.

(3) Identify any essential information that is lacking and request that it be made available at the earliest possible time.

(4) Send copies of such advice to the Council.

(b) The referring agency shall deliver its referral to the Council not later than twenty-five (25) days after the final environmental impact statement has been made available to the Environmental Protection Agency, commenting agencies, and the public. Except when an extension of this period has been granted by the lead agency, the Council will not accept a referral after that date.

(c) The referral shall consist of:

(1) A copy of the letter signed by the head of the referring agency and delivered to the lead agency informing the lead agency of the referral and the reasons for it, and requesting that no action be taken to implement the matter until the Council acts upon the referral. The letter shall include a copy of the statement referred to in (c)(2) of this section.

(2) A statement supported by factual evidence leading to the conclusion that the matter is unsatisfactory from the standpoint of public health or welfare or environmental quality. The statement shall:

(i) Identify any material facts in controversy and incorporate (by reference if appropriate) agreed upon facts,

(ii) Identify any existing environmental requirements or policies which would be violated by the matter,

(iii) Present the reasons why the referring agency believes the matter is environmentally unsatisfactory,

(iv) Contain a finding by the agency whether the issue raised is of national importance because of the threat to national environmental resources or policies or for some other reason,

(v) Review the steps taken by the referring agency to bring its concerns to the attention of the lead agency at the earliest possible time, and

(vi) Give the referring agency's recommendations as to what mitigation alternative, further study, or other course of action (including abandonment of the matter) are necessary to remedy the situation.

(d) Not later than twenty-five (25) days after the referral to the Council the lead agency may deliver a response to the Council, and the referring agency. If the lead agency requests more time and gives assurance that the matter will not go forward in the interim, the Council may grant an extension. The response shall:

(1) Address fully the issues raised in the referral.

(2) Be supported by evidence.

(3) Give the lead agency's response to the referring agency's recommendations.

(e) Interested persons (including the applicant) may deliver their views in writing to the Council. Views in support of the referral should be delivered not later than the referral. Views in support of the response shall be delivered not later than the response.

(f) Not later than twenty-five (25) days after receipt of both the referral and any response or upon being informed that there will be no response (unless the lead agency agrees to a longer time), the Council may take one or more of the following actions:

(1) Conclude that the process of referral and response has successfully resolved the problem.

(2) Initiate discussions with the agencies with the objective of mediation with referring and lead agencies.

(3) Hold public meetings or hearings to obtain additional views and information.

(4) Determine that the issue is not one of national importance and request the referring and lead agencies to pursue their decision process.

(5) Determine that the issue should be further negotiated by the referring and lead agencies and is not appropriate for Council consideration until one or more heads of agencies report to the Council that the agencies' disagreements are irreconcilable.

(6) Publish its findings and recommendations (including where appropriate a finding that the submitted evidence does not support the position of an agency).

(7) When appropriate, submit the referral and the response together with the Council's recommendation to the President for action.

(g) The Council shall take no longer than 60 days to complete the actions specified in paragraph (f)(2), (3), or (5) of this section.

(h) When the referral involves an action required by statute to be determined on the record after opportunity for agency hearing, the referral shall be conducted in a manner consistent with 5 U.S.C. 557(d) (Administrative Procedure Act).

(43 FR 55998, Nov. 29, 1978; 44 FR 873, Jan. 3, 1979)

40 CFR PART 1505 -- NEPA AND AGENCY DECISIONMAKING

Sec.
1505.1 Agency decisionmaking procedures.
1505.2 Record of decision in cases requiring environmental impact statements.
1505.3 Implementing the decision.

Authority: NEPA, the Environmental Quality Improvement Act of 1970, as amended (42 U.S.C. 4371 et seq.), sec. 309 of the Clean Air Act, as amended (42 U.S.C. 7609), and E.O. 11514 (Mar. 5, 1970, as amended by E.O. 11991, May 24, 1977).

Source: 43 FR 55998, Nov. 29, 1978, unless otherwise noted.

40 CFR 1505.1 Agency decisionmaking procedures.

Agencies shall adopt procedures (Section 1507.3) to ensure that decisions are made in accordance with the policies and purposes of the Act. Such procedures shall include but not be limited to:

(a) Implementing procedures under section 102(2) to achieve the requirements of sections 101 and 102(1).

(b) Designating the major decision points for the agency's principal programs likely to have a significant effect on the human environment and assuring that the NEPA process corresponds with them.

(c) Requiring that relevant environmental documents, comments, and responses be part of the record in formal rulemaking or adjudicatory proceedings.

(d) Requiring that relevant environmental documents, comments, and responses accompany the proposal through existing agency review processes so that agency officials use the statement in making decisions.

(e) Requiring that the alternatives considered by the decisionmaker are encompassed by the range of alternatives discussed in the relevant environmental documents and that the decisionmaker consider the alternatives described in the environmental impact statement. If another decision document accompanies the relevant environmental documents to the decisionmaker, agencies are encouraged to make available to the public before the decision is made any part of that document that relates to the comparison of alternatives.

40 CFR 1505.2 Record of decision in cases requiring environmental impact statements.

At the time of its decision (Section 1506.10) or, if appropriate, its recommendation to Congress, each agency shall prepare a concise public record of decision. The record, which may be integrated into any other record prepared by the agency, including that required by OMB Circular A-95 (Revised), part I, sections 6(c) and (d), and Part II, section 5(b)(4), shall:

(a) State what the decision was.

(b) Identify all alternatives considered by the agency in reaching its decision, specifying the alternative or alternatives which were considered to be environmentally preferable. An agency may discuss preferences among alternatives based on relevant factors including economic and technical considerations and agency statutory missions. An agency shall identify and discuss all such factors including any essential considerations of national policy which were balanced by the agency in making its decision and state how those considerations entered into its decision.

(c) State whether all practicable means to avoid or minimize environmental harm from the alternative selected have been adopted, and if not, why they were not. A monitoring and enforcement program shall be adopted and summarized where applicable for any mitigation.

40 CFR 1505.3 Implementing the decision.

Agencies may provide for monitoring to assure that their decisions are carried out and should do so in important cases. Mitigation (Section 1505.2(c)) and other conditions established in the environmental impact statement or during its review and committed as part of the decision shall be implemented by the lead agency or other appropriate consenting agency. The lead agency shall:

(a) Include appropriate conditions in grants, permits or other approvals.

(b) Condition funding of actions on mitigation.

(c) Upon request, inform cooperating or commenting agencies on progress in carrying out mitigation measures which they have proposed and which were adopted by the agency making the decision.

(d) Upon request, make available to the public the results of relevant monitoring.

40 CFR PART 1506

Sec.
1506.1 Limitations on actions during NEPA process.
1506.2 Elimination of duplication with State and local procedures.
1506.3 Adoption.
1506.4 Combining documents.
1506.5 Agency responsibility.
1506.6 Public involvement.
1506.7 Further guidance.
1506.8 Proposals for legislation.
1506.9 Filing requirements.
1506.10 Timing of agency action.
1506.11 Emergencies.
1506.12 Effective date.

Authority: NEPA, the Environmental Quality Improvement Act of 1970, as amended (42 U.S.C. 4371 et seq.), sec. 309 of the Clean Air Act, as amended (42 U.S.C. 7609), and E.O. 11514 (Mar. 5, 1970, as amended by E.O. 11991, May 24, 1977).

Source: 43 FR 56000, Nov. 29, 1978, unless otherwise noted.

40 CFR 1506.1 Limitations on actions during NEPA process.

(a) Until an agency issues a record of decision as provided in Section 1505.2 (except as provided in paragraph (c) of this section), no action concerning the proposal shall be taken which would:

    (1) Have an adverse environmental impact; or

    (2) Limit the choice of reasonable alternatives.

(b) If any agency is considering an application from a non-Federal entity, and is aware that the applicant is about to take an action within the agency's jurisdiction that would meet either of the criteria in paragraph (a) of this section, then the agency shall promptly notify the applicant that the agency will take appropriate action to insure that the objectives and procedures of NEPA are achieved.

(c) While work on a required program environmental impact statement is in progress and the action is not covered by an existing program statement, agencies shall not undertake in the interim any major Federal action covered by the program which may significantly affect the quality of the human environment unless such action:

    (1) Is justified independently of the program;

    (2) Is itself accompanied by an adequate environmental impact statement; and

    (3) Will not prejudice the ultimate decision on the program. Interim action prejudices the ultimate decision on the program when it tends to determine subsequent development or limit alternatives.

(d) This section does not preclude development by applicants of plans or designs or performance of other work necessary to support an application for Federal, State or local permits or assistance. Nothing in this section shall preclude Rural Electrification Administration approval of minimal expenditures not affecting the environment (e.g. long leadtime equipment and purchase options) made by non-governmental entities seeking loan guarantees from the Administration.

40 CFR 1506.2 Elimination of duplication with State and local procedures.

(a) Agencies authorized by law to cooperate with State agencies of statewide jurisdiction pursuant to section 102(2)(D) of the Act may do so.

(b) Agencies shall cooperate with State and local agencies to the fullest extent possible to reduce duplication between NEPA and State and local requirements, unless the agencies are specifically barred from doing so by some other law. Except for cases covered by paragraph (a) of this section, such cooperation shall to the fullest extent possible include:

    (1) Joint planning processes.

    (2) Joint environmental research and studies.

    (3) Joint public hearings (except where otherwise provided by statute).

    (4) Joint environmental assessments.

(c) Agencies shall cooperate with State and local agencies to the fullest extent possible to reduce duplication between NEPA and comparable State and local requirements, unless the agencies are specifically barred from doing so by some other law. Except for cases covered by paragraph (a) of this section, such cooperation shall to the fullest extent possible include joint environmental impact statements. In such cases one or more Federal agencies and one or more State or local agencies shall be joint lead agencies. Where State laws or local ordinances have environmental impact statement requirements in addition to but not in conflict with those in NEPA, Federal agencies shall cooperate in fulfilling these requirements as well as those of Federal laws so that one document will comply with all applicable laws.

(d) To better integrate environmental impact statements into State or local planning processes, statements shall discuss any inconsistency of a proposed action with any approved State or local plan and laws (whether or not federally sanctioned). Where an inconsistency exists, the statement should describe the extent to which the agency would reconcile its proposed action with the plan or law.

40 CFR 1506.3 Adoption.

(a) An agency may adopt a Federal draft or final environmental impact statement or portion thereof provided that the statement or portion thereof meets the standards for an adequate statement under these regulations.

(b) If the actions covered by the original environmental impact statement and the proposed action are substantially the same, the agency adopting another agency's statement is not required to recirculate it except as a final statement. Otherwise the adopting agency shall treat the statement as a draft and recirculate it (except as provided in paragraph (c) of this section).

(c) A cooperating agency may adopt without recirculating the environmental impact statement of a lead agency when, after an independent review of the statement, the cooperating agency concludes that its comments and suggestions have been satisfied.

(d) When an agency adopts a statement which is not final within the agency that prepared it, or when the action it assesses is the subject of a referral under Part 1504, or when the statement's adequacy is the subject of a judicial action which is not final, the agency shall so specify.

40 CFR 1506.4 Combining documents.

Any environmental document in compliance with NEPA may be combined with any other agency document to reduce duplication and paperwork.

40 CFR 1506.5 Agency responsibility.

(a) Information. If an agency requires an applicant to submit environmental information for possible use by the agency in preparing an environmental impact statement, then the agency should assist the applicant by outlining the types of information required. The agency shall independently evaluate the information submitted and shall be responsible for its accuracy. If the agency chooses to use the information submitted by the applicant in the environmental impact statement, either directly or by reference, then the names of the persons responsible for the independent evaluation shall be included in the list of preparers (Section 1502.17). It is the intent of this paragraph that acceptable work not be redone, but that it be verified by the agency.

(b) Environmental assessments. If an agency permits an applicant to prepare an environmental assessment, the agency, besides fulfilling the requirements of paragraph (a) of this section, shall make its own evaluation of the environmental issues and take responsibility for the scope and content of the environmental assessment.

(c) Environmental impact statements. Except as provided in Section 1506.2 and Section 1506.3 any environmental impact statement prepared pursuant to the requirements of NEPA shall be prepared directly by or by a contractor selected by the lead agency or where appropriate under Section 1501.6(b), a cooperating agency. It is the intent of these regulations that the contractor be chosen solely by the lead agency, or by the lead agency in cooperation with cooperating agencies, or where appropriate by a cooperating agency to avoid any conflict of interest. Contractors shall execute a disclosure statement prepared by the lead agency, or where appropriate the cooperating agency, specifying that they have no financial or other interest in the outcome of the project. If the document is prepared by contract, the responsible Federal official shall furnish guidance and participate in the preparation and shall independently evaluate the statement prior to its approval and take responsibility for its scope and contents. Nothing in this section is intended to prohibit any agency from requesting any person to submit information to it or to prohibit any person from submitting information to any agency.

40 CFR 1506.6 Public involvement.

Agencies shall:

(a) Make diligent efforts to involve the public in preparing and implementing their NEPA procedures.

(b) Provide public notice of NEPA-related hearings, public meetings, and the availability of environmental documents so as to inform those persons and agencies who may be interested or affected.

 (1) In all cases the agency shall mail notice to those who have requested it on an individual action.

 (2) In the case of an action with effects of national concern notice shall include publication in the Federal Register and notice by mail to national organizations reasonably expected to be interested in the matter and may include listing in the 102 Monitor. An agency engaged in rulemaking may provide notice by mail to national organizations who have requested that notice regularly be provided. Agencies shall maintain a list of such organizations.

 (3) In the case of an action with effects primarily of local concern the notice may include:

  (i) Notice to State and areawide clearinghouses pursuant to OMB Circular A-95 (Revised).

  (ii) Notice to Indian tribes when effects may occur on reservations.

  (iii) Following the affected State's public notice procedures for comparable actions.

  (iv) Publication in local newspapers (in papers of general circulation rather than legal papers).

  (v) Notice through other local media.

  (vi) Notice to potentially interested community organizations including small business associations.

  (vii) Publication in newsletters that may be expected to reach potentially interested persons.

  (viii) Direct mailing to owners and occupants of nearby or affected property.

  (ix) Posting of notice on and off site in the area where the action is to be located.

(c) Hold or sponsor public hearings or public meetings whenever appropriate or in accordance with statutory requirements applicable to the agency.

Criteria shall include whether there is:

(1) Substantial environmental controversy concerning the proposed action or substantial interest in holding the hearing.

(2) A request for a hearing by another agency with jurisdiction over the action supported by reasons why a hearing will be helpful. If a draft environmental impact statement is to be considered at a public hearing, the agency should make the statement available to the public at least 15 days in advance (unless the purpose of the hearing is to provide information for the draft environmental impact statement).

(d) Solicit appropriate information from the public.

(e) Explain in its procedures where interested persons can get information or status reports on environmental impact statements and other elements of the NEPA process.

(f) Make environmental impact statements, the comments received, and any underlying documents available to the public pursuant to the provisions of the Freedom of Information Act (5 U.S.C. 552), without regard to the exclusion for interagency memoranda where such memoranda transmit comments of Federal agencies on the environmental impact of the proposed action. Materials to be made available to the public shall be provided to the public without charge to the extent practicable, or at a fee which is not more than the actual costs of reproducing copies required to be sent to other Federal agencies, including the Council.

40 CFR 1506.7 Further guidance.

The Council may provide further guidance concerning NEPA and its procedures including:

(a) A handbook which the Council may supplement from time to time, which shall in plain language provide guidance and instructions concerning the application of NEPA and these regulations.

(b) Publication of the Council's Memoranda to Heads of Agencies.

(c) In conjunction with the Environmental Protection Agency and the publication of the 102 Monitor, notice of:

(1) Research activities;

(2) Meetings and conferences related to NEPA; and

(3) Successful and innovative procedures used by agencies to implement NEPA.

40 CFR 1506.8 Proposals for legislation.

(a) The NEPA process for proposals for legislation (Section 1508.17) significantly affecting the quality of the human environment shall be integrated with the legislative process of the Congress. A legislative environmental impact statement is the detailed statement required by law to be included in a recommendation or report on a legislative proposal to Congress. A legislative environmental impact statement shall be considered part of the formal transmittal of a legislative proposal to Congress; however, it may be transmitted to Congress up to 30 days later in order to allow time for completion of an accurate statement which can serve as the basis for public and Congressional debate. The statement must be available in time for Congressional hearings and deliberations.

(b) Preparation of a legislative environmental impact statement shall conform to the requirements of these regulations except as follows:

(1) There need not be a scoping process.

(2) The legislative statement shall be prepared in the same manner as a draft statement, but shall be considered the "detailed statement" required by statute; Provided, That when any of the following conditions exist both the draft and final environmental impact statement on the legislative proposal shall be prepared and circulated as provided by Section 1503.1 and Section 1506.10.

    (i) A Congressional Committee with jurisdiction over the proposal has a rule requiring both draft and final environmental impact statements.

    (ii) The proposal results from a study process required by statute (such as those required by the Wild and Scenic Rivers Act (16 U.S.C. 1271 et seq.) and the Wilderness Act (16 U.S.C. 1131 et seq.)).

    (iii) Legislative approval is sought for Federal or federally assisted construction or other projects which the agency recommends be located at specific geographic locations. For proposals requiring an environmental impact statement for the acquisition of space by the General Services Administration, a draft statement shall accompany the Prospectus or the 11(b) Report of Building Project Surveys to the Congress, and a final statement shall be completed before site acquisition.

    (iv) The agency decides to prepare draft and final statements.

(c) Comments on the legislative statement shall be given to the lead agency which shall forward them along with its own responses to the Congressional committees with jurisdiction.

40 CFR 1506.9 Filing requirements.

Environmental impact statements together with comments and responses shall be filed with the Environmental Protection Agency, attention Office of Federal Activities (A-104), 401 M Street SW., Washington, DC 20460. Statements shall be filed with EPA no earlier than they are also transmitted to commenting agencies and made available to the public. EPA shall deliver one copy of each statement to the Council, which shall satisfy the requirement of availability to the President. EPA may issue guidelines to agencies to implement its responsibilities under this section and Section 1506.10.

40 CFR 1506.10 Timing of agency action.

(a) The Environmental Protection Agency shall publish a notice in the Federal Register each week of the environmental impact statements filed during the preceding week. The minimum time periods set forth in this section shall be calculated from the date of publication of this notice.

(b) No decision on the proposed action shall be made or recorded under Section 1505.2 by a Federal agency until the later of the following dates:

(1) Ninety (90) days after publication of the notice described above in paragraph (a) of this section for a draft environmental impact statement.

(2) Thirty (30) days after publication of the notice described above in paragraph (a) of this section for a final environmental impact statement.

An exception to the rules on timing may be made in the case of an agency decision which is subject to a formal internal appeal. Some agencies have a formally established appeal process which allows other agencies or the public to take appeals on a decision and make their views known, after publication of the final environmental impact statement. In such cases, where a real opportunity exists to alter the decision, the decision may be made and recorded at the same time the environmental impact statement is published. This means that the period for appeal of the decision and the 30-day period prescribed in paragraph (b)(2) of this section may run concurrently. In such cases the environmental impact statement shall explain the timing and the public's right of appeal. An agency engaged in rulemaking under the Administrative Procedure Act or other statute for the purpose of protecting the public health or safety, may waive the time period in paragraph (b)(2) of this section and publish a decision on the final rule simultaneously with publication of the notice of the availability of the final environmental impact statement as described in paragraph (a) of this section.

(c) If the final environmental impact statement is filed within ninety (90) days after a draft environmental impact statement is filed with the Environmental Protection Agency, the minimum thirty (30) day period and the minimum ninety (90) day period may run concurrently. However, subject to paragraph (d) of this section agencies shall allow not less than 45 days for comments on draft statements.

(d) The lead agency may extend prescribed periods. The Environmental Protection Agency may upon a showing by the lead agency of compelling reasons of national policy reduce the prescribed periods and may upon a showing by any other Federal agency of compelling reasons of national policy also extend prescribed periods, but only after consultation with the lead agency. (Also see Section 1507.3(d).) Failure to file timely comments shall not be a sufficient reason for extending a period. If the lead agency does not concur with the extension of time, EPA may not extend it for more than 30 days. When the Environmental Protection Agency reduces or extends any period of time it shall notify the Council.

(43 FR 56000, Nov. 29, 1978; 44 FR 874, Jan. 3, 1979)

40 CFR 1506.11 Emergencies.

Where emergency circumstances make it necessary to take an action with significant environmental impact without observing the provisions of these regulations, the Federal agency taking the action should consult with the Council about alternative arrangements. Agencies and the Council will limit such arrangements to actions necessary to control the immediate impacts of the emergency. Other actions remain subject to NEPA review.

40 CFR 1506.12 Effective date.

The effective date of these regulations is July 30, 1979, except that for agencies that administer programs that qualify under section 102(2)(D) of the Act or under section 104(h) of the Housing and Community Development Act of 1974 an additional four months shall be allowed for the State or local agencies to adopt their implementing procedures.

(a) These regulations shall apply to the fullest extent practicable to ongoing activities and environmental documents begun before the effective date. These regulations do not apply to an environmental impact statement or supplement if the draft statement was filed before the effective date of these regulations. No completed environmental documents need be redone by reasons of these regulations. Until these regulations are applicable, the Council's guidelines published in the Federal Register of August 1, 1973, shall continue to be applicable. In cases where these regulations are applicable the guidelines are superseded. However, nothing shall prevent an agency from proceeding under these regulations at an earlier time.

(b) NEPA shall continue to be applicable to actions begun before January 1, 1970, to the fullest extent possible.

40 CFR PART 1507 -- AGENCY COMPLIANCE

Sec.
1507.1 Compliance.
1507.2 Agency capability to comply.
1507.3 Agency procedures.

Authority: NEPA, the Environmental Quality Improvement Act of 1970, as amended (42 U.S.C. 4371 et seq.), sec. 309 of the Clean Air Act, as amended (42 U.S.C. 7609), and E.O. 11514 (Mar. 5, 1970, as amended by E.O. 11991, May 24, 1977).

Source: 43 FR 56002, Nov. 29, 1978, unless otherwise noted.

40 CFR 1507.1 Compliance.

All agencies of the Federal Government shall comply with these regulations. It is the intent of these regulations to allow each agency flexibility in adapting its implementing procedures authorized by Section 1507.3 to the requirements of other applicable laws.

40 CFR 1507.2 Agency capability to comply.

Each agency shall be capable (in terms of personnel and other resources) of complying with the requirements enumerated below. Such compliance may include use of other's resources, but the using agency shall itself have sufficient capability to evaluate what others do for it. Agencies shall:

(a) Fulfill the requirements of section 102(2)(A) of the Act to utilize a systematic, interdisciplinary approach which will insure the integrated use of the natural and social sciences and the environmental design arts in planning and in decisionmaking which may have an impact on the human environment. Agencies shall designate a person to be responsible for overall review of agency NEPA compliance.

(b) Identify methods and procedures required by section 102(2)(B) to insure that presently unquantified environmental amenities and values may be given appropriate consideration.

(c) Prepare adequate environmental impact statements pursuant to section 102(2)(C) and comment on statements in the areas where the agency has jurisdiction by law or special expertise or is authorized to develop and enforce environmental standards.

(d) Study, develop, and describe alternatives to recommended courses of action in any proposal which involves unresolved conflicts concerning alternative uses of available resources. This requirement of section 102(2)(E) extends to all such proposals, not just the more limited scope of section 102(2)(C)(iii) where the discussion of alternatives is confined to impact statements.

(e) Comply with the requirements of section 102(2)(H) that the agency initiate and utilize ecological information in the planning and development of resource-oriented projects.

(f) Fulfill the requirements of sections 102(2)(F), 102(2)(G), and 102(2)(I), of the Act and of Executive Order 11514, Protection and Enhancement of Environmental Quality, Sec. 2.

40 CFR 1507.3 Agency procedures.

(a) Not later than eight months after publication of these regulations as finally adopted in the Federal Register, or five months after the establishment of an agency, whichever shall come later, each agency shall as necessary adopt procedures to supplement these regulations. When the agency is a department, major subunits are encouraged (with the consent of the department) to adopt their own procedures. Such procedures shall not paraphrase these regulations. They shall confine themselves to implementing procedures. Each agency shall consult with the Council while developing its procedures and before publishing them in the Federal Register for comment. Agencies with similar programs should consult with each other and the Council to coordinate their procedures, especially for programs requesting similar information from applicants. The procedures shall be adopted only after an opportunity for public review and after review by the Council for conformity with the Act and these regulations. The Council shall complete its review within 30 days. Once in effect they shall be filed with the Council and made readily available to the public. Agencies are encouraged to publish explanatory guidance for these regulations and their own procedures. Agencies shall continue to review their policies and procedures and in consultation with the Council to revise them as necessary to ensure full compliance with the purposes and provisions of the Act.

(b) Agency procedures shall comply with these regulations except where compliance would be inconsistent with statutory requirements and shall include:

(1) Those procedures required by Sections 1501.2(d), 1502.9(c)(3), 1505.1, 1506.6(e), and 1508.4.

(2) Specific criteria for and identification of those typical classes of action:

(i) Which normally do require environmental impact statements.

(ii) Which normally do not require either an environmental impact statement or an environmental assessment (categorical exclusions (Section 1508.4)).

(iii) Which normally require environmental assessments but not necessarily environmental impact statements.

(c) Agency procedures may include specific criteria for providing limited exceptions to the provisions of these regulations for classified proposals. They are proposed actions which are specifically authorized under criteria established by an Executive Order or statute to be kept secret in the interest of national defense or foreign policy and are in fact properly classified pursuant to such Executive Order or statute. Environmental assessments and environmental impact statements which address classified proposals may be safeguarded and restricted from public dissemination in accordance with agencies' own regulations applicable to classified information. These documents may be organized so that classified portions can be included as annexes, in order that the unclassified portions can be made available to the public.

(d) Agency procedures may provide for periods of time other than those presented in Section 1506.10 when necessary to comply with other specific statutory requirements.

(e) Agency procedures may provide that where there is a lengthy period between the agency's decision to prepare an environmental impact statement and the time of actual preparation, the notice of intent required by Section 1501.7 may be published at a reasonable time in advance of preparation of the draft statement.

32 CFR 989.7 Classified actions. (40 CFR 1507.3)

The fact that a proposed action is classified does not relieve the proponent from complying with NEPA. In such cases, necessary classified environmental documents must be prepared, safeguarded, and disseminated to the decision-maker or others according to requirements that apply to classified information.

40 CFR Part 1508 -- TERMINOLOGY AND INDEX

Sec.
1508.1 Terminology.
1508.2 Act.
1508.3 Affecting.
1508.4 Categorical exclusion.
1508.5 Cooperating agency.
1508.6 Council.
1508.7 Cumulative impacts.
1508.8 Effects.
1508.9 Environmental assessment.
1508.10 Environmental document.
1508.11 Environmental impact statement.
1508.12 Federal Agency.
1508.13 Finding of no significant impact.
1508.14 Human environment.
1508.15 Jurisdiction by law.
1508.16 Lead agency.
1508.17 Legislation.
1508.18 Major Federal action.
1508.19 Matter.
1508.20 Mitigation.
1508.21 NEPA process.
1508.22 Notice of intent.
1508.23 Proposal.
1508.24 Referring agency.
1508.25 Scope.
1508.26 Special expertise.
1508.27 Significantly.
1508.28 Tiering.

Authority: NEPA, the Environmental Quality Improvement Act of 1970, as amended (42 U.S.C. 4371 et seq.), sec.309 of the Clean Air Act, as amended (42 U.S.C. 7609), and E.O. 11514 (Mar.5, 1970, as amended by E.O. 11991, May 24, 1977).

Source: 43 FR 56003, Nov. 29, 1978, unless otherwise noted.

40 CFR 1508.1 Terminology.

The terminology of this part shall be uniform throughout the Federal Government.

40 CFR 1508.2 Act.

"Act" means the National Environmental Policy Act, as amended (42 U.S.C. 4321, et seq.) which is also referred to as "NEPA."

40 CFR 1508.3 Affecting.

"Affecting" means will or may have an effect on.

40 CFR 1508.4 Categorical exclusion.

"Categorical exclusion" means a category of actions which do not individually or cumulatively have a significant effect on the human environment and which have been found to have no such effect in procedures adopted by a Federal agency in implementation of these regulations (Section 1507.3) and for which, therefore, neither an environmental assessment nor an environmental impact statement is required. An agency may decide in its procedures or otherwise, to prepare environmental assessments for the reasons stated in Section 1508.9 even though it is not required to do so. Any procedures under this section shall provide for extraordinary circumstances in which a normally excluded action may have a significant environmental effect.

40 CFR 1508.5 Cooperating agency.

"Cooperating agency" means any Federal agency other than a lead agency which has jurisdiction by law or special expertise with respect to any environmental impact involved in a proposal (or a reasonable alternative) for legislation or other major Federal action significantly affecting the quality of the human environment. The selection and responsibilities of a cooperating agency are described in 1501.6. A State or local agency of similar qualifications or, when the effects are on a reservation, an Indian Tribe, may by agreement with the lead agency become a cooperating agency.

40 CFR 1508.6 Council.

"Council" means the Council on Environmental Quality established by Title II of the Act.

40 CFR 1508.7 Cumulative impact.

"Cumulative impact" is the impact on the environment which results from the incremental impact of the action when added to other past, present, and reasonably foreseeable future actions regardless of what agency (Federal or non-Federal) or person undertakes such other actions. Cumulative impacts can result from individually minor but collectively significant actions taking place over a period of time.

40 CFR 1508.8 Effects.

"Effects" include:

(a) Direct effects, which are caused by the action and occur at the same time and place.

(b) Indirect effects, which are caused by the action and are later in time or farther removed in distance, but are still reasonably foreseeable. Indirect effects may include growth inducing effects and other effects related to induced changes in the pattern of land use, population density or growth rate, and related effects on air and water and other natural systems, including ecosystems.

Effects and impacts as used in these regulations are synonymous. Effects includes ecological (such as the effects on natural resources and on the components, structures, and functioning of affected ecosystems), aesthetic, historic, cultural, economic, social, or health, whether direct, indirect, or cumulative. Effects may also include those resulting from actions which may have both beneficial and detrimental effects, even if on balance the agency believes that the effect will be beneficial.

40 CFR 1508.9 Environmental assessment.

"Environmental assessment":

(a) Means a concise public document for which a Federal agency is responsible that serves to:

(1) Briefly provide sufficient evidence and analysis for determining whether to prepare an environmental impact statement or a finding of no significant impact.

(2) Aid an agency's compliance with the Act when no environmental impact statement is necessary.

(3) Facilitate preparation of a statement when one is necessary.

(b) Shall include brief discussions of the need for the proposal, of alternatives as required by section 102(2)(E), of the environmental impacts of the proposed action and alternatives, and a listing of agencies and persons consulted.

40 CFR 1508.10 Environmental document.

"Environmental document" includes the documents specified in Section 1508.9 (environmental assessment), Section 1508.11 (environmental impact statement), Section 1508.13 (finding of no significant impact), and Section 1508.22 (notice of intent).

40 CFR 1508.11 Environmental impact statement.

"Environmental impact statement" means a detailed written statement as required by section 102(2)(C) of the Act.

40 CFR 1508.12 Federal agency.

"Federal agency" means all agencies of the Federal Government. It does not mean the Congress, the Judiciary, or the President, including the performance of staff functions for the President in his Executive Office. It also includes for purposes of these regulations States and units of general local government and Indian tribes assuming NEPA responsibilities under section 104(h) of the Housing and Community Development Act of 1974.

40 CFR 1508.13 Finding of no significant impact.

"Finding of no significant impact" means a document by a Federal agency briefly presenting the reasons why an action, not otherwise excluded (Section 1508.4), will not have a significant effect on the human environment and for which an environmental impact statement therefore will not be prepared. It shall include the environmental assessment or a summary of it and shall note any other environmental documents related to it (Section 1501.7(a)(5)). If the assessment is included, the finding need not repeat any of the discussion in the assessment but may incorporate it by reference.

40 CFR 1508.14 Human environment.

"Human environment" shall be interpreted comprehensively to include the natural and physical environment and the relationship of people with that environment. (See the definition of "effects" (Section 1508.8).) This means that economic or social effects are not intended by themselves to require preparation of an environmental impact statement. When an environmental impact statement is prepared and economic or social and natural or physical environmental effects are interrelated, then the environmental impact statement will discuss all of these effects on the human environment.

40 CFR 1508.15 Jurisdiction by law.

''Jurisdiction by law'' means agency authority to approve, veto, or finance all or part of the proposal.

40 CFR 1508.16 Lead agency.

''Lead agency'' means the agency or agencies preparing or having taken primary responsibility for preparing the environmental impact statement.

40 CFR 1508.17 Legislation.

''Legislation'' includes a bill or legislative proposal to Congress developed by or with the significant cooperation and support of a Federal agency, but does not include requests for appropriations. The test for significant cooperation is whether the proposal is in fact predominantly that of the agency rather than another source. Drafting does not by itself constitute significant cooperation. Proposals for legislation include requests for ratification of treaties. Only the agency which has primary responsibility for the subject matter involved will prepare a legislative environmental impact statement.

40 CFR 1508.18 Major Federal action.

''Major Federal action'' includes actions with effects that may be major and which are potentially subject to Federal control and responsibility. Major reinforces but does not have a meaning independent of significantly (Section 1508.27). Actions include the circumstance where the responsible officials fail to act and that failure to act is reviewable by courts or administrative tribunals under the Administrative Procedure Act or other applicable law as agency action.

(a) Actions include new and continuing activities, including projects and programs entirely or partly financed, assisted, conducted, regulated, or approved by federal agencies; new or revised agency rules, regulations, plans, policies, or procedures; and legislative proposals (Section 1506.8, Section 1508.17). Actions do not include funding assistance solely in the form of general revenue sharing funds, distributed under the State and Local Fiscal Assistance Act of 1972, 31 U.S.C. 1221 et seq., with no Federal agency control over the subsequent use of such funds. Actions do not include bringing judicial or administrative civil or criminal enforcement actions.

(b) Federal actions tend to fall within one of the following categories:

(1) Adoption of official policy, such as rules, regulations, and interpretations adopted pursuant to the Administrative Procedure Act, 5 U.S.C. 551 et seq.; treaties and international conventions or agreements; formal documents establishing an agency's policies which will result in or substantially alter agency programs.

(2) Adoption of formal plans, such as official documents prepared or approved by federal agencies which guide or prescribe alternative uses of Federal resources, upon which future agency actions will be based.

(3) Adoption of programs, such as a group of concerted actions to implement a specific policy or plan; systematic and connected agency decisions allocating agency resources to implement a specific statutory program or executive directive.

(4) Approval of specific projects, such as construction or management activities located in a defined geographic area. Projects include actions approved by permit or other regulatory decision as well as federal and federally assisted activities.

40 CFR 1508.19 Matter.

"Matter" includes for purposes of Part 1504:

(a) With respect to the Environmental Protection Agency, any proposed legislation, project, action or regulation as those terms are used in section 309(a) of the Clean Air Act (42 U.S.C. 7609).

(b) With respect to all other agencies, any proposed major federal action to which section 102(2)(C) of NEPA applies.

40 CFR 1508.20 Mitigation.

"Mitigation" includes:

(a) Avoiding the impact altogether by not taking a certain action or parts of an action.

(b) Minimizing impacts by limiting the degree or magnitude of the action and its implementation.

(c) Rectifying the impact by repairing, rehabilitating, or restoring the affected environment.

(d) Reducing or eliminating the impact over time by preservation and maintenance operations during the life of the action.

(e) Compensating for the impact by replacing or providing substitute resources or environments.

40 CFR 1508.21 NEPA process.

"NEPA process" means all measures necessary for compliance with the requirements of section 2 and Title I of NEPA.

40 CFR 1508.22 Notice of intent.

"Notice of intent" means a notice that an environmental impact statement will be prepared and considered. The notice shall briefly:

(a) Describe the proposed action and possible alternatives.

(b) Describe the agency's proposed scoping process including whether, when, and where any scoping meeting will be held.

(c) State the name and address of a person within the agency who can answer questions about the proposed action and the environmental impact statement.

40 CFR 1508.23 Proposal.

"Proposal" exists at that stage in the development of an action when an agency subject to the Act has a goal and is actively preparing to make a decision on one or more alternative means of accomplishing that goal and the effects can be meaningfully evaluated. Preparation of an environmental impact statement on a proposal should be timed (Section 1502.5) so that the final statement may be completed in time for the statement to be included in any recommendation or report on the proposal. A proposal may exist in fact as well as by agency declaration that one exists.

40 CFR 1508.24 Referring agency.

"Referring agency" means the federal agency which has referred any matter to the Council after a determination that the matter is unsatisfactory from the standpoint of public health or welfare or environmental quality.

40 CFR 1508.25 Scope.

Scope consists of the range of actions, alternatives, and impacts to be considered in an environmental impact statement. The scope of an individual statement may depend on its relationships to other statements (Section 1502.20 and Section 1508.28). To determine the scope of environmental impact statements, agencies shall consider 3 types of actions, 3 types of alternatives, and 3 types of impacts. They include:

(a) Actions (other than unconnected single actions) which may be:

    (1) Connected actions, which means that they are closely related and therefore should be discussed in the same impact statement. Actions are connected if they:

        (i) Automatically trigger other actions which may require environmental impact statements.

        (ii) Cannot or will not proceed unless other actions are taken previously or simultaneously.

        (iii) Are interdependent parts of a larger action and depend on the larger action for their justification.

    (2) Cumulative actions, which when viewed with other proposed actions have cumulatively significant impacts and should therefore be discussed in the same impact statement.

    (3) Similar actions, which when viewed with other reasonably foreseeable or proposed agency actions, have similarities that provide a basis for evaluating their environmental consequences together, such as common timing or geography. An agency may wish to analyze these actions in the same impact statement. It should do so when the best way to assess adequately the combined impacts of similar actions or reasonable alternatives to such actions is to treat them in a single impact statement.

(b) Alternatives, which include:

    (1) No action alternative.

    (2) Other reasonable courses of actions.

    (3) Mitigation measures (not in the proposed action).

(c) Impacts, which may be: (1) Direct; (2) indirect; (3) cumulative.

40 CFR 1508.26 Special expertise.

"Special expertise" means statutory responsibility, agency mission, or related program experience.

40 CFR 1508.27 Significantly.

"Significantly" as used in NEPA requires considerations of both context and intensity:

(a) Context. This means that the significance of an action must be analyzed in several contexts such as society as a whole (human, national), the affected region, the affected interests, and the locality. Significance varies with the setting of the proposed action. For instance, in the case of a site-specific action, significance would usually depend upon the effects in the locale rather than in the world as a whole. Both short- and long-term effects are relevant.

(b) Intensity. This refers to the severity of impact. Responsible officials must bear in mind that more than one agency may make decisions about partial aspects of a major action. The following should be considered in evaluating intensity:

(1) Impacts that may be both beneficial and adverse. A significant effect may exist even if the Federal agency believes that on balance the effect will be beneficial.

(2) The degree to which the proposed action affects public health or safety.

(3) Unique characteristics of the geographic area such as proximity to historic or cultural resources, park lands, prime farmlands, wetlands, wild and scenic rivers, or ecologically critical areas.

(4) The degree to which the effects on the quality of the human environment are likely to be highly controversial.

(5) The degree to which the possible effects on the human environment are highly uncertain or involve unique or unknown risks.

(6) The degree to which the action may establish a precedent for future actions with significant effects or represents a decision in principle about a future consideration.

(7) Whether the action is related to other actions with individually insignificant but cumulatively significant impacts. Significance exists if it is reasonable to anticipate a cumulatively significant impact on the environment. Significance cannot be avoided by terming an action temporary or by breaking it down into small component parts.

(8) The degree to which the action may adversely affect districts, sites, highways, structures, or objects listed in or eligible for listing in the National Register of Historic Places or may cause loss or destruction of significant scientific, cultural, or historical resources.

(9) The degree to which the action may adversely affect an endangered or threatened species or its habitat that has been determined to be critical under the Endangered Species Act of 1973.

(10) Whether the action threatens a violation of Federal, State, or local law or requirements imposed for the protection of the environment.

(43 FR 56003, Nov. 29, 1978; 44 FR 874, Jan. 3, 1979)

40 CFR 1508.28 Tiering.

"Tiering" refers to the coverage of general matters in broader environmental impact statements (such as national program or policy statements) with subsequent narrower statements or environmental analyses (such as regional or basinwide program statements or ultimately site-specific statements) incorporating by reference the general discussions and concentrating solely on the issues specific to the statement subsequently prepared. Tiering is appropriate when the sequence of statements or analyses is:

(a) From a program, plan, or policy environmental impact statement to a program, plan, or policy statement or analysis of lesser scope or to a site-specific statement or analysis.

(b) From an environmental impact statement on a specific action at an early stage (such as need and site selection) to a supplement (which is preferred) or a subsequent statement or analysis at a later stage (such as environmental mitigation). Tiering in such cases is appropriate when it helps the lead agency to focus on the issues which are ripe for decision and exclude from consideration issues already decided or not yet ripe.

INDEX TO PARTS 1500 THROUGH 1508 OF CEQ NEPA REGULATIONS

APPENDIX 3 MEMORANDUM: FORTY MOST ASKED QUESTIONS CONCERNING CEQ'S NEPA REGULATIONS (40 QUESTIONS)*

MEMORANDUM: QUESTIONS AND ANSWERS ABOUT THE NEPA REGULATIONS

INDEX

---

* **Source:** 46 Fed. Reg. 18026 (March 23, 1981), as amended, 51 Fed. Reg. 15618 (April 25, 1986)

31. Application of Regulations to Independent Regulatory Agencies
32. Supplements to Old EISs
33. Referrals
34. Records of Decision
35. Time Required for the NEPA Process
36. Environmental Assessments (EA)
37. Findings of No Significant Impact (FONSI)
38. Public Availability of EAs v. FONSIs
39. Mitigation Measures Imposed in EAs and FONSIs
40. Propriety of Issuing EA When Mitigation Reduces Impacts

1a. Range of Alternatives. What is meant by "range of alternatives" as referred to in Sec. 1505.1(e)? [1]

    A. The phrase "range of alternatives" refers to the alternatives discussed in environmental documents. It includes all reasonable alternatives, which must be rigorously explored and objectively evaluated, as well as those other alternatives, which are eliminated from detailed study with a brief discussion of the reasons for eliminating them. Section 1502.14. A decisionmaker must not consider alternatives beyond the range of alternatives discussed in the relevant environmental documents. Moreover, a decisionmaker must, in fact, consider all the alternatives discussed in an EIS. Section 1505.1(e).

1b. How many alternatives have to be discussed when there is an infinite number of possible alternatives?

    A. For some proposals there may exist a very large or even an infinite number of possible reasonable alternatives. For example, a proposal to designate wilderness areas within a National Forest could be said to involve an infinite number of alternatives from 0 to 100 percent of the forest. When there are potentially a very large number of alternatives, only a reasonable number of examples, covering the full spectrum of alternatives, must be analyzed and compared in the EIS. An appropriate series of alternatives might include dedicating 0, 10, 30, 50, 70, 90, or 100 percent of the forest to wilderness. What constitutes a reasonable range of alternatives depends on the nature of the proposal and the facts in each case.

2a. Alternatives Outside the Capability of Applicant or Jurisdiction of Agency. If an EIS is prepared in connection with an application for a permit or other federal approval, must the EIS rigorously analyze and discuss alternatives that are outside the capability of the applicant or can it be limited to reasonable alternatives that can be carried out by the applicant?

    A. Section 1502.14 requires the EIS to examine all reasonable alternatives to the proposal. In determining the scope of alternatives to be considered, the emphasis is on what is "reasonable" rather than on whether the proponent or applicant likes or is itself capable of carrying out a particular alternative. Reasonable alternatives include those that are practical or feasible from the technical and economic standpoint and using common sense, rather than simply desirable from the standpoint of the applicant.

2b. Must the EIS analyze alternatives outside the jurisdiction or capability of the agency or beyond what Congress has authorized?

    A. An alternative that is outside the legal jurisdiction of the lead agency must still be analyzed in the EIS if it is reasonable. A potential conflict with local or federal law does not necessarily render an alternative unreasonable, although such conflicts must be considered. Section 1506.2(d). Alternatives that are outside the scope of what Congress has approved or funded must still be evaluated in the EIS if they are reasonable, because the EIS may serve as the basis for modifying the Congressional approval or funding in light of NEPA's goals and policies. Section 1500.1(a).

3. **No-Action Alternative. What does the "no action" alternative include? If an agency is under a court order or legislative command to act, must the EIS address the "no action" alternative?**

A. Section 1502.14(d) requires the alternatives analysis in the EIS to "include the alternative of no action." There are two distinct interpretations of "no action" that must be considered, depending on the nature of the proposal being evaluated. The first situation might involve an action such as updating a land management plan where ongoing programs initiated under existing legislation and regulations will continue, even as new plans are developed. In these cases "no action" is "no change" from current management direction or level of management intensity. To construct an alternative that is based on no management at all would be a useless academic exercise. Therefore, the "no action" alternative may be thought of in terms of continuing with the present course of action until that action is changed. Consequently, projected impacts of alternative management schemes would be compared in the EIS to those impacts projected for the existing plan. In this case, alternatives would include management plans of both greater and lesser intensity, especially greater and lesser levels of resource development.

The second interpretation of "no action" is illustrated in instances involving federal decisions on proposals for projects. "No action" in such cases would mean the proposed activity would not take place, and the resulting environmental effects from taking no action would be compared with the effects of permitting the proposed activity or an alternative activity to go forward.

Where a choice of "no action" by the agency would result in predictable actions by others, this consequence of the "no action" alternative should be included in the analysis. For example, if denial of permission to build a railroad to a facility would lead to construction of a road and increased truck traffic, the EIS should analyze this consequence of the "no action" alternative.

In light of the above, it is difficult to think of a situation where it would not be appropriate to address a "no action" alternative. Accordingly, the regulations require the analysis of the no action alternative even if the agency is under a court order or legislative command to act. This analysis provides a benchmark, enabling decisionmakers to compare the magnitude of environmental effects of the action alternatives. It is also an example of a reasonable alternative outside the jurisdiction of the agency which must be analyzed. Section 1502.14(c). See Question 2 above. Inclusion of such an analysis in the EIS is necessary to inform the Congress, the public, and the President as intended by NEPA. Section 1500.1(a).

4a. **Agency's Preferred Alternative. What is the "agency's preferred alternative"?**

A. The "agency's preferred alternative" is the alternative which the agency believes would fulfill its statutory mission and responsibilities, giving consideration to economic, environmental, technical and other factors. The concept of the "agency's preferred alternative" is different from the "environmentally preferable alternative," although in some cases one alternative may be both. See Question 6 below. It is identified so that agencies and the public can understand the lead agency's orientation.

4b. Does the "preferred alternative" have to be identified in the Draft EIS and the Final EIS or just in the Final EIS?

    A. Section 1502.14(e) requires the section of the EIS on alternatives to "identify the agency's preferred alternative if one or more exists, in the draft statement, and identify such alternative in the final statement . . ." This means that if the agency has a preferred alternative at the Draft EIS stage, that alternative must be labeled or identified as such in the Draft EIS. If the responsible federal official in fact has no preferred alternative at the Draft EIS stage, a preferred alternative need not be identified there. By the time the Final EIS is filed, Section 1502.14(e) presumes the existence of a preferred alternative and requires its identification in the Final EIS "unless another law prohibits the expression of such a preference."

4c. Who recommends or determines the "preferred alternative?"

    A. The lead agency's official with line responsibility for preparing the EIS and assuring its adequacy is responsible for identifying the agency's preferred alternative(s). The NEPA regulations do not dictate which official in an agency shall be responsible for preparation of EISs, but agencies can identify this official in their implementing procedures, pursuant to Section 1507.3.

    Even though the agency's preferred alternative is identified by the EIS preparer in the EIS, the statement must be objectively prepared and not slanted to support the choice of the agency's preferred alternative over the other reasonable and feasible alternatives.

5. Proposed Action v. Preferred Alternative. Is the "proposed action" the same thing as the "preferred alternative"?

    A. The "proposed action" may be, but is not necessarily, the agency's "preferred alternative." The proposed action may be a proposal in its initial form before undergoing analysis in the EIS process. If the proposed action is internally generated, such as preparing a land management plan, the proposed action might end up as the agency's preferred alternative. On the other hand the proposed action may be granting an application to a non-federal entity for a permit. The agency may or may not have a "preferred alternative" at the Draft EIS stage (see Question 4 above). In that case the agency may decide at the Final EIS stage, on the basis of the Draft EIS and the public and agency comments, that an alternative other than the proposed action is the agency's "preferred alternative."

5b. Is the analysis of the "proposed action" in an EIS to be treated differently from the analysis of alternatives?

    A. The degree of analysis devoted to each alternative in the EIS is to be substantially similar to that devoted to the "proposed action." Section 1502.14 is titled "Alternatives including the proposed action" to reflect such comparable treatment. Section 1502.14(b) specifically requires "substantial treatment" in the EIS of each alternative including the proposed action. This regulation does not dictate an amount of information to be provided, but rather, prescribes a level of treatment, which may in turn require varying amounts of information, to enable a reviewer to evaluate and compare alternatives.

6a. **Environmentally Preferable Alternative. What is the meaning of the term "environmentally preferable alternative" as used in the regulations with reference to Records of Decision? How is the term "environment" used in the phrase?**

A. Section 1505.2(b) requires that, in cases where an EIS has been prepared, the Record of Decision (ROD) must identify all alternatives that were considered, ". . . specifying the alternative or alternatives which were considered to be environmentally preferable." The environmentally preferable alternative is the alternative that will promote the national environmental policy as expressed in NEPA's Section 101. Ordinarily, this means the alternative that causes the least damage to the biological and physical environment; it also means the alternative which best protects, preserves, and enhances historic, cultural, and natural resources.

The Council recognizes that the identification of the environmentally preferable alternative may involve difficult judgments, particularly when one environmental value must be balanced against another. The public and other agencies reviewing a Draft EIS can assist the lead agency to develop and determine environmentally preferable alternatives by providing their views in comments on the Draft EIS. Through the identification of the environmentally preferable alternative, the decisionmaker is clearly faced with a choice between that alternative and others, and must consider whether the decision accords with the Congressionally declared policies of the Act.

6b. **Who recommends or determines what is environmentally preferable?**

A. The agency EIS staff is encouraged to make recommendations of the environmentally preferable alternative(s) during EIS preparation. In any event the lead agency official responsible for the EIS is encouraged to identify the environmentally preferable alternative(s) in the EIS. In all cases, commentors from other agencies and the public are also encouraged to address this question. The agency must identify the environmentally preferable alternative in the ROD.

7. **Difference Between Sections of EIS on Alternatives and Environmental Consequences. What is the difference between the sections in the EIS on "alternatives" and "environmental consequences"? How do you avoid duplicating the discussion of alternatives in preparing these two sections?**

A. The "alternatives" section is the heart of the EIS. This section rigorously explores and objectively evaluates all reasonable alternatives including the proposed action. Section 1502.14. It should include relevant comparisons on environmental and other grounds. The "environmental consequences" section of the EIS discusses the specific environmental impacts or effects of each of the alternatives including the proposed action. Section 1502.16. In order to avoid duplication between these two sections, most of the "alternatives" section should be devoted to describing and comparing the alternatives. Discussion of the environmental impacts of these alternatives should be limited to a concise descriptive summary of such impacts in a comparative form, including charts or tables, thus sharply defining the issues and providing a clear basis for choice among options. Section 1502.14. The "environmental consequences" section should be devoted largely to a scientific analysis of the direct and indirect environmental effects of the proposed action and of each of the alternatives. It forms the analytic basis for the concise comparison in the "alternatives" section.

8. **Early Application of NEPA. Section 1501.2(d) of the NEPA regulations requires agencies to provide for the early application of NEPA to cases where actions are planned by private**

applicants or non-Federal entities and are, at some stage, subject to federal approval of permits, loans, loan guarantees, insurance or other actions. What must and can agencies do to apply NEPA early in these cases?

A. Section 1501.2(d) requires federal agencies to take steps toward ensuring that private parties and state and local entities initiate environmental studies as soon as federal involvement in their proposals can be foreseen. This section is intended to ensure that environmental factors are considered at an early stage in the planning process and to avoid the situation where the applicant for a federal permit or approval has completed planning and eliminated all alternatives to the proposed action by the time the EIS process commences or before the EIS process has been completed.

Through early consultation, business applicants and approving agencies may gain better appreciation of each other's needs and foster a decisionmaking process which avoids later unexpected confrontations.

Federal agencies are required by Section 1507.3(b) to develop procedures to carry out Section 1501.2(d). The procedures should include an "outreach program", such as a means for prospective applicants to conduct pre-application consultations with the lead and cooperating agencies. Applicants need to find out, in advance of project planning, what environmental studies or other information will be required, and what mitigation requirements are likely, in connection with the later federal NEPA process. Agencies should designate staff to advise potential applicants of the agency's NEPA information requirements and should publicize their pre-application procedures and information requirements in newsletters or other media used by potential applicants.

Complementing Section 1501.2(d), Section 1506.5(a) requires agencies to assist applicants by outlining the types of information required in those cases where the agency requires the applicant to submit environmental data for possible use by the agency in preparing an EIS.

Section 1506.5(b) allows agencies to authorize preparation of environmental assessments by applicants. Thus, the procedures should also include a means for anticipating and utilizing applicants' environmental studies or "early corporate environmental assessments" to fulfill some of the federal agency's NEPA obligations. However, in such cases the agency must still evaluate independently the environmental issues and take responsibility for the environmental assessment.

These provisions are intended to encourage and enable private and other non-federal entities to build environmental considerations into their own planning processes in a way that facilitates the application of NEPA and avoids delay.

9. **Applicant Who Needs Other Permits.** To what extent must an agency inquire into whether an applicant for a federal permit, funding or other approval of a proposal will also need approval from another agency for the same proposal or some other related aspect of it?

A. Agencies must integrate the NEPA process into other planning at the earliest possible time to insure that planning and decisions reflect environmental values, to avoid delays later in the process, and to head off potential conflicts. Specifically, the agency must "provide for cases where actions are planned by . . . applicants," so that designated staff are available to advise potential applicants of studies or other information that will foreseeably be required for the later federal action; the agency shall consult with the applicant if the agency foresees its own involvement in the proposal; and it shall insure that the NEPA process commences at the earliest possible time. Section 1501.2(d). (See Question 8.)

The regulations emphasize agency cooperation early in the NEPA process. Section 1501.6. Section 1501.7 on "scoping" also provides that all affected Federal agencies are to be invited to participate in scoping the environmental issues and to identify the various environmental review and consultation requirements that may apply to the proposed action. Further, Section 1502.25(b) requires that the draft EIS list all the federal permits, licenses and other entitlements that are needed to implement the proposal.

These provisions create an affirmative obligation on federal agencies to inquire early, and to the maximum degree possible, to ascertain whether an applicant is or will be seeking other federal assistance or approval, or whether the applicant is waiting until a proposal has been substantially developed before requesting federal aid or approval.

Thus, a federal agency receiving a request for approval or assistance should determine whether the applicant has filed separate requests for federal approval or assistance with other federal agencies. Other federal agencies that are likely to become involved should then be contacted, and the NEPA process coordinated, to insure an early and comprehensive analysis of the direct and indirect effects of the proposal and any related actions. The agency should inform the applicant that action on its application may be delayed unless it submits all other federal applications (where feasible to do so), so that all the relevant agencies can work together on the scoping process and preparation of the EIS.

10a. Limitations on Action During 30-Day Review Period for Final EIS. What actions by agencies and/or applicants are allowed during EIS preparation and during the 30-day review period after publication of a final EIS?

   A. No federal decision on the proposed action shall be made or recorded until at least 30 days after the publication by EPA of notice that the particular EIS has been filed with EPA. Sections 1505.2 and 1506.10. Section 1505.2 requires this decision to be stated in a public Record of Decision.

   Until the agency issues its Record of Decision, no action by an agency or an applicant concerning the proposal shall be taken which would have an adverse environmental impact or limit the choice of reasonable alternatives. Section 1506.1(a). But this does not preclude preliminary planning or design work which is needed to support an application for permits or assistance. Section 1506.1(d).

   When the impact statement in question is a program EIS, no major action concerning the program may be taken which may significantly affect the quality of the human environment, unless the particular action is justified independently of the program, is accompanied by its own adequate environmental impact statement and will not prejudice the ultimate decision on the program. Section 1506.1(c).

10b. Do these limitations on action (described in Question 10a) apply to state or local agencies that have statutorily delegated responsibility for preparation of environmental documents required by NEPA, for example, under the HUD Block Grant program?

   A. Yes, these limitations do apply, without any variation from their application to federal agencies.

11. **Limitations on Actions by an Applicant During EIS Process.** What actions must a lead agency take during the NEPA process when it becomes aware that a non-federal applicant is about to take an action within the agency's jurisdiction that would either have an adverse environmental impact or limit the choice of reasonable alternatives (e.g., prematurely commit money or other resources towards the completion of the proposal)?

A. The federal agency must notify the applicant that the agency will take strong affirmative steps to insure that the objectives and procedures of NEPA are fulfilled. Section 1506.1(b). These steps could include seeking injunctive measures under NEPA, or the use of sanctions available under either the agency's permitting authority or statutes setting forth the agency's statutory mission. For example, the agency might advise an applicant that if it takes such action the agency will not process its application.

12a. **Effective Date and Enforceability of the Regulations.** What actions are subject to the Council's new regulations, and what actions are grandfathered under the old guidelines?

A. The effective date of the Council's regulations was July 30, 1979 (except for certain HUD programs under the Housing and Community Development Act, 42 U.S.C. 5304(h), and certain state highway programs that qualify under Section 102(2)(D) of NEPA for which the regulations became effective on November 30, 1979). All the provisions of the regulations are binding as of that date, including those covering decisionmaking, public participation, referrals, limitations on actions, EIS supplements, etc. For example, a Record of Decision would be prepared even for decisions where the draft EIS was filed before July 30, 1979.

But in determining whether or not the new regulations apply to the preparation of a particular environmental document, the relevant factor is the date of filing of the draft of that document. Thus, the new regulations do not require the redrafting of an EIS or supplement if the draft EIS or supplement was filed before July 30, 1979. However, a supplement prepared after the effective date of the regulations for an EIS issued in final before the effective date of the regulations would be controlled by the regulations.

Even though agencies are not required to apply the regulations to an EIS or other document for which the draft was filed prior to July 30, 1979, the regulations encourage agencies to follow the regulations "to the fullest extent practicable," i.e., if it is feasible to do so, in preparing the final document. Section 1506.12(a).

12b. **Are projects authorized by Congress before the effective date of the Council's regulations grandfathered?**

A. No. The date of Congressional authorization for a project is not determinative of whether the Council's regulations or former Guidelines apply to the particular proposal. No incomplete projects or proposals of any kind are grandfathered in whole or in part. Only certain environmental documents, for which the draft was issued before the effective date of the regulations, are grandfathered and subject to the Council's former Guidelines.

12c. **Can a violation of the regulations give rise to a cause of action?**

A. While a trivial violation of the regulations would not give rise to an independent cause of action, such a cause of action would arise from a substantial violation of the regulations. Section 1500.3.

13. **Use of Scoping Before Notice of Intent to Prepare EIS.** Can the scoping process be used in connection with preparation of an environmental assessment, i.e., before both the decision to proceed with an EIS and publication of a notice of intent?

   A. Yes. Scoping can be a useful tool for discovering alternatives to a proposal, or significant impacts that may have been overlooked. In cases where an environmental assessment is being prepared to help an agency decide whether to prepare an EIS, useful information might result from early participation by other agencies and the public in a scoping process.

   The regulations state that the scoping process is to be preceded by a Notice of Intent (NOI) to prepare an EIS. But that is only the minimum requirement. Scoping may be initiated earlier, as long as there is appropriate public notice and enough information available on the proposal so that the public and relevant agencies can participate effectively.

   However, scoping that is done before the assessment, and in aid of its preparation, cannot substitute for the normal scoping process after publication of the NOI, unless the earlier public notice stated clearly that this possibility was under consideration, and the NOI expressly provides that written comments on the scope of alternatives and impacts will still be considered.

14a. **Rights and Responsibilities of Lead and Cooperating Agencies.** What are the respective rights and responsibilities of lead and cooperating agencies? What letters and memoranda must be prepared?

   A. After a lead agency has been designated (Sec. 1501.5), that agency has the responsibility to solicit cooperation from other federal agencies that have jurisdiction by law or special expertise on any environmental issue that should be addressed in the EIS being prepared. Where appropriate, the lead agency should seek the cooperation of state or local agencies of similar qualifications. When the proposal may affect an Indian reservation, the agency should consult with the Indian tribe. Section 1508.5. The request for cooperation should come at the earliest possible time in the NEPA process.

   After discussions with the candidate cooperating agencies, the lead agency and the cooperating agencies are to determine by letter or by memorandum which agencies will undertake cooperating responsibilities. To the extent possible at this stage, responsibilities for specific issues should be assigned. The allocation of responsibilities will be completed during scoping. Section 1501.7(a)(4).

   Cooperating agencies must assume responsibility for the development of information and the preparation of environmental analyses at the request of the lead agency. Section 1501.6(b)(3). Cooperating agencies are now required by Section 1501.6 to devote staff resources that were normally primarily used to critique or comment on the Draft EIS after its preparation, much earlier in the NEPA process -- primarily at the scoping and Draft EIS preparation stages. If a cooperating agency determines that its resource limitations preclude any involvement, or the degree of involvement (amount of work) requested by the lead agency, it must so inform the lead agency in writing and submit a copy of this correspondence to the Council. Section 1501.6(c).

   In other words, the potential cooperating agency must decide early if it is able to devote any of its resources to a particular proposal. For this reason the regulation states that an agency may reply to a request for cooperation that "other program commitments preclude any involvement or the degree of involvement requested in the action that is the subject of the environmental impact statement." (Emphasis added). The regulation refers to the "action," rather than to the EIS, to clarify that the agency is taking itself out of all phases of the federal action, not just draft EIS preparation. This means that the agency has determined that it cannot be involved in the later stages of EIS review and comment, as well as decisionmaking on the proposed action. For this reason, cooperating agencies with jurisdiction by law (those which have permitting or other approval authority) cannot opt out entirely of the duty to cooperate on the EIS. See also Question 15, relating specifically to the responsibility of EPA.

14b. How are disputes resolved between lead and cooperating agencies concerning the scope and level of detail of analysis and the quality of data in impact statements?

A. Such disputes are resolved by the agencies themselves. A lead agency, of course, has the ultimate responsibility for the content of an EIS. But it is supposed to use the environmental analysis and recommendations of cooperating agencies with jurisdiction by law or special expertise to the maximum extent possible, consistent with its own responsibilities as lead agency. Section 1501.6(a)(2).

If the lead agency leaves out a significant issue or ignores the advice and expertise of the cooperating agency, the EIS may be found later to be inadequate. Similarly, where cooperating agencies have their own decisions to make and they intend to adopt the environmental impact statement and base their decisions on it, one document should include all of the information necessary for the decisions by the cooperating agencies. Otherwise they may be forced to duplicate the EIS process by issuing a new, more complete EIS or Supplemental EIS, even though the original EIS could have sufficed if it had been properly done at the outset. Thus, both lead and cooperating agencies have a stake in producing a document of good quality. Cooperating agencies also have a duty to participate fully in the scoping process to ensure that the appropriate range of issues is determined early in the EIS process.

Because the EIS is not the Record of Decision, but instead constitutes the information and analysis on which to base a decision, disagreements about conclusions to be drawn from the EIS need not inhibit agencies from issuing a joint document, or adopting another agency's EIS, if the analysis is adequate. Thus, if each agency has its own "preferred alternative," both can be identified in the EIS. Similarly, a cooperating agency with jurisdiction by law may determine in its own ROD that alternative A is the environmentally preferable action, even though the lead agency has decided in its separate ROD that Alternative B is environmentally preferable.

14c. What are the specific responsibilities of federal and state cooperating agencies to review draft EISs?

A. Cooperating agencies (i.e., agencies with jurisdiction by law or special expertise) and agencies that are authorized to develop or enforce environmental standards, must comment on environmental impact statements within their jurisdiction, expertise or authority. Sections 1503.2, 1508.5. If a cooperating agency is satisfied that its views are adequately reflected in the environmental impact statement, it should simply comment accordingly. Conversely, if the cooperating agency determines that a draft EIS is incomplete, inadequate or inaccurate, or it has other comments, it should promptly make such comments, conforming to the requirements of specificity in section 1503.3.

14d. How is the lead agency to treat the comments of another agency with jurisdiction by law or special expertise which has failed or refused to cooperate or participate in scoping or EIS preparation?

A. A lead agency has the responsibility to respond to all substantive comments raising significant issues regarding a draft EIS. Section 1503.4. However, cooperating agencies are generally under an obligation to raise issues or otherwise participate in the EIS process during scoping and EIS preparation if they reasonably can do so. In practical terms, if a cooperating agency fails to cooperate at the outset, such as during scoping, it will find that its comments at a later stage will not be as persuasive to the lead agency.

15. Commenting Responsibilities of EPA. Are EPA's responsibilities to review and comment on the environmental effects of agency proposals under Section 309 of the Clean Air Act independent of its responsibility as a cooperating agency?

A. Yes. EPA has an obligation under Section 309 of the Clean Air Act to review and comment in writing on the environmental impact of any matter relating to the authority of the Administrator contained in proposed legislation, federal construction projects, other federal actions requiring EISs, and new regulations. 42 U.S.C. Sec. 7609. This obligation is independent of its role as a cooperating agency under the NEPA regulations.

16. Third Party Contracts. What is meant by the term "third party contracts" in connection with the preparation of an EIS? See Section 1506.5(c). When can "third party contracts" be used?

A. As used by EPA and other agencies, the term "third party contract" refers to the preparation of EISs by contractors paid by the applicant. In the case of an EIS for a National Pollution Discharge Elimination System (NPDES) permit, the applicant, aware in the early planning stages of the proposed project of the need for an EIS, contracts directly with a consulting firm for its preparation. See 40 C.F.R. 6.604(g). The "third party" is EPA which, under Section 1506.5(c), must select the consulting firm, even though the applicant pays for the cost of preparing the EIS. The consulting firm is responsible to EPA for preparing an EIS that meets the requirements of the NEPA regulations and EPA's NEPA procedures. It is in the applicant's interest that the EIS comply with the law so that EPA can take prompt action on the NPDES permit application. The "third party contract" method under EPA's NEPA procedures is purely voluntary, though most applicants have found it helpful in expediting compliance with NEPA.

If a federal agency uses "third party contracting," the applicant may undertake the necessary paperwork for the solicitation of a field of candidates under the agency's direction, so long as the agency complies with Section 1506.5(c). Federal procurement requirements do not apply to the agency because it incurs no obligations or costs under the contract, nor does the agency procure anything under the contract.

17a. Disclosure Statement to Avoid Conflict of Interest. If an EIS is prepared with the assistance of a consulting firm, the firm must execute a disclosure statement. What criteria must the firm follow in determining whether it has any "financial or other interest in the outcome of the project" which would cause a conflict of interest?

A. Section 1506.5(c), which specifies that a consulting firm preparing an EIS must execute a disclosure statement, does not define "financial or other interest in the outcome of the project." The Council interprets this term broadly to cover any known benefits other than general enhancement of professional reputation. This includes any financial benefit such as a promise of future construction or design work on the project, as well as indirect benefits the consultant is aware of (e.g., if the project would aid proposals sponsored by the firm's other clients). For example, completion of a highway project may encourage construction of a shopping center or industrial park from which the consultant stands to benefit. If a consulting firm is aware that it has such an interest in the decision on the proposal, it should be disqualified from preparing the EIS, to preserve the objectivity and integrity of the NEPA process.

When a consulting firm has been involved in developing initial data and plans for the project, but does not have any financial or other interest in the outcome of the decision, it need not be disqualified from preparing the EIS. However, a disclosure statement in the draft EIS should clearly state the scope and extent of the firm's prior involvement to expose any potential conflicts of interest that may exist.

17b. If the firm in fact has no promise of future work or other interest in the outcome of the proposal, may the firm later bid in competition with others for future work on the project if the proposed action is approved?

    A. Yes.

18. Uncertainties About Indirect Effects of A Proposal. How should uncertainties about indirect effects of a proposal be addressed, for example, in cases of disposal of federal lands, when the identity or plans of future landowners is unknown?

    A. The EIS must identify all the indirect effects that are known, and make a good faith effort to explain the effects that are not known but are "reasonably foreseeable." Section 1508.8(b). In the example, if there is total uncertainty about the identity of future land owners or the nature of future land uses, then of course, the agency is not required to engage in speculation or contemplation about their future plans. But, in the ordinary course of business, people do make judgments based upon reasonably foreseeable occurrences. It will often be possible to consider the likely purchasers and the development trends in that area or similar areas in recent years; or the likelihood that the land will be used for an energy project, shopping center, subdivision, farm or factory. The agency has the responsibility to make an informed judgment, and to estimate future impacts on that basis, especially if trends are ascertainable or potential purchasers have made themselves known. The agency cannot ignore these uncertain, but probable, effects of its decisions.

19a. Mitigation Measures. What is the scope of mitigation measures that must be discussed?

    A. The mitigation measures discussed in an EIS must cover the range of impacts of the proposal. The measures must include such things as design alternatives that would decrease pollution emissions, construction impacts, esthetic intrusion, as well as relocation assistance, possible land use controls that could be enacted, and other possible efforts. Mitigation measures must be considered even for impacts that by themselves would not be considered "significant." Once the proposal itself is considered as a whole to have significant effects, all of its specific effects on the environment (whether or not "significant") must be considered, and mitigation measures must be developed where it is feasible to do so. Sections 1502.14(f), 1502.16(h), 1508.14.

19b. How should an EIS treat the subject of available mitigation measures that are (1) outside the jurisdiction of the lead or cooperating agencies, or (2) unlikely to be adopted or enforced by the responsible agency?

A. All relevant, reasonable mitigation measures that could improve the project are to be identified, even if they are outside the jurisdiction of the lead agency or the cooperating agencies, and thus would not be committed as part of the RODs of these agencies. Sections 1502.16(h), 1505.2(c). This will serve to alert agencies or officials who can implement these extra measures, and will encourage them to do so. Because the EIS is the most comprehensive environmental document, it is an ideal vehicle in which to lay out not only the full range of environmental impacts but also the full spectrum of appropriate mitigation.

However, to ensure that environmental effects of a proposed action are fairly assessed, the probability of the mitigation measures being implemented must also be discussed. Thus the EIS and the Record of Decision should indicate the likelihood that such measures will be adopted or enforced by the responsible agencies. Sections 1502.16(h), 1505.2. If there is a history of nonenforcement or opposition to such measures, the EIS and Record of Decision should acknowledge such opposition or nonenforcement. If the necessary mitigation measures will not be ready for a long period of time, this fact, of course, should also be recognized.

20. Worst Case Analysis. [Withdrawn.] [2]

21. Combining Environmental and Planning Documents. Where an EIS or an EA is combined with another project planning document (sometimes called "piggybacking"), to what degree may the EIS or EA refer to and rely upon information in the project document to satisfy NEPA's requirements?

A. Section 1502.25 of the regulations requires that draft EISs be prepared concurrently and integrated with environmental analyses and related surveys and studies required by other federal statutes. In addition, Section 1506.4 allows any environmental document prepared in compliance with NEPA to be combined with any other agency document to reduce duplication and paperwork. However, these provisions were not intended to authorize the preparation of a short summary or outline EIS, attached to a detailed project report or land use plan containing the required environmental impact data. In such circumstances, the reader would have to refer constantly to the detailed report to understand the environmental impacts and alternatives which should have been found in the EIS itself.

The EIS must stand on its own as an analytical document which fully informs decision-makers and the public of the environmental effects of the proposal and those of the reasonable alternatives. Section 1502.1. But, as long as the EIS is clearly identified and is self-supporting, it can be physically included in or attached to the project report or land use plan, and may use attached report material as technical backup.

Forest Service environmental impact statements for forest management plans are handled in this manner. The EIS identifies the agency's preferred alternative, which is developed in detail as the proposed management plan. The detailed proposed plan accompanies the EIS through the review process, and the documents are appropriately cross-referenced. The proposed plan is useful for EIS readers as an example, to show how one choice of management options translates into effects on natural resources. This procedure permits initiation of the 90-day public review of proposed forest plans, which is required by the National Forest Management Act.

All the alternatives are discussed in the EIS, which can be read as an independent document. The details of the management plan are not repeated in the EIS, and vice versa. This is a reasonable functional separation of the documents: the EIS contains information relevant to the choice among alternatives; the plan is a detailed description of proposed management activities suitable for use by the land managers. This procedure provides for concurrent compliance with the public review requirements of both NEPA and the National Forest Management Act.

Under some circumstances, a project report or management plan may be totally merged with the EIS, and the one document labeled as both "EIS" and "management plan" or "project report." This may be reasonable where the documents are short, or where the EIS format and the regulations for clear, analytical EISs also satisfy the requirements for a project report.

22. **State and Federal Agencies as Joint Lead Agencies. May state and federal agencies serve as joint lead agencies? If so, how do they resolve law, policy and resource conflicts under NEPA and the relevant state environmental policy act? How do they resolve differences in perspective where, for example, national and local needs may differ?**

A. Under Section 1501.5(b), federal, state or local agencies, as long as they include at least one federal agency, may act as joint lead agencies to prepare an EIS. Section 1506.2 also strongly urges state and local agencies and the relevant federal agencies to cooperate fully with each other. This should cover joint research and studies, planning activities, public hearings, environmental assessments and the preparation of joint EISs under NEPA and the relevant "little NEPA" state laws, so that one document will satisfy both laws.

The regulations also recognize that certain inconsistencies may exist between the proposed federal action and any approved state or local plan or law. The joint document should discuss the extent to which the federal agency would reconcile its proposed action with such plan or law. Section 1506.2(d). (See Question 23).

Because there may be differences in perspective as well as conflicts among federal, state and local goals for resources management, the Council has advised participating agencies to adopt a flexible, cooperative approach. The joint EIS should reflect all of their interests and missions, clearly identified as such. The final document would then indicate how state and local interests have been accommodated, or would identify conflicts in goals (e.g., how a hydroelectric project, which might induce second home development, would require new land use controls). The EIS must contain a complete discussion of scope and purpose of the proposal, alternatives, and impacts so that the discussion is adequate to meet the needs of local, state and federal decisionmakers.

23a. **Conflicts of Federal Proposal With Land Use Plans, Policies or Controls. How should an agency handle potential conflicts between a proposal and the objectives of Federal, state or local land use plans, policies and controls for the area concerned? See Sec. 1502.16(c).**

A. The agency should first inquire of other agencies whether there are any potential conflicts. If there would be immediate conflicts, or if conflicts could arise in the future when the plans are finished (see Question 23(b) below), the EIS must acknowledge and describe the extent of those conflicts. If there are any possibilities of resolving the conflicts, these should be explained as well. The EIS should also evaluate the seriousness of the impact of the proposal on the land use plans and policies, and whether, or how much, the proposal will impair the effectiveness of land use control mechanisms for the area. Comments from officials of the affected area should be solicited early and should be carefully acknowledged and answered in the EIS.

23b. What constitutes a "land use plan or policy" for purposes of this discussion?

A. The term "land use plans," includes all types of formally adopted documents for land use planning, zoning and related regulatory requirements. Local general plans are included, even though they are subject to future change. Proposed plans should also be addressed if they have been formally proposed by the appropriate government body in a written form, and are being actively pursued by officials of the jurisdiction. Staged plans, which must go through phases of development such as the Water Resources Council's Level A, B and C planning process should also be included even though they are incomplete.

The term "policies" includes formally adopted statements of land use policy as embodied in laws or regulations. It also includes proposals for action such as the initiation of a planning process, or a formally adopted policy statement of the local, regional or state executive branch, even if it has not yet been formally adopted by the local, regional or state legislative body.

23c. What options are available for the decisionmaker when conflicts with such plans or policies are identified?

A. After identifying any potential land use conflicts, the decisionmaker must weigh the significance of the conflicts, among all the other environmental and non-environmental factors that must be considered in reaching a rational and balanced decision. Unless precluded by other law from causing or contributing to any inconsistency with the land use plans, policies or controls, the decisionmaker retains the authority to go forward with the proposal, despite the potential conflict. In the Record of Decision, the decisionmaker must explain what the decision was, how it was made, and what mitigation measures are being imposed to lessen adverse environmental impacts of the proposal, among the other requirements of Section 1505.2. This provision would require the decisionmaker to explain any decision to override land use plans, policies or controls for the area.

24a. Environmental Impact Statements on Policies, Plans or Programs. When are EISs required on policies, plans or programs?

A. An EIS must be prepared if an agency proposes to implement a specific policy, to adopt a plan for a group of related actions, or to implement a specific statutory program or executive directive. Section 1508.18. In addition, the adoption of official policy in the form of rules, regulations and interpretations pursuant to the Administrative Procedure Act, treaties, conventions, or other formal documents establishing governmental or agency policy which will substantially alter agency programs, could require an EIS. Section 1508.18. In all cases, the policy, plan, or program must have the potential for significantly affecting the quality of the human environment in order to require an EIS. It should be noted that a proposal "may exist in fact as well as by agency declaration that one exists." Section 1508.23.

24b. When is an area-wide or overview EIS appropriate?

A. The preparation of an area-wide or overview EIS may be particularly useful when similar actions, viewed with other reasonably foreseeable or proposed agency actions, share common timing or geography. For example, when a variety of energy projects may be located in a single watershed, or when a series of new energy technologies may be developed through federal funding, the overview or area-wide EIS would serve as a valuable and necessary analysis of the affected environment and the potential cumulative impacts of the reasonably foreseeable actions under that program or within that geographical area.

24c. What is the function of tiering in such cases?

A. Tiering is a procedure which allows an agency to avoid duplication of paperwork through the incorporation by reference of the general discussions and relevant specific discussions from an environmental impact statement of broader scope into one of lesser scope or vice versa. In the example given in Question 24b, this would mean that an overview EIS would be prepared for all of the energy activities reasonably foreseeable in a particular geographic area or resulting from a particular development program. This impact statement would be followed by site-specific or project-specific EISs. The tiering process would make each EIS of greater use and meaning to the public as the plan or program develops, without duplication of the analysis prepared for the previous impact statement.

25a. Appendices and Incorporation by Reference. When is it appropriate to use appendices instead of including information in the body of an EIS?

A. The body of the EIS should be a succinct statement of all the information on environmental impacts and alternatives that the decisionmaker and the public need, in order to make the decision and to ascertain that every significant factor has been examined. The EIS must explain or summarize methodologies of research and modeling, and the results of research that may have been conducted to analyze impacts and alternatives.

Lengthy technical discussions of modeling methodology, baseline studies, or other work are best reserved for the appendix. In other words, if only technically trained individuals are likely to understand a particular discussion then it should go in the appendix, and a plain language summary of the analysis and conclusions of that technical discussion should go in the text of the EIS.

The final statement must also contain the agency's responses to comments on the draft EIS. These responses will be primarily in the form of changes in the document itself, but specific answers to each significant comment should also be included. These specific responses may be placed in an appendix. If the comments are especially voluminous, summaries of the comments and responses will suffice. (See Question 29 regarding the level of detail required for responses to comments.)

25b. How does an appendix differ from incorporation by reference?

A. First, if at all possible, the appendix accompanies the EIS, whereas the material which is incorporated by reference does not accompany the EIS. Thus the appendix should contain information that reviewers will be likely to want to examine. The appendix should include material that pertains to preparation of a particular EIS. Research papers directly relevant to the proposal, lists of affected species, discussion of the methodology of models used in the analysis of impacts, extremely detailed responses to comments, or other information, would be placed in the appendix.

The appendix must be complete and available at the time the EIS is filed. Five copies of the appendix must be sent to EPA with five copies of the EIS for filing. If the appendix is too bulky to be circulated, it instead must be placed in conveniently accessible locations or furnished directly to commentors upon request. If it is not circulated with the EIS, the Notice of Availability published by EPA must so state, giving a telephone number to enable potential commentors to locate or request copies of the appendix promptly.

Material that is not directly related to preparation of the EIS should be incorporated by reference. This would include other EISs, research papers in the general literature, technical background papers or other material that someone with technical training could use to evaluate the analysis of the proposal. These must be made available, either by citing the literature, furnishing copies to central locations, or sending copies directly to commentors upon request.

Care must be taken in all cases to ensure that material incorporated by reference, and the occasional appendix that does not accompany the EIS, are in fact available for the full minimum public comment period.

26a. Index and Keyword Index in EISs. How detailed must an EIS index be?

A. The EIS index should have a level of detail sufficient to focus on areas of the EIS of reasonable interest to any reader. It cannot be restricted to the most important topics. On the other hand, it need not identify every conceivable term or phrase in the EIS. If an agency believes that the reader is reasonably likely to be interested in a topic, it should be included.

26b. Is a keyword index required?

A. No. A keyword index is a relatively short list of descriptive terms that identifies the key concepts or subject areas in a document. For example it could consist of 20 terms which describe the most significant aspects of an EIS that a future researcher would need: type of proposal, type of impacts, type of environment, geographical area, sampling or modeling methodologies used. This technique permits the compilation of EIS data banks, by facilitating quick and inexpensive access to stored materials. While a keyword index is not required by the regulations, it could be a useful addition for several reasons. First, it can be useful as a quick index for reviewers of the EIS, helping to focus on areas of interest. Second, if an agency keeps a listing of the keyword indexes of the EISs it produces, the EIS preparers themselves will have quick access to similar research data and methodologies to aid their future EIS work. Third, a keyword index will be needed to make an EIS available to future researchers using EIS data banks that are being developed. Preparation of such an index now when the document is produced will save a later effort when the data banks become operational.

27a. List of Preparers. If a consultant is used in preparing an EIS, must the list of preparers identify members of the consulting firm as well as the agency NEPA staff who were primarily responsible?

A. Section 1502.17 requires identification of the names and qualifications of persons who were primarily responsible for preparing the EIS or significant background papers, including basic components of the statement. This means that members of a consulting firm preparing material that is to become part of the EIS must be identified. The EIS should identify these individuals even though the consultant's contribution may have been modified by the agency.

27b. Should agency staff involved in reviewing and editing the EIS also be included in the list of preparers?

A. Agency personnel who wrote basic components of the EIS or significant background papers must, of course, be identified. The EIS should also list the technical editors who reviewed or edited the statements.

27c. How much information should be included on each person listed?

A. The list of preparers should normally not exceed two pages. Therefore, agencies must determine which individuals had primary responsibility and need not identify individuals with minor involvement. The list of preparers should include a very brief identification of the individuals involved, their qualifications (expertise, professional disciplines) and the specific portion of the EIS for which they are responsible. This may be done in tabular form to cut down on length. A line or two for each person's qualifications should be sufficient.

28. Advance or Xerox Copies of EIS. May an agency file xerox copies of an EIS with EPA pending the completion of printing the document?

A. Xerox copies of an EIS may be filed with EPA prior to printing only if the xerox copies are simultaneously made available to other agencies and the public. Section 1506.9 of the regulations, which governs EIS filing, specifically requires Federal agencies to file EISs with EPA no earlier than the EIS is distributed to the public. However, this section does not prohibit xeroxing as a form of reproduction and distribution. When an agency chooses xeroxing as the reproduction method, the EIS must be clear and legible to permit ease of reading and ultimate microfiching of the EIS. Where color graphs are important to the EIS, they should be reproduced and circulated with the xeroxed copy.

29a. Responses to Comments. What response must an agency provide to a comment on a draft EIS which states that the EIS's methodology is inadequate or inadequately explained? For example, what level of detail must an agency include in its response to a simple postcard comment making such an allegation?

A. Appropriate responses to comments are described in Section 1503.4. Normally the responses should result in changes in the text of the EIS, not simply a separate answer at the back of the document. But, in addition, the agency must state what its response was, and if the agency decides that no substantive response to a comment is necessary, it must explain briefly why.

An agency is not under an obligation to issue a lengthy reiteration of its methodology for any portion of an EIS if the only comment addressing the methodology is a simple complaint that the EIS methodology is inadequate. But agencies must respond to comments, however brief, which are specific in their criticism of agency methodology. For example, if a commentor on an EIS said that an agency's air quality dispersion analysis or methodology was inadequate, and the agency had included a discussion of that analysis in the EIS, little if anything need be added in response to such a comment. However, if the commentor said that the dispersion analysis was inadequate because of its use of a certain computational technique, or that a dispersion analysis was inadequately explained because computational techniques were not included or referenced, then the agency would have to respond in a substantive and meaningful way to such a comment.

If a number of comments are identical or very similar, agencies may group the comments and prepare a single answer for each group. Comments may be summarized if they are especially voluminous. The comments or summaries must be attached to the EIS regardless of whether the agency believes they merit individual discussion in the body of the final EIS.

29b. How must an agency respond to a comment on a draft EIS that raises a new alternative not previously considered in the draft EIS?

A.   This question might arise in several possible situations. First, a commentor on a draft EIS may indicate that there is a possible alternative which, in the agency's view, is not a reasonable alternative. Section 1502.14(a). If that is the case, the agency must explain why the comment does not warrant further agency response, citing authorities or reasons that support the agency's position and, if appropriate, indicate those circumstances which would trigger agency reappraisal or further response. Section 1503.4(a). For example, a commentor on a draft EIS on a coal fired power plant may suggest the alternative of using synthetic fuel. The agency may reject the alternative with a brief discussion (with authorities) of the unavailability of synthetic fuel within the time frame necessary to meet the need and purpose of the proposed facility.

A second possibility is that an agency may receive a comment indicating that a particular alternative, while reasonable, should be modified somewhat, for example, to achieve certain mitigation benefits, or for other reasons. If the modification is reasonable, the agency should include a discussion of it in the final EIS. For example, a commentor on a draft EIS on a proposal for a pumped storage power facility might suggest that the applicant's proposed alternative should be enhanced by the addition of certain reasonable mitigation measures, including the purchase and setaside of a wildlife preserve to substitute for the tract to be destroyed by the project. The modified alternative including the additional mitigation measures should be discussed by the agency in the final EIS.

A third slightly different possibility is that a comment on a draft EIS will raise an alternative which is a minor variation of one of the alternatives discussed in the draft EIS, but this variation was not given any consideration by the agency. In such a case, the agency should develop and evaluate the new alternative, if it is reasonable, in the final EIS. If it is qualitatively within the spectrum of alternatives that were discussed in the draft, a supplemental draft will not be needed. For example, a commentor on a draft EIS to designate a wilderness area within a National Forest might reasonably identify a specific tract of the forest, and urge that it be considered for designation. If the draft EIS considered designation of a range of alternative tracts which encompassed forest area of similar quality and quantity, no supplemental EIS would have to be prepared. The agency could fulfill its obligation by addressing that specific alternative in the final EIS.

As another example, an EIS on an urban housing project may analyze the alternatives of constructing 2,000, 4,000, or 6,000 units. A commentor on the draft EIS might urge the consideration of constructing 5,000 units utilizing a different configuration of buildings. This alternative is within the spectrum of alternatives already considered, and, therefore, could be addressed in the final EIS.

A fourth possibility is that a commentor points out an alternative which is not a variation of the proposal or of any alternative discussed in the draft impact statement, and is a reasonable alternative that warrants serious agency response. In such a case, the agency must issue a supplement to the draft EIS that discusses this new alternative. For example, a commentor on a draft EIS on a nuclear power plant might suggest that a reasonable alternative for meeting the projected need for power would be through peak load management and energy conservation programs. If the permitting agency has failed to consider that approach in the Draft EIS, and the approach cannot be dismissed by the agency as unreasonable, a supplement to the Draft EIS, which discusses that alternative, must be prepared. (If necessary, the same supplement should also discuss substantial changes in the proposed action or significant new circumstances or information, as required by Section 1502.9(c)(1) of the Council's regulations.)

If the new alternative was not raised by the commentor during scoping, but could have been, commentors may find that they are unpersuasive in their efforts to have their suggested alternative analyzed in detail by the agency. However, if the new alternative is discovered or developed later, and it could not reasonably have been raised during the scoping process, then the agency must address it in a supplemental draft EIS. The agency is, in any case, ultimately responsible for preparing an adequate EIS that considers all alternatives.

30. **Adoption of EISs. When a cooperating agency with jurisdiction by law intends to adopt a lead agency's EIS and it is not satisfied with the adequacy of the document, may the cooperating agency adopt only the part of the EIS with which it is satisfied? If so, would a cooperating agency with jurisdiction by law have to prepare a separate EIS or EIS supplement covering the areas of disagreement with the lead agency?**

A.   Generally, a cooperating agency may adopt a lead agency's EIS without recirculating it if it concludes that its NEPA requirements and its comments and suggestions have been satisfied. Section 1506.3(a), (c). If necessary, a cooperating agency may adopt only a portion of the lead agency's EIS and may reject that part of the EIS with which it disagrees, stating publicly why it did so. Section 1506.3(a).

A cooperating agency with jurisdiction by law (e.g., an agency with independent legal responsibilities with respect to the proposal) has an independent legal obligation to comply with NEPA. Therefore, if the cooperating agency determines that the EIS is wrong or inadequate, it must prepare a supplement to the EIS, replacing or adding any needed information, and must circulate the supplement as a draft for public and agency review and comment. A final supplemental EIS would be required before the agency could take action. The adopted portions of the lead agency EIS should be circulated with the supplement. Section 1506.3(b). A cooperating agency with jurisdiction by law will have to prepare its own Record of Decision for its action, in which it must explain how it reached its conclusions. Each agency should explain how and why its conclusions differ, if that is the case, from those of other agencies which issued their Records of Decision earlier.

An agency that did not cooperate in preparation of an EIS may also adopt an EIS or portion thereof. But this would arise only in rare instances, because an agency adopting an EIS for use in its own decision normally would have been a cooperating agency. If the proposed action for which the EIS was prepared is substantially the same as the proposed action of the adopting agency, the EIS may be adopted as long as it is recirculated as a final EIS and the agency announces what it is doing. This would be followed by the 30-day review period and issuance of a Record of Decision by the adopting agency. If the proposed action by the adopting agency is not substantially the same as that in the EIS (i.e., if an EIS on one action is being adapted for use in a decision on another action), the EIS would be treated as a draft and circulated for the normal public comment period and other procedures. Section 1506.3(b).

31a. Application of Regulations to Independent Regulatory Agencies. Do the Council's NEPA regulations apply to independent regulatory agencies like the Federal Energy Regulatory Commission (FERC) and the Nuclear Regulatory Commission?

A. The statutory requirements of NEPA's Section 102 apply to "all agencies of the federal government." The NEPA regulations implement the procedural provisions of NEPA as set forth in NEPA's Section 102(2) for all agencies of the federal government. The NEPA regulations apply to independent regulatory agencies, however, they do not direct independent regulatory agencies or other agencies to make decisions in any particular way or in a way inconsistent with an agency's statutory charter. Sections 1500.3, 1500.6, 1507.1, and 1507.3.

31b. Can an Executive Branch agency like the Department of the Interior adopt an EIS prepared by an independent regulatory agency such as FERC?

A. If an independent regulatory agency such as FERC has prepared an EIS in connection with its approval of a proposed project, an Executive Branch agency (e.g., the Bureau of Land Management in the Department of the Interior) may, in accordance with Section 1506.3, adopt the EIS or a portion thereof for its use in considering the same proposal. In such a case the EIS must, to the satisfaction of the adopting agency, meet the standards for an adequate statement under the NEPA regulations (including scope and quality of analysis of alternatives) and must satisfy the adopting agency's comments and suggestions. If the independent regulatory agency fails to comply with the NEPA regulations, the cooperating or adopting agency may find that it is unable to adopt the EIS, thus forcing the preparation of a new EIS or EIS Supplement for the same action. The NEPA regulations were made applicable to all federal agencies in order to avoid this result, and to achieve uniform application and efficiency of the NEPA process.

32. Supplements to Old EISs. Under what circumstances do old EISs have to be supplemented before taking action on a proposal?

A. As a rule of thumb, if the proposal has not yet been implemented, or if the EIS concerns an ongoing program, EISs that are more than 5 years old should be carefully reexamined to determine if the criteria in Section 1502.9 compel preparation of an EIS supplement.

If an agency has made a substantial change in a proposed action that is relevant to environmental concerns, or if there are significant new circumstances or information relevant to environmental concerns and bearing on the proposed action or its impacts, a supplemental EIS must be prepared for an old EIS so that the agency has the best possible information to make any necessary substantive changes in its decisions regarding the proposal. Section 1502.9(c).

33a. Referrals. When must a referral of an interagency disagreement be made to the Council?

A. The Council's referral procedure is a pre-decision referral process for interagency disagreements. Hence, Section 1504.3 requires that a referring agency must deliver its referral to the Council not later than 25 days after publication by EPA of notice that the final EIS is available (unless the lead agency grants an extension of time under Section 1504.3(b)).

33b. May a referral be made after this issuance of a Record of Decision?

A. No, except for cases where agencies provide an internal appeal procedure which permits simultaneous filing of the final EIS and the record of decision (ROD). Section 1506.10(b)(2). Otherwise, as stated above, the process is a pre-decision referral process. Referrals must be made within 25 days after the notice of availability of the final EIS, whereas the final decision (ROD) may not be made or filed until after 30 days from the notice of availability of the EIS. Sections 1504.3(b), 1506.10(b). If a lead agency has granted an extension of time for another agency to take action on a referral, the ROD may not be issued until the extension has expired.

34a. Records of Decision. Must Records of Decision (RODs) be made public? How should they be made available?

A. Under the regulations, agencies must prepare a "concise public record of decision," which contains the elements specified in Section 1505.2. This public record may be integrated into any other decision record prepared by the agency, or it may be separate if decision documents are not normally made public. The Record of Decision is intended by the Council to be an environmental document (even though it is not explicitly mentioned in the definition of "environmental document" in Section 1508.10). Therefore, it must be made available to the public through appropriate public notice as required by Section 1506.6(b). However, there is no specific requirement for publication of the ROD itself, either in the Federal Register or elsewhere.

34b. May the summary section in the final Environmental Impact Statement substitute for or constitute an agency's Record of Decision?

A. No. An environmental impact statement is supposed to inform the decisionmaker before the decision is made. Sections 1502.1, 1505.2. The Council's regulations provide for a 30-day period after notice is published that the final EIS has been filed with EPA before the agency may take final action. During that period, in addition to the agency's own internal final review, the public and other agencies can comment on the final EIS prior to the agency's final action on the proposal. In addition, the Council's regulations make clear that the requirements for the summary in an EIS are not the same as the requirements for a ROD. Sections 1502.12 and 1505.2.

34c. What provisions should Records of Decision contain pertaining to mitigation and monitoring?

A. Lead agencies "shall include appropriate conditions [including mitigation measures and monitoring and enforcement programs] in grants, permits or other approvals" and shall "condition funding of actions on mitigation." Section 1505.3. Any such measures that are adopted must be explained and committed in the ROD.

The reasonable alternative mitigation measures and monitoring programs should have been addressed in the draft and final EIS. The discussion of mitigation and monitoring in a Record of Decision must be more detailed than a general statement that mitigation is being required, but not so detailed as to duplicate discussion of mitigation in the EIS. The Record of Decision should contain a concise summary identification of the mitigation measures which the agency has committed itself to adopt.

The Record of Decision must also state whether all practicable mitigation measures have been adopted, and if not, why not. Section 1505.2(c). The Record of Decision must identify the mitigation measures and monitoring and enforcement programs that have been selected and plainly indicate that they are adopted as part of the agency's decision. If the proposed action is the issuance of a permit or other approval, the specific details of the mitigation measures shall then be included as appropriate conditions in whatever grants, permits, funding or other approvals are being made by the federal agency. Section 1505.3 (a), (b). If the proposal is to be carried out by the federal agency itself, the Record of Decision should delineate the mitigation and monitoring measures in sufficient detail to constitute an enforceable commitment, or incorporate by reference the portions of the EIS that do so.

34d. What is the enforceability of a Record of Decision?

A. Pursuant to generally recognized principles of federal administrative law, agencies will be held accountable for preparing Records of Decision that conform to the decisions actually made and for carrying out the actions set forth in the Records of Decision. This is based on the principle that an agency must comply with its own decisions and regulations once they are adopted. Thus, the terms of a Record of Decision are enforceable by agencies and private parties. A Record of Decision can be used to compel compliance with or execution of the mitigation measures identified therein.

35. Time Required for the NEPA Process. How long should the NEPA process take to complete?

A. When an EIS is required, the process obviously will take longer than when an EA is the only document prepared. But the Council's NEPA regulations encourage streamlined review, adoption of deadlines, elimination of duplicative work, eliciting suggested alternatives and other comments early through scoping, cooperation among agencies, and consultation with applicants during project planning. The Council has advised agencies that under the new NEPA regulations even large complex energy projects would require only about 12 months for the completion of the entire EIS process. For most major actions, this period is well within the planning time that is needed in any event, apart from NEPA.

The time required for the preparation of program EISs may be greater. The Council also recognizes that some projects will entail difficult long-term planning and/or the acquisition of certain data which of necessity will require more time for the preparation of the EIS. Indeed, some proposals should be given more time for the thoughtful preparation of an EIS and development of a decision which fulfills NEPA's substantive goals.

For cases in which only an environmental assessment will be prepared, the NEPA process should take no more than 3 months, and in many cases substantially less, as part of the normal analysis and approval process for the action.

36a. Environmental Assessments (EA). How long and detailed must an environmental assessment (EA) be?

A. The environmental assessment is a concise public document which has three defined functions. (1) It briefly provides sufficient evidence and analysis for determining whether to prepare an EIS; (2) it aids an agency's compliance with NEPA when no EIS is necessary, i.e., it helps to identify better alternatives and mitigation measures; and (3) it facilitates preparation of an EIS when one is necessary. Section 1508.9(a).

Since the EA is a concise document, it should not contain long descriptions or detailed data which the agency may have gathered. Rather, it should contain a brief discussion of the need for the proposal, alternatives to the proposal, the environmental impacts of the proposed action and alternatives, and a list of agencies and persons consulted. Section 1508.9(b).

While the regulations do not contain page limits for EA's, the Council has generally advised agencies to keep the length of EAs to not more than approximately 10-15 pages. Some agencies expressly provide page guidelines (e.g., 10-15 pages in the case of the Army Corps). To avoid undue length, the EA may incorporate by reference background data to support its concise discussion of the proposal and relevant issues.

36b. Under what circumstances is a lengthy EA appropriate?

A. Agencies should avoid preparing lengthy EAs except in unusual cases, where a proposal is so complex that a concise document cannot meet the goals of Section 1508.9 and where it is extremely difficult to determine whether the proposal could have significant environmental effects. In most cases, however, a lengthy EA indicates that an EIS is needed.

37a. Findings of No Significant Impact (FONSI). What is the level of detail of information that must be included in a finding of no significant impact (FONSI)?

A. The FONSI is a document in which the agency briefly explains the reasons why an action will not have a significant effect on the human environment and, therefore, why an EIS will not be prepared. Section 1508.13. The finding itself need not be detailed, but must succinctly state the reasons for deciding that the action will have no significant environmental effects, and, if relevant, must show which factors were weighted most heavily in the determination. In addition to this statement, the FONSI must include, summarize, or attach and incorporate by reference, the environmental assessment.

37b. What are the criteria for deciding whether a FONSI should be made available for public review for 30 days before the agency's final determination whether to prepare an EIS?

A. Public review is necessary, for example, (a) if the proposal is a borderline case, i.e., when there is a reasonable argument for preparation of an EIS; (b) if it is an unusual case, a new kind of action, or a precedent setting case such as a first intrusion of even a minor development into a pristine area; (c) when there is either scientific or public controversy over the proposal; or (d) when it involves a proposal which is or is closely similar to one which normally requires preparation of an EIS. Sections 1501.4(e)(2), 1508.27. Agencies also must allow a period of public review of the FONSI if the proposed action would be located in a floodplain or wetland. E.O. 11988, Sec. 2(a)(4); E.O. 11990, Sec. 2(b).

38. Public Availability of EAs v. FONSIs. Must (EAs) and FONSIs be made public? If so, how should this be done?

A. Yes, they must be available to the public. Section 1506.6 requires agencies to involve the public in implementing their NEPA procedures, and this includes public involvement in the preparation of EAs and FONSIs. These are public "environmental documents" under Section 1506.6(b), and, therefore, agencies must give public notice of their availability. A combination of methods may be used to give notice, and the methods should be tailored to the needs of particular cases. Thus, a Federal Register notice of availability of the documents, coupled with notices in national publications and mailed to interested national groups might be appropriate for proposals that are national in scope. Local newspaper notices may be more appropriate for regional or site-specific proposals.

The objective, however, is to notify all interested or affected parties. If this is not being achieved, then the methods should be reevaluated and changed. Repeated failure to reach the interested or affected public would be interpreted as a violation of the regulations.

39. **Mitigation Measures Imposed in EAs and FONSIs. Can an EA and FONSI be used to impose enforceable mitigation measures, monitoring programs, or other requirements, even though there is no requirement in the regulations in such cases for a formal Record of Decision?**

    A. Yes. In cases where an environmental assessment is the appropriate environmental document, there still may be mitigation measures or alternatives that would be desirable to consider and adopt even though the impacts of the proposal will not be "significant." In such cases, the EA should include a discussion of these measures or alternatives to "assist agency planning and decisionmaking" and to "aid an agency's compliance with [NEPA] when no environmental impact statement is necessary." Section 1501.3(b), 1508.9(a)(2). The appropriate mitigation measures can be imposed as enforceable permit conditions, or adopted as part of the agency final decision in the same manner mitigation measures are adopted in the formal Record of Decision that is required in EIS cases.

40. **Propriety of Issuing EA When Mitigation Reduces Impacts. If an environmental assessment indicates that the environmental effects of a proposal are significant but that, with mitigation, those effects may be reduced to less than significant levels, may the agency make a finding of no significant impact rather than prepare an EIS? Is that a legitimate function of an EA and scoping?**

    [N.B.: The 1987-88 CEQ Annual Report stated that CEQ intended to issue additional guidance on this topic. Ed. note.]

    A Mitigation measures may be relied upon to make a finding of no significant impact only if they are imposed by statute or regulation, or submitted by an applicant or agency as part of the original proposal. As a general rule, the regulations contemplate that agencies should use a broad approach in defining significance and should not rely on the possibility of mitigation as an excuse to avoid the EIS requirement. Sections 1508.8, 1508.27.

    If a proposal appears to have adverse effects which would be significant, and certain mitigation measures are then developed during the scoping or EA stages, the existence of such possible mitigation does not obviate the need for an EIS. Therefore, if scoping or the EA identifies certain mitigation possibilities without altering the nature of the overall proposal itself, the agency should continue the EIS process and submit the proposal, and the potential mitigation, for public and agency review and comment. This is essential to ensure that the final decision is based on all the relevant factors and that the full NEPA process will result in enforceable mitigation measures through the Record of Decision.

    In some instances, where the proposal itself so integrates mitigation from the beginning that it is impossible to define the proposal without including the mitigation, the agency may then rely on the mitigation measures in determining that the overall effects would not be significant (e.g., where an application for a permit for a small hydro dam is based on a binding commitment to build fish ladders, to permit adequate down stream flow, and to replace any lost wetlands, wildlife habitat and recreational potential). In those instances, agencies should make the FONSI and EA available for 30 days of public comment before taking action. Section 1501.4(e)(2).

Similarly, scoping may result in a redefinition of the entire project, as a result of mitigation proposals. In that case, the agency may alter its previous decision to do an EIS, as long as the agency or applicant resubmits the entire proposal and the EA and FONSI are available for 30 days of review and comment. One example of this would be where the size and location of a proposed industrial park are changed to avoid affecting a nearby wetland area.

[This memorandum was filed in the Federal Register and appears at 46 Fed. Reg. 18026 (Mar. 23, 1981).]

ENDNOTES

The first endnote appeared in the original Federal Register. The other endnote, which refers to subsequent CEQ actions, is for information only.

1. References throughout the document are to the Council on Environmental Quality's Regulations For Implementing The Procedural Provisions of the National Environmental Policy Act. 40 CFR Parts 1500-1508.

2. Q20 Worst Case Analysis was withdrawn by final rule issued at 51 Fed. Reg. 15618 (Apr. 25. 1986); textual errors corrected 51 F.R. p. 16,846 (May 7, 1986). The preamble to this rule is published at ELR Admin. Mat. 35055.

MEMORANDUM: GUIDANCE REGARDING NEPA REGULATIONS

40 CFR Part 1500

48 Fed. Reg. 34263 July 28, 1983

MEMORANDUM

For: Heads of Federal Agencies
From: A. Alan Hill, Chairman, Council on Environmental Quality

Re: Guidance Regarding NEPA Regulations

The Council on Environmental Quality (CEQ) regulations implementing the National Environmental Policy Act (NEPA) were issued on November 29, 1978. These regulations became effective for, and binding upon, most federal agencies on July 30, 1979, and for all remaining federal agencies on November 30, 1979.

As part of the Council's NEPA oversight responsibilities it solicited through an August 14, 1981, notice in the Federal Register public and agency comments regarding a series of questions that were developed to provide information on the manner in which federal agencies were implementing the CEQ regulations. On July 12, 1982, the Council announced the availability of a document summarizing the comments received from the public and other agencies and also identifying issue areas which the Council intended to review. On August 12, 1982, the Council held a public meeting to address those issues and hear any other comments which the public or other interested agencies might have about the NEPA process. The issues addressed in this guidance were identified during this process.

There are many ways in which agencies can meet their responsibilities under NEPA and the 1978 regulations. The purpose of this document is to provide the Council's guidance on various ways to carry out activities under the regulations.

Scoping

The Council on Environmental Quality (CEQ) regulations direct federal agencies which have made a decision to prepare an environmental impact statement to engage in a public scoping process. Public hearings or meetings, although often held, are not required; instead the manner in which public input will be sought is left to the discretion of the agency.

The purpose of this process is to determine the scope of the EIS so that preparation of the document can be effectively managed. Scoping is intended to ensure that problems are identified early and properly studied, that issues of little significance do not consume time and effort, that the draft EIS is thorough and balanced, and that delays occasioned by an inadequate draft EIS are avoided. The scoping process should identify the public and agency concerns; clearly define the environmental issues and alternatives to be examined in the EIS including the elimination of non-significant issues; identify related issues which originate from separate legislation, regulation, or Executive Order (e.g. historic preservation or endangered species concerns); and identify state and local agency requirements which must be addressed. An effective scoping process can help reduce unnecessary paperwork and time delays in preparing and processing the EIS by clearly identifying all relevant procedural requirements.

In April 1981, the Council issued a "Memorandum for General Counsels, NEPA Liaisons and Participants in Scoping" on the subject of Scoping Guidance. The purpose of this guidance was to give agencies suggestions as to how to more effectively carry out the CEQ scoping requirement. The availability of this document was announced in the Federal Register at 46 FR 25461. It is still available upon request from the CEQ General Counsel's office.

The concept of lead agency (§1508.16) and cooperating agency (§1508.5) can be used effectively to help manage the scoping process and prepare the environmental impact statement. The lead agency should identify the potential cooperating agencies. It is incumbent upon the lead agency to identify any agency which may ultimately be involved in the proposed action, including any subsequent permitting actions. Once cooperating agencies have been identified they have specific responsibility under the NEPA regulations (40 CFR 1501.6). Among other things cooperating agencies have responsibilities to participate in the scoping process and to help identify issues which are germane to any subsequent action it must take on the proposed action. The ultimate goal of this combined agency effort is to produce an EIS which in addition to fulfilling the basic intent of NEPA, also encompasses to the maximum extent possible all the environmental and public involvement requirements of state and federal laws, Executive Orders, and administrative policies of the involved agencies. Examples of these requirements include the Fish and Wildlife Coordination Act, the Clean Air Act, the Endangered Species Act, the National Historic Preservation Act, the Wild and Scenic Rivers Act, the Farmland Protection Policy Act, Executive Order 11990 (Protection of Wetlands), and Executive Order 11998 (Floodplain Management).

It is emphasized that cooperating agencies have the responsibility and obligation under the CEQ regulations to participate in the scoping process. Early involvement leads to early identification of significant issues, better decisionmaking, and avoidance of possible legal challenges. Agencies with "jurisdiction by law" must accept designation as a cooperating agency if requested (40 CFR 1501.6).

One of the functions of scoping is to identify the public involvement/public hearing procedures of all appropriate state and federal agencies that will ultimately act upon the proposed action. To the maximum extent possible, such procedures should be integrated into the EIS process so that joint public meetings and hearings can be conducted. Conducting joint meetings and hearings eliminates duplication and should significantly reduce the time and cost of processing an EIS and any subsequent approvals. The end result will be a more informed public cognizant of all facets of the proposed action.

It is important that the lead agency establish a process to properly manage scoping. In appropriate situations the lead agency should consider designating a project coordinator and forming an interagency project review team. The project coordinator would be the key person in monitoring time schedules and responding to any problems which may arise in both scoping and preparing the EIS. The project review team would be established early in scoping and maintained throughout the process of preparing the EIS. This review team would include state and local agency representatives. The review team would meet periodically to ensure that the EIS is complete, concise, and prepared in a timely manner.

A project review team has been used effectively on many projects. Some of the more important functions this review team can serve include: (1) A source of information, (2) a coordination mechanism, and (3) a professional review group. As an information source, the review team can identify all federal, state, and local environmental requirements, agency public meeting and hearing procedures, concerned citizen groups, data needs and sources of existing information, and the significant issues and reasonable alternatives for detailed analysis, excluding the non-significant issues. As a coordination mechanism, the team can ensure the rapid distribution of appropriate information or environmental studies, and can reduce the time required for formal consultation on a number of issues (e.g., endangered species or historic preservation). As a professional review group the team can assist in establishing and monitoring a tight time schedule for preparing the EIS by identifying critical points in the process, discussing and recommending solutions to the lead agency as problems arise, advising whether a requested analysis or information item is relevant to the issues under consideration, and providing timely and substantive review comments on any preliminary reports or analyses that may be prepared during the process. The presence of professionals from all scientific disciplines which have a significant role in the proposed action could greatly enhance the value of the team.

The Council recognizes that there may be some problems with the review team concept such as limited agency travel funds and the amount of work necessary to coordinate and prepare for the periodic team meetings. However, the potential benefits of the team concept are significant and the Council encourages agencies to consider utilizing interdisciplinary project review teams to aid in EIS preparation. A regularly scheduled meeting time and location should reduce coordination problems. In some instances, meetings can be arranged so that many projects are discussed at each session. The benefits of the concept are obvious: timely and effective preparation of the EIS, early identification and resolution of any problems which may arise, and elimination, or at least reduction of, the need for additional environmental studies subsequent to the approval of the EIS.

Since the key purpose of scoping is to identify the issues and alternatives for consideration, the scoping process should "end" once the issues and alternatives to be addressed in the EIS have been clearly identified. Normally this would occur during the final stages of preparing the draft EIS and before it is officially circulated for public and agency review.

The Council encourages the lead agency to notify the public of the results of the scoping process to ensure that all issues have been identified. The lead agency should document the results of the scoping process in its administrative record.

The NEPA regulations place a new and significant responsibility on agencies and the public alike during the scoping process to identify all significant issues and reasonable alternatives to be addressed in the EIS. Most significantly, the Council has found that scoping is an extremely valuable aid to better decisionmaking. Thorough scoping may also have the effect of reducing the frequency with which proposed actions are challenged in court on the basis of an inadequate EIS. Through the techniques identified in this guidance, the lead agency will be able to document that an open public involvement process was conducted, that all reasonable alternatives were identified, that significant issues were identified and non-significant issues eliminated, and that the environmental public involvement requirements of all agencies were met, to the extent possible, in a single "one-stop" process.

Categorical Exclusions

Section 1507 of the CEQ regulations directs federal agencies when establishing implementing procedures to identify those actions which experience has indicated will not have a significant environmental effect and to categorically exclude them from NEPA review. In our August 1981 request for public comments, we asked the question "Have categorical exclusions been adequately identified and defined?".

The responses the Council received indicated that there was considerable belief that categorical exclusions were not adequately identified and defined. A number of commentators indicated that agencies had not identified all categories of actions that meet the categorical exclusion definition (§1508.4) or that agencies were overly restrictive in their interpretations of categorical exclusions. Concerns were expressed that agencies were requiring too much documentation for projects that were not major federal actions with significant effects and also that agency procedures to add categories of actions to their existing lists of categorical exclusions were too cumbersome.

The National Environmental Policy Act and the CEQ regulations are concerned primarily with those "major federal actions significantly affecting the quality of the human environment" (42 U.S.C. 4332). Accordingly, agency procedures, resources, and efforts should focus on determining whether the proposed federal action is a major federal action significantly affecting the quality of the human environment. If the answer to this question is yes, an environmental impact statement must be prepared. If there is insufficient information to answer the question, an environmental assessment is needed to assist the agency in determining if the environmental impacts are significant and require an EIS. If the assessment shows that the impacts are not significant, the agency must prepare a finding of no significant impact. Further stages of this federal action may be excluded from requirements to prepare NEPA documents.

The CEQ regulations were issued in 1978 and most agency implementing regulations and procedures were issued shortly thereafter. In recognition of the experience with the NEPA process that agencies have had since the CEQ regulations were issued, the Council believes that it is appropriate for agencies to examine their procedures to insure that the NEPA process utilizes this additional knowledge and experience. Accordingly, the Council strongly encourages agencies to re-examine their environmental procedures and specifically those portions of the procedures where "categorical exclusions" are discussed to determine if revisions are appropriate. The specific issues which the Council is concerned about are (1) the use of detailed lists of specific activities for categorical exclusions, (2) the excessive use of environmental assessments/findings of no significant impact and (3) excessive documentation.

The Council has noted some agencies have developed lists of specific activities which qualify as categorical exclusions. The Council believes that if this approach is applied narrowly it will not provide the agency with sufficient flexibility to make decisions on a project-by-project basis with full consideration to the issues and impacts that are unique to a specific project. The Council encourages the agencies to consider broadly defined criteria which characterize types of actions that, based on the agency's experience, do not cause significant environmental effects. If this technique is adopted, it would be helpful for the agency to offer several examples of activities frequently performed by that agency's personnel which would normally fall in these categories. Agencies also need to consider whether the cumulative effects of several small actions would cause sufficient environmental impact to take the actions out of the categorically excluded class.

The Council also encourages agencies to examine the manner in which they use the environmental assessment process in relation to their process for identifying projects that meet the categorical exclusion definition. A report(1) to the Council indicated that some agencies have a very high ratio of findings of no significant impact to environmental assessments each year while producing only a handful of EIS's. Agencies should examine their decisionmaking process to ascertain if some of these actions do not, in fact, fall within the categorical exclusion definition, or, conversely, if they deserve full EIS treatment.

As previously noted, the Council received a number of comments that agencies require an excessive amount of environmental documentation for projects that meet the categorical exclusion definition. The Council believes that sufficient information will usually be available during the course of normal project development to determine the need for an EIS and further that the agency's administrative record will clearly document the basis for its decision. Accordingly, the Council strongly discourages procedures that would require the preparation of additional paperwork to document that an activity has been categorically excluded.

Categorical exclusions promulgated by an agency should be reviewed by the Council at the draft stage. After reviewing comments received during the review period and prior to publication in final form, the Council will determine whether the categorical exclusions are consistent with the NEPA regulations.

Adoption Procedures

During the recent effort undertaken by the Council to review the current NEPA regulations, several participants indicated federal agencies were not utilizing the adoption procedures as authorized by the CEQ regulations. The concept of adoption was incorporated into the Council's NEPA Regulations (40 CFR 1506.3) to reduce duplicative EISs prepared by Federal agencies. The experiences gained during the 1970's revealed situations in which two or more agencies had an action relating to the same project; however, the timing of the actions was different. In the early years of NEPA implementation, agencies independently approached their activities and decisions. This procedure lent itself to two or even three EISs on the same project. In response to this situation the CEQ regulations authorized agencies, in certain instances, to adopt environmental impact statements prepared by other agencies.

In general terms, the regulations recognize three possible situations in which adoption is appropriate. One is where the federal agency participated in the process as a cooperating agency. (40 CFR 1506.3(c)). In this case, the cooperating agency may adopt a final EIS and simply issue its record of decision.(2) However, the cooperating agency must independently review the EIS and determine that its own NEPA procedures have been satisfied.

A second case concerns the federal agency which was not a cooperating agency, but is, nevertheless, undertaking an activity which was the subject of an EIS. (40 CFR 1506.3(b)). This situation would arise because an agency did not anticipate that it would be involved in a project which was the subject of another agency's EIS. In this instance where the proposed action is substantially the same as that action described in the EIS, the agency may adopt the EIS and recirculate (file with EPA and distribute to agencies and the public) it as a final EIS. However, the agency must independently review the EIS to determine that it is current and that its own NEPA procedures have been satisfied. When recirculating the final EIS the agency should provide information which identifies what federal action is involved.

The third situation is one in which the proposed action is not substantially the same as that covered by the EIS. In this case, any agency may adopt an EIS or a portion thereof by circulating the EIS as a draft or as a portion of the agency's draft and preparing a final EIS. (40 CFR 1506.3(a)). Repetitious analysis and time consuming data collection can be easily eliminated utilizing this procedure.

The CEQ regulations specifically address the question of adoption only in terms of preparing EIS's. However, the objectives that underlie this portion of the regulations -- i.e., reducing delays and eliminating duplication -- apply with equal force to the issue of adopting other environmental documents. Consequently, the Council encourages agencies to put in place a mechanism for adopting environmental assessments prepared by other agencies. Under such procedures the agency could adopt the environmental assessment and prepare a Finding of No Significant Impact based on that assessment. In doing so, the agency should be guided by several principles:

-- First, when an agency adopts such an analysis it must independently evaluate the information contained therein and take full responsibility for its scope and content.

-- Second, if the proposed action meets the criteria set out in 40 CFR 1501.4(e)(2), a Finding of No Significant Impact would be published for 30 days of public review before a final determination is made by the agency on whether to prepare an environmental impact statement.

Contracting Provisions

Section 1506.5(c) of the NEPA regulations contains the basic rules for agencies which choose to have an environmental impact statement prepared by a contractor. That section requires the lead or cooperating agency to select the contractor, to furnish guidance and to participate in the preparation of the environmental impact statement. The regulation requires contractors who are employed to prepare an environmental impact statement to sign a disclosure statement stating that they have no financial or other interest in the outcome of the project. The responsible federal official must independently evaluate the statement prior to its approval and take responsibility for its scope and contents.

During the recent evaluation of comments regarding agency implementation of the NEPA process, the Council became aware of confusion and criticism about the provisions of Section 1506.5(c). It appears that a great deal of misunderstanding exists regarding the interpretation of the conflict of interest provision. There is also some feeling that the conflict of interest provision should be completely eliminated.(3)

Applicability of §1506.5(c)

This provision is only applicable when a federal lead agency determines that it needs contractor assistance in preparing an EIS. Under such circumstances, the lead agency or a cooperating agency should select the contractor to prepare the EIS.(4)

This provision does not apply when the lead agency is preparing the EIS based on information provided by a private applicant. In this situation, the private applicant can obtain its information from any source. Such sources could include a contractor hired by the private applicant to do environmental, engineering, or other studies necessary to provide sufficient information to the lead agency to prepare an EIS. The agency must independently evaluate the information and is responsible for its accuracy.

Conflict of Interest Provisions

The purpose of the disclosure statement requirement is to avoid situations in which the contractor preparing the environmental impact statement has an interest in the outcome of the proposal. Avoidance of this situation should, in the Council's opinion, ensure a better and more defensible statement for the federal agencies. This requirement also serves to assure the public that the analysis in the environmental impact statement has been prepared free of subjective, self-serving research and analysis.

Some persons believe these restrictions are motivated by undue and unwarranted suspicion about the bias of contractors. The Council is aware that many contractors would conduct their studies in a professional and unbiased manner. However, the Council has the responsibility of overseeing the administration of the National Environmental Policy Act in a manner most consistent with the statute's directives and the public's expectations of sound government. The legal responsibilities for carrying out NEPA's objectives rest solely with federal agencies. Thus, if any delegation of work is to occur, it should be arranged to be performed in as objective a manner as possible.

Preparation of environmental impact statements by parties who would suffer financial losses if, for example, a "no action" alternative were selected, could easily lead to a public perception of bias. It is important to maintain the public's faith in the integrity of the EIS process, and avoidance of conflicts in the preparation of environmental impact statements is an important means of achieving this goal.

The Council has discovered that some agencies have been interpreting the conflicts provision in an overly burdensome manner. In some instances, multidisciplinary firms are being excluded from environmental impact statements preparation contracts because of links to a parent company which has design and/or construction capabilities. Some qualified contractors are not bidding on environmental impact statement contracts because of fears that their firm may be excluded from future design or construction contracts. Agencies have also applied the selection and disclosure provisions to project proponents who wish to have their own contractor for providing environmental information. The result of these misunderstandings has been reduced competition in bidding for EIS preparation contracts, unnecessary delays in selecting a contractor and preparing the EIS, and confusion and resentment about the requirement. The Council believes that a better understanding of the scope of §1506.5(c) by agencies, contractors and project proponents will eliminate these problems.

Section 1506.5(c) prohibits a person or entity entering into a contract with a federal agency to prepare an EIS when that party has at that time and during the life of the contract pecuniary or other interests in the outcomes of the proposal. Thus, a firm which has an agreement to prepare an EIS for a construction project cannot, at the same time, have an agreement to perform the construction, nor could it be the owner of the construction site. However, if there are no such separate interests or arrangements, and if the contract for EIS preparation does not contain any incentive clauses or guarantees of any future work on the project, it is doubtful that an inherent conflict of interest will exist. Further, §1506.5(c) does not prevent an applicant from submitting information to an agency. The lead federal agency should evaluate potential conflicts of interest prior to entering into any contract for the preparation of environmental documents.

Selection of Alternatives in Licensing and Permitting Situations

Numerous comments have been received questioning an agency's obligation, under the National Environmental Policy Act, to evaluate alternatives to a proposed action developed by an applicant for a federal permit or license. This concern arises from a belief that projects conceived and developed by private parties should not be questioned or second-guessed by the government. There has been discussion of developing two standards to determining the range of alternatives to be evaluated: The "traditional" standard for projects which are initiated and developed by a Federal agency, and a second standard of evaluating only those alternatives presented by an applicant for a permit or license.

Neither NEPA nor the CEQ regulations make a distinction between actions initiated by a Federal agency and by applicants. Early NEPA case law, while emphasizing the need for a rigorous examination of alternatives, did not specifically address this issue. In 1981, the Council addressed the question in its document, "Forty Most Asked Questions Concerning CEQ's National

Environmental Policy Act Regulations".(5) The answer indicated that the emphasis in determining the scope of alternatives should be on what is "reasonable". The Council said that, "Reasonable alternatives include those that are practical or feasible from the technical and economic standpoint and using common sense rather than simply desirable from the standpoint of the applicant."

Since issuance of that guidance, the Council has continued to receive requests for further clarification of this question. Additional interest has been generated by a recent appellate court decision. Roosevelt Campobello International Park Commission v. E.P.A. (6) dealt with EPA's decision of whether to grant a permit under the National Pollutant Discharge Elimination System to a company proposing a refinery and deep-water terminal in Maine. The court discussed both the criteria used by EPA in its selecting of alternative sites to evaluate, and the substantive standard used to evaluate the sites. The court determined that EPA's choice of alternative sites was "focused by the primary objectives of the permit applicant . . ." and that EPA had limited its consideration of sites to only those sites which were considered feasible, given the applicant's stated goals. The court found that EPA's criteria for selection of alternative sites was sufficient to meet its NEPA responsibilities.

This decision is in keeping with the concept that an agency's responsibilities to examine alternative sites has always been "bounded by some notion of feasibility" to avoid NEPA from becoming "an exercise in frivolous boilerplate".(7) NEPA has never been interpreted to require examination of purely conjectural possibilities whose implementation is deemed remote and speculative. Rather, the agency's duty is to consider "alternatives as they exist and are likely to exist."(8) In the Roosevelt Campobello case, for example, EPA examined three alternative sites and two alternative modifications of the project at the preferred alternative site. Other factors to be developed during the scoping process -- comments received from the public, other government agencies and institutions, and development of the agency's own environmental data -- should certainly be incorporated into the decision of which alternatives to seriously evaluate in the EIS. There is, however, no need to disregard the applicant's purposes and needs and the common sense realities of a given situation in the development of alternatives.

Tiering

Tiering of environmental impact statements refers to the process of addressing a broad, general program, policy or proposal in an initial environmental impact statement (EIS), and analyzing a narrower site-specific proposal, related to the initial program, plan or policy in a subsequent EIS. The concept of tiering was promulgated in the 1978 CEQ regulations; the preceding CEQ guidelines had not addressed the concept. The Council's intent in formalizing the tiering concept was to encourage agencies, "to eliminate repetitive discussions and to focus on the actual issues ripe for decisions at each level of environmental review."(9)

Despite these intentions, the Council perceives that the concept of tiering has caused a certain amount of confusion and uncertainty among individuals involved in the NEPA process. This confusion is by no means universal; indeed, approximately half of those commenting in response to our question about tiering (10) indicated that tiering is effective and should be used more frequently. Approximately one-third of the commentators responded that they had no experience with tiering upon which to base their comments. The remaining commentators were critical of tiering. Some commentators believed that tiering added an additional layer of paperwork to the process and encouraged, rather than discouraged, duplication. Some commentators thought that the inclusion of tiering in the CEQ regulations added an extra legal requirement to the NEPA process. Other commentators said that an initial EIS could be prepared when issues were too broad to analyze properly for any meaningful consideration. Some commentators believed that the concept was simply not applicable to the types of projects with which they worked; others were concerned about the need to supplement a tiered EIS. Finally, some who responded to our inquiry questioned the courts' acceptance of tiered EISs.

The Council believes that misunderstanding of tiering and its place in the NEPA process is the cause of much of this criticism. Tiering, of course, is by no means the best way to handle all proposals which are subject to NEPA analysis and documentation. The regulations do not require tiering; rather, they authorize its use when an agency determines it is appropriate. It is an option for an agency to use when the nature of the proposal lends itself to tiered EIS(s).

Tiering does not add an additional legal requirement to the NEPA process. An environmental impact statement is required for proposals for legislation and other major Federal actions significantly affecting the quality of the human environment. In the context of NEPA, "major Federal actions" include adoption of official policy, formal plans, and programs as well as approval of specific projects, such as construction activities in a particular location or approval of permits to an outside applicant. Thus, where a Federal agency adopts a formal plan which will be executed throughout a particular region, and later proposes a specific activity to implement that plan in the same region, both actions need to be analyzed under NEPA to determine whether they are major actions which will significantly affect the environment. If the answer is yes in both cases, both actions will be subject to the EIS requirement, whether tiering is used or not. The agency then has one of two alternatives: Either preparation of two environmental impact statements, with the second repeating much of the analysis and information found in the first environmental impact statement, or tiering the two documents. If tiering is utilized, the site-specific EIS contains a summary of the issues discussed in the first statement and the agency will incorporate by reference discussions from the first statement. Thus, the second, or site-specific statement, would focus primarily on the issues relevant to the specific proposal, and would not duplicate material found in the first EIS. It is difficult to understand, given this scenario, how tiering can be criticized for adding an unnecessary layer to the NEPA process; rather, it is intended to streamline the existing process.

The Council agrees with commentators who stated that there are stages in the development of a proposal for a program, plan or policy when the issues are too broad to lend themselves to meaningful analysis in the framework of an EIS. The CEQ regulations specifically define a "proposal" as existing at, "that stage in the development of an action when an agency subject to [NEPA] has a goal and is actively preparing to make a decision on one or more alternative means of accomplishing the goal and the effects can be meaningfully evaluated." (11) Tiering is not intended to force an agency to prepare an EIS before this stage is reached; rather, it is a technique to be used once meaningful analysis can be performed. An EIS is not required before that stage in the development of a proposal, whether tiering is used or not.

The Council also realizes that tiering is not well suited to all agency programs. Again, this is why tiering has been established as an option for the agency to use, as opposed to a requirement.

A supplemental EIS is required when an agency makes substantial changes in the proposed action relevant to environmental concerns, or when there are significant new circumstances or information relevant to environmental concerns bearing on the proposed action, and is optional when an agency otherwise determines to supplement an EIS.(12) The standard for supplementing an EIS is not changed by the use of tiering; there will no doubt be occasions when a supplement is needed, but the use of tiering should reduce the number of those occasions.

Finally, some commentators raised the question of courts' acceptability of tiering. This concern is understandable, given several cases which have reversed agency decisions in regard to a particular programmatic EIS. However, these decisions have never invalidated the concept of tiering, as stated in the CEQ regulations and discussed above. Indeed, the courts recognized the usefulness of the tiering approach in case law before the promulgation of the tiering regulation. Rather, the problems appear when an agency determines not to prepare a site-specific EIS based on the fact that a programmatic EIS was prepared. In this situation, the courts carefully examine the analysis contained in the programmatic EIS. A court may or may not find that the programmatic EIS contains appropriate analysis of impacts and alternatives to meet the adequacy test for the site-specific proposal. A recent decision by the Ninth Circuit Court of Appeals (13) invalidated an attempt by the Forest Service to make a determination regarding wilderness and non-wilderness designations on the basis of a programmatic EIS for this reason. However, it should be stressed that this and other decisions are not a repudiation of the tiering concept. In these instances, in fact, tiering has not been used; rather, the agencies have attempted to rely exclusively on programmatic or "first level" EISs which did not have site-specific information. No court has found that the tiering process as provided for in the CEQ regulations is an improper manner of implementing the NEPA process.

In summary, the Council believes that tiering can be a useful method of reducing paperwork and duplication when used carefully for appropriate types of plans, programs and policies which will later be translated into site-specific projects. Tiering should not be viewed as an additional substantive requirement, but rather a means of accomplishing the NEPA requirements in an efficient manner as possible.

Footnotes

(1) Environmental Law Institute, NEPA In Action Environmental Offices in Nineteen Federal Agencies, A Report To the Council on Environmental Quality, October 1981.

(2) Records of decision must be prepared by each agency responsible for making a decision, and cannot be adopted by another agency.

(3) The Council also received requests for guidance on effective management of the third-party environmental impact statement approach. However, the Council determined that further study regarding the policies behind this technique is warranted, and plans to undertake that task in the future.

(4) There is no bar against the agency considering candidates suggested by the applicant, although the Federal agency must retain its independence. If the applicant is seen as having a major role in the selection of the contractor, contractors may feel the need to please both the agency and the applicant. An applicant's suggestion, if any, to the agency regarding the choice of contractors should be one of many factors involved in the selection process.

(5) 46 FR 18026 (1981).

(6) 684 F.2d 1041 (1st Cir. 1982).

(7) Vermont Yankee Nuclear Power Corp. v. NRDC, 435 U.S. 519, 551 (1978).

(8) Monarch Chemical Works, Inc. v. Exon, 466 F.Supp. 639, 650 (1979), quoting Carolina Environmental Study Group v. U.S., 510 F.2d 796, 801 (1975).

(9) Preamble, FR, Vol. 43, No. 230, p. 55984, 11/29/78.

(10) "Is tiering being used to minimizes repetition in an environmental assessment and in environmental impact statements?", 46 FR 41131, August 14, 1981.

(11) 40 CFR 1508.23 (emphasis added).

(12) 40 CFR 1502.9(c).

(13) California v. Block, 18 ERC 1149 (1982). [FR Doc. 83-20522 Filed 7-27-83; 8:45 am]

APPENDIX 5   SCOPING GUIDANCE

MEMORANDUM: SCOPING GUIDANCE
(Council on Environmental Quality Apr. 30, 1981)

I. Introduction

A. Background of this document

In 1978, with the publication of the proposed NEPA regulations (since adopted as formal rules, 40 C.F.R. Parts 1500-1508), the Council on Environmental Quality gave formal recognition to an increasingly used term—scoping. Scoping is an idea that has long been familiar to those involved in NEPA compliance: In order to manage effectively the preparation of an environmental impact statement (EIS), one must determine the scope of the document—that is, what will be covered, and in what detail. Planning of this kind was a normal component of EIS preparation. But the consideration of issues and choice of alternatives to be examined was in too many cases completed outside of public view. The innovative approach to scoping in the regulations is that the process is open to the public and state and local governments, as well as to affected federal agencies. This open process gives rise to important new opportunities for better and more efficient NEPA analyses, and simultaneously places new responsibilities on public and agency participants alike to surface their concerns early. Scoping helps insure hat real problems are identified early and properly studied, that issues that are of no concern do not consume time and effort; that the draft statement when first made public is balanced and thorough; and that the delays occasioned by redoing an inadequate draft are avoided. Scoping does not create problems that did not already exist, it ensures that problems that would have been raised anyway are identified early in the process.

Many members of the public as well as agency staffs engaged in the NEPA process have told the Council that the open scoping requirement is one of the most far-reaching changes engendered by the NEPA regulations. They have predicted that scoping could have a profound positive effect on environmental analyses, on the impact statement process itself, and ultimately on decision making.

Because the concept of open scoping was new, the Council decided to encourage agencies' innovation without unduly restrictive guidance. Thus the regulations relating to scoping are very simple. They state that "there shall be an early and open process for determining the scope of issues to be addressed" which "shall be termed scoping," but they lay down few specific requirements. (Section 1501.7*). They require an open process with public notice; identification of significant and insignificant issues; allocation of EIS preparation assignments; identification of

---

related analysis requirements in order to avoid duplication of work; and the planning of a schedule for EIS preparation that meshes with the agency's decision making schedule. (Section 1501.7(a)). The regulations encourage, but do not require, setting time limits and page limits for the EIS, and holding scoping meetings. (Section 1501 .7(b)). Aside from these general outlines, the regulations left the agencies on their own. The Council did not believe, and still does not, that it is necessary or appropriate to dictate the specific manner in which over 100 federal agencies should deal with the public. However, the Council has received several requests for more guidance. In 1980 we decided to investigate the agency and public response to the scoping requirement, to find out what was working and what was not, and to share this with all agencies and the public.

The Council first conducted its own survey, asking federal agencies to report some of their scoping experiences The Council then contracted with the American Arbitration Association and Clark McGlennon Associates to survey the scoping techniques of major agencies and to study several innovative methods in detail.* Council staff conducted a two-day workshop in Atlanta in June 1980, to discuss with federal agency NEPA staff and several EIS contractors what seems to work best in scoping of different types of proposals, and discussed scoping with federal, state and local officials in meetings in all 10 federal regions.

This document is a distillation of all the work that has been done so far by many people to identify valuable scoping techniques. It is offered as a guide to encourage success and to help avoid pitfalls. Since scoping methods are still evolving, the Council welcomes any comments on this guide, and may add to it or revise it in coming years.

B. What scoping is and what it can do

Scoping is often the first contact between proponents of a proposal and the public. This fact is the source of the power of scoping and of the trepidation that it sometimes evokes. If a scoping meeting is held, people on both sides of an issue will be in the same room and, if all goes well, will speak to each other. The possibilities that flow from this situation are vast. Therefore, a large portion of this document is devoted to the productive management of meetings and the de-fusing of possible heated disagreements.

Even if a meeting is not held, the scoping process leads EIS preparers to think about the proposal early on, in order to explain it to the public and affected agencies. The participants respond with their own concerns about significant issues and suggestions of alternatives. Thus as the draft EIS is prepared, it will include, from the beginning, a reflection or at least an acknowledgment of the cooperating agencies' and the public's concerns. This reduces the need for changes after the draft is finished, because it reduces the chances of overlooking a significant issue or reasonable alternative. It also in many cases increases public confidence in NEPA and the decision making process, thereby reducing delays, such as from litigation, later on when implementing the decisions. As we will discuss further in this document, the public generally responds positively when its views are taken seriously, even if they cannot be wholly accommodated.

But scoping is not simply another "public relations" meeting requirement. It has specific and fairly limited objectives: (a) to identify the affected public and agency concerns; (b) to facilitate an efficient EIS preparation process, through assembling the cooperating agencies, assigning EIS writing tasks, ascertaining all the related permits and reviews that must be scheduled concurrently, and setting time or page limits; (c) to define the issues and alternatives that will be examined in detail in the EIS while simultaneously devoting less attention and time to issues

---

* The results of this examination arc reported in ''Scoping the Content of EISs: An Evaluation of Agencies' Experiences," which is available from the Council or the Resource Planning Analysis Office of the U.S. Geological Survey, 750 National Center, Reston, Va. 22092

which cause no concern; and (d) to save time in the overall process by helping to ensure that draft statements adequately address relevant issues, reducing the possibility that new comments will cause a statement to be rewritten or supplemented.

Sometimes the scoping process enables early identification of a few serious problems with a proposal, which can be changed or solved because the proposal is still being developed. In these cases, scoping the EIS can actually lead to the solution of a conflict over the proposed action itself. We have found that this extra benefit of scoping occurs fairly frequently. But it cannot be expected in most cases, and scoping can still be considered successful when conflicts are clarified but not solved. This guide does not presume that resolution of conflicts over proposals is a principal goal of scoping, because it is only possible in limited circumstances. Instead, the Council views the principal goal of .scoping to be an adequate and efficiently prepared EIS. Our suggestions and recommendations are aimed at reducing the conflicts among affected interests that impede this limited objective. But we are aware of the possibilities of more general conflict resolution that are inherent in any productive discussions among interested parties. We urge all participants in scoping processes to be alert to this larger context, in which scoping could prove to be the first step in environmental problem-solving.

Scoping can lay a firm foundation for the rest of the decision making process. If the EIS can be relied upon to include all the necessary information for formulating policies and making rational choices, the agency will be better able to make a sound and prompt decision. In addition, if it is clear that all reasonable alternatives are being seriously considered, the public will usually be more satisfied with the choice among them.

II. Advice for Government Agencies Conducting Scoping

A. General context

Scoping is a process, not an event or a meeting. It continues throughout the planning for an EIS, and may involve a series of meetings, telephone conversations, or written comments from different interested groups. Because it is a process, participants must remain flexible. The scope of an EIS occasionally may need to be modified later if a new issue surfaces. no matter how thorough the scoping was. But it makes sense to try to set the scope of the statement as early as possible.

Scoping may identify people who already have knowledge about a site or an alternative proposal or a relevant study, and induce them to make it available. This can save a lot of research time and money. But people will not come forward unless they believe their views and materials will receive serious consideration. Thus scoping is a crucial first step toward building public confidence in a fair environmental analysis and ultimately a fair decision making process.

One further point to remember: the lead agency cannot shed its responsibility to assess each significant impact or alternative even if one is found after scoping. But anyone who hangs back and fails to raise something that reasonably could have been raised earlier on will have a hard time prevailing during later stages Or the NEPA process or if litigation ensues. Thus a thorough scoping process does provide some protection against subsequent lawsuits.

B. Step-by-step through the process

1. Start scoping after you have enough information

Scoping cannot be useful until the agency knows enough about the proposed action to identify most of the affected parties, and to present a coherent proposal and a suggested initial list of environmental issues and alternatives. Until that time there is no way to explain to the public or other agencies *what* you want them to get involved *in. So* the first stage is to gather preliminary information from the applicant, or to compose a clear picture of your proposal, if it is being developed by the agency.

2. *Prepare an information packet*

In many cases, scoping of the EIS has been preceded by preparation of an environmental assessment (EA) as the basis for the decision to proceed with an EIS. In such cases, the EA will, of course, include the preliminary information that is needed.

If you have not prepared an EA, you should put together a brief information packet consisting of a description of the proposal, an initial list of impacts and alternatives, maps, drawings, and any other material or references that can help the interested public to understand what is being proposed. The proposed work plan of the EIS is not usually sufficient for this purpose. Such documents rarely contain a description of the goals of the proposal to enable readers to develop alternatives.

At this stage, the purpose of the information is to enable participants to make an intelligent contribution to scoping the EIS. Because they will be helping to plan what will be examined during the environmental review, they need to know where you are now in that planning process.

Include in the packet a brief explanation of what scoping is and what procedure will be used, to give potential participants a context for their involvement. Be sure to point out that you want comments from participants on very specific matters. Also reiterate that no decision has yet been made on the contents of the EIS, much less on the proposal itself. Thus, explain that you do not yet have a preferred alternative, but that you may identify the preferred alternative in the draft EIS. (See Section 1502.14(e)). This should reduce the tendency of participants to perceive the proposal as already a definite plan. Encourage them to focus on recommendations for improvements to the various alternatives.

Some of the complaints alleging that scoping can be a waste of time stem from the fact that the participants may not know what the proposal is until they arrive at a meeting. Even the most intelligent among us can rarely make useful, substantive comments on the spur of the moment. Don't expect helpful suggestions to result if participants are put in such a position.

3. *Design the scoping process for each project*

There is no established or required procedure for scoping. The process can be carried out by meetings, telephone conversations, written comments, or a combination of all three. It is important to tailor the type, the timing and the location of public and agency comments to the proposal at hand.

For example, a proposal to adopt a land management plan for a National Forest in a sparsely populated region may not lend itself to calling a single meeting in a central location. While people living in the area and elsewhere may be interested, any meeting place will be inconvenient for most of the potential participants. One solution is to distribute the information packet, solicit written comments, list a telephone number with the name of the scoping coordinator, and invite comments to be phoned in. Otherwise, small meetings in several locations may be necessary when face-to-face communications is important.

In another case, a site-specific construction project may be proposed. This would be a better candidate for a central scoping meeting. But you must first find out if anyone would be interested in attending such a meeting. If you simply assume that a meeting is necessary, you may hire a hall and a stenographer, assemble your staff for a meeting, and find that nobody shows up.

There are many proposals that just do not generate sufficient public interest to cause people to attend another public meeting. So a wise early step is to contact known local citizens groups and civic leaders.

In addition, you may suggest in your initial scoping notice and information packet that all those who desire a meeting should call to request one. That way you will only hear from those who are seriously interested in attending.

The question of where to hold a meeting is a difficult one in many cases. Except for site specific construction projects, it may be unclear where the interested parties can be found. For example, an EIS on a major energy development program may involve policy issues and alternatives to the program that are of interest to public groups all over the nation, and to agencies headquartered in Washington, D.C., while the physical impacts might be expected to be felt most strongly in a particular region of the country. In such a case, if personal contact is desired, several meetings would be necessary, especially in the affected region and in Washington, to enable all interests to be heard.

As a general guide, unless a proposal has no site specific impacts, scoping meetings should not be *confined* to Washington. Agencies should try to elicit the views of people who are closer to the affected regions.

The key is to be flexible. It may not be possible to plan the whole scoping process at the outset, unless you know who all the potential players are. You can start with written comments, move on to an informal meeting, and hold further meetings if desired.

There are several reasons to hold a scoping meeting. First, some of the best effects of scoping stem from the fact that all parties have the opportunity to meet one another and to listen to the concerns of the others. There is no satisfactory substitute for personal contact to achieve this result. If there is any possibility that resolution of underlying conflicts over a proposal may be achieved, this is always enhanced by the development of personal and working relationships among the parties.

Second, even in a conflict situation people usually respond positively when they are treated as partners in the project review process. If they feel confident that their views were actually heard and taken seriously, they will be more likely to be satisfied that the decision making process was fair even if they disagree with the outcome. It is much easier to show people that you are listening to them if you hold a face-to-face meeting where they can see you writing down their points, than if their only contact is through written comments.

If you suspect that a particular proposal could benefit from a meeting with the affected public at any time during its review, the best time to have the meeting is during this early scoping stage. The fact that you are willing to discuss openly a proposal before you have committed substantial resources to it will often enhance the chances for reaching an accord.

If you decide that a public meeting is appropriate, you still must decide what type of meeting, or how many meetings, to hold. We will discuss meetings in detail below in "Conducting a Public Meeting." But as part of designing the scoping process, you must decide between a single meeting and multiple ones for different interest groups, and whether to hold a separate meeting for government agency participants.

The single large public meeting brings together all the interested parties, which has both advantages and disadvantages. If the meeting is efficiently run, you can cover a lot of interests and issues in a short time. And a single meeting does reduce agency travel time and expense. In some cases it may be an advantage to have all interest groups hear each others' concerns, possibly promoting compromise. It is definitely important to have the staffs of the cooperating agencies, as well as the lead agency, hear the public views of what the significant issues are, and it will be difficult and expensive for the cooperating agencies to attend several meetings. But if there are opposing groups of citizens who feel strongly on both sides of an issue, the setting of the large meeting may needlessly create tension and an emotional confrontation between the groups. Moreover, some people may feel intimidated in such a setting, and won't express themselves at all.

The principal drawback of the large meeting, however, is that it is generally unwieldy. To keep order, discussion is limited, dialogue is difficult, and often all participants are frustrated, agency and public alike. Large meetings can serve to identify the interest groups for future discussion, but often little else is accomplished. Large meetings often become "events" where grandstanding substitutes for substantive comments. Many agencies resort to a formal hearing-type format to maintain control, and this can cause resentments among participants who come to the meeting expecting a responsive discussion.

For these reasons, we recommend that meetings be kept small and informal, and that you hold several, if necessary, to accommodate the different interest groups. The other solution is to break a large gathering into small discussion groups, which is discussed below. Using either method increases the likelihood that participants will level with you and communicate their underlying concerns rather than make an emotional statement just for effect.

Moreover, in our experience, a separate meeting for cooperating agencies is quite productive. Working relationships can be forged for the effective participation of all involved in the preparation of the EIS. Work assignments are made by the lead agency, a schedule may be set for production of parts of the draft EIS, and information gaps can be identified early. But a productive meeting such as this is not possible at the very beginning of the process. It can only result from the same sort of planning and preparation that goes into the public meetings. We discuss below the special problems of cooperating agencies, and their information needs for effective participation in scoping.

4. Issuing the public notice

The preliminary look at the proposal, in which you develop the information packet discussed above, will enable you to tell what kind of public notice will be most appropriate and effective.

Section 1501.7 of the NEPA regulations requires that a notice of intent to prepare an EIS must be published in the Federal Register prior to initiating scoping.* This means that one of the appropriate means of giving public notice of the upcoming scoping process could be the same Federal Register notice. And because the notice of intent must be published anyway, the scoping notice would be essentially free. But use of the Federal Register is not an absolute requirement, and other means of public notice often are more effective, including local newspapers, radio and TV, posting notice in public places, etc. (See Section 1506.6 of the regulations.)

---

* Several agencies have found it useful to conduct scoping for environmental assessments. EAs are prepared where answering the question of whether an EIS is necessary requires identification of significant environmental issues; and consideration of alternatives in an EA can often be useful even where an EIS is not necessary. In both situations scoping can be valuable Thus the Council has stated that scoping may be used in connection with preparation of an EA, that is, before publishing any notice of intent to prepare an EIS. As in normal scoping. appropriate public notice is required, as well as adequate information on the proposal to make scoping worthwhile. But scoping at this early stage cannot substitute for the normal scoping process unless the earlier public notice stated clearly that this would be the case, and the notice of intent expressly provides that written comments suggesting impacts and alternatives for study will still be considered.

What is important is that the notice actually reach the affected public. If the proposal is an important new national policy in which national environmental groups can be expected to be interested, these groups can be contacted by form letter with ease. (See the *Conservation Directory* for a list of national groups.*) Similarly, for proposals that may have major implications for the business community, trade associations can be helpful means of alerting affected groups. The Federal Register notice can be relied upon to notify others that you did not know about. But the Federal Register is of little use for reaching individuals or local groups interested in a site specific proposal. Therefore notices in local papers, letters to local government officials and personal contact with a few known interested individuals would be more appropriate. Land owners abutting any proposed project site should be notified individually.

Remember that issuing press releases to newspapers, and radio and TV stations is not enough, because they may not be used by the media unless the proposal is considered "newsworthy." If the proposal is controversial, you can try alerting reporters or editors to an upcoming scoping meeting for coverage in special weekend sections used by many papers. But placing a notice in the legal notices section of the paper is the only guarantee that it will be published.

5. *Conducting a public meeting*

In our study of agency practice in conducting scoping, the most interesting information on what works and doesn't work involves the conduct of meetings. Innovative techniques have been developed, and experience shows that these can be successful.

One of the most important factors turns out to be the training and experience of the moderator. The U.S. Office of Personnel Management and others give training courses on how to run a meeting effectively. Specific techniques are taught to keep the meeting on course and to deal with confrontations. These techniques are sometimes called "meeting facilitation skills."

When holding a meeting, the principle thing to remember about scoping is that it is a process to initiate preparation of an EIS. It is not concerned with the ultimate decision on the proposal. A fruitful scoping process leads to an adequate environmental analysis, including all reasonable alternatives and mitigation measures. This limited goal is in the interest of all the participants, and thus offers the possibility of agreement by the parties on this much at least. To run a successful meeting you must keep the focus on this *positive* purpose .

At the point of scoping therefore, in one sense all the parties involved have a common goal, which is a thorough environmental review. If you emphasize this in the meeting you can stop any grandstanding speeches without a heavy hand, by simply asking the speaker if he or she has any concrete suggestions for the group on issues to be covered in the EIS. By frequently drawing the meeting back to this central purpose of scoping, the opponents of a proposal will see that you have not already made a decision, and they will be forced to deal with the real issues. In addition, when people see that you are genuinely seeking their opinion, some will volunteer useful information about a particular subject or site that they may know better than anyone on your staff.

As we stated above, we found that informal meetings in small groups are the most satisfactory for eliciting useful issues and information. Small groups can be formed in two ways: you can invite different interest groups to different meetings, or you can break a large number into small groups for discussion.

---

* The Conservation Directory is a publication of the National Wildlife Federation, 1421 16th St., N.W., Washington, D.C. 20036, $4.00.

One successful model is used by the Army Corps of Engineers, among others. In cases where a public meeting is desired, it is publicized and scheduled for a location that will be convenient for as many potential participants as possible. The information packet is made available in several ways, by sending it to those known to be interested, giving a telephone number in the public notices for use in requesting one, and providing more at the door of the meeting place as well. As participants enter the door, each is given a number. Participants are asked to register their name, address and/or telephone number for use in future contact during scoping and the rest of the NEPA process.

The first part of the meeting is devoted to a discussion of the proposal in general, covering its purpose, proposed location, design, and any other aspects that can be presented in a lecture format. A question and answer period concerning this information is often held at this time. Then if there are more than 15 or 20 attendees at the meeting, the next step is to break it into small groups for more intensive discussion. At this point, the numbers held by the participants are used to assign them to small groups by sequence, random drawing, or any other method. Each group should be no larger than 12, and 8-10 is better. The groups are informed that their task is to prepare a list of significant environmental issues and reasonable alternatives for analysis in the EIS. These lists will be presented to the main group and combined into a master list, after the discussion groups are finished. The rules for how priorities are to be assigned to the issues identified by each group should be made clear before the large group breaks up.

Some agencies ask each group member to vote for the 5 or 10 most important issues. After tallying the votes of individual members, each group would only report out those issues that received a certain number of votes. In this way only those items of most concern to the members would even make the list compiled by each group. Some agencies go further, and only let each group report out the top few issues identified. But you must be careful not to ignore issues that may be considered a medium priority by many people. They may still be important, even if not in the top rank. Thus instead of simply voting, the members of the groups should rank the listed issues in order of perceived importance. Points may be assigned to each item on the basis of the rankings by each member, so that the group can compile a list of its issues in priority order. Each group should then be asked to assign cut-off numbers to separate high, medium and low priority items. Each group should then report out to the main meeting all of its issues, but with priorities clearly assigned.

One member of the lead agency or cooperating agency staff should join each group to answer questions and to listen to the participants' expressions of concern. It has been the experience of many of those who have tried this method that it is better not to have the agency person lead the group discussions. There does need to be a leader, who should be chosen by the group members. In this way, the agency staff member will not be perceived as forcing his opinions on the others.

If the agency has a sufficient staff of formally trained "meeting facilitators," they may be able to achieve the same result even where agency staff people lead the discussion groups. But absent such training, the staff should not lead the discussion groups. A good technique is to have the agency person serve as the recording secretary for the group, writing down each impact and alternative that is suggested for study by the participants. This enhances the neutral status of the agency representative, and ensures that he is perceived as listening and reacting to the views of the group. Frequently, the recording of issues is done with a large pad mounted on the wall like a blackboard, which has been well received by agency and public alike, because all can see that the views expressed actually have been heard and understood.

When the issues are listed, each must be clarified or combined with others to eliminate duplication or fuzzy concepts. The agency staff person can actually lead in this effort because of his need to reflect on paper exactly what the issues are. After the group has listed all the environmental impacts and alternatives and any other issues that the members wish to have considered, they are asked to discuss the relative merits and importance of each listed item. The group should be reminded that one of its tasks is to eliminate insignificant issues. Following this, the members assign priorities or vote using one of the methods described above.

The discussion groups are then to return to the large meeting to report on the results of their ranking. At this point further discussion may be useful to seek a consensus on which issues are really insignificant. But the moderator must not appear to be ruthlessly eliminating issues that the participants ranked of high or medium importance. The best that can usually be achieved is to "de-emphasize" some of them, by placing them in the low priority category.

6. What to do with the comments

After you have comments from the cooperating agencies and the interested public, you must evaluate them and make judgments about which issues are in fact significant and which ones are not. The decision of what the EIS should contain is ultimately made by the lead agency. But you will now know what the interested participants consider to be the principal areas for study and analysis. You should be guided by these concerns, or be prepared to briefly explain why you do not agree. Every issue that is raised as a priority matter during scoping should be addressed in some manner in the EIS, either by in-depth analysis, or at least a short explanation showing that the issue was examined, but not considered significant for one or more reasons.

Some agencies have complained that the time savings claimed for scoping have not been realized because after public groups raise numerous minor matters, they cannot focus the EIS on the significant issues. It is true that it is always easier to add issues than it is to subtract them during scoping. And you should realize that trying to *eliminate* a particular environmental impact or alternative from study may arouse the suspicions of some people. Cooperating agencies may be even more reluctant to eliminate issues in their areas of special expertise than the public participants. But the way to approach it is to seek consensus on which issues are less important. These issues may then be de-emphasized in the EIS by a brief discussion of why they were not examined in depth.

If no consensus can be reached, it is still your responsibility to select the significant issues. The lead agency cannot abdicate its role and simply defer to the public. Thus a group of participants at a scoping meeting should not be able to "vote" an insignificant matter into a big issue. If a certain issue is raised and in your professional judgment you believe it is not significant, explain clearly and briefly in the EIS why it is not significant. There is no need to devote time and pages to it in the EIS if you can show that it is not relevant or important to the proposed action. But you should address in some manner all matters that were raised in the scoping process, either by an extended analysis or a brief explanation showing that you acknowledge the concern.

Several agencies have made a practice of sending out a postscoping document to make public the decisions that have been made on what issues to cover in the EIS. This is not a requirement, but in certain controversial cases it can be worthwhile. Especially when scoping has been conducted by written comments, and there has been no face-to-face contact, a post-scoping document is the only assurance to the participants that they were heard and understood until the draft EIS comes out. Agencies have acknowledged to us that "letters instead of meetings seem to get disregarded easier." Thus a reasonable quid pro quo for relying on comment letters would be to send out a post-scoping document as feedback to the commentors.

The post-scoping document may be as brief as a list of impacts and alternatives selected for analysis; it may consist of the "scope of work" produced by the lead and cooperating agencies for their own EIS work or for the contractor; or it may be a special document that describes all the issues and explains why they were selected.

7. *Allocating work assignments and setting schedules*

Following the public participation in whatever form, and the selection of issues to be covered, the lead agency must allocate the EIS preparation work among the available resources. If there are no cooperating agencies, the lead agency allocates work among its own personnel or contractors. If there are cooperating agencies involved, they may be assigned specific research or writing tasks. The NEPA regulations require that they normally devote their own resources to the issues in which they have special expertise or jurisdiction by law. (Sections 1501.6(b)(3), (5), and 1501.7(a)(4)).

In all cases, the lead agency should set a schedule for completion of the work, designate a project manager and assign the reviewers, and must set a time limit for the entire NEPA analysis if requested to do so by an applicant. (Section 1501.8).

8. *A few ideas to try*

a. Route design workshop

As part of a scoping process, a successful innovation by one agency involved route selection for a railroad. The agency invited representatives of the interested groups (identified at a previous public meeting) to try their hand at designing alternative routes for a proposed rail segment. Agency staff explained design constraints and evaluation criteria such as the desire to minimize damage to prime agricultural land and valuable wildlife habitat. The participants were divided in to small groups for a few hours of intensive work. After learning of the real constraints on alternative routes, the participants had a better understanding of the agency's and applicant's viewpoints. Two of the participants actually supported alternative routes that affected their own land because the overall impacts of these routes appeared less adverse.

The participants were asked to rank the five alternatives they had devised and the top two were included in the EIS. But the agency did not permit the groups to apply the same evaluation criteria to the routes proposed by the applicant or the agency. Thus public confidence in the process was not as high as it could have been, and probably was reduced when the applicant's proposal was ultimately selected.

The Council recommends that when a hands-on design workshop is used, the assignment of the group be expanded to include evaluation of the reasonableness of all the suggested alternatives.

b. Hotline

Several agencies have successfully used a special telephone number, essentially a hotline, to take public comments before, after, or instead of a public meeting. It helps to designate a named staff member to receive these calls so that some continuity and personal relationships can be developed.

c. Videotape of sites

A videotape of proposed sites is an excellent tool for explaining site differences and limitations during the lecture-format part of a scoping meeting.

d. Videotape meetings

One agency has videotaped whole scoping meetings. Staff found that the participants took their roles more seriously and the taping appeared not to precipitate grandstanding tactics.

e. Review committee

Success has been reported from one agency which sets up review committees, representing all interested groups, to oversee the scoping process. The committees help to design the scoping process. In cooperation with the lead agency, the committee reviews the materials generated by the scoping meeting. Again, however, the final decision on EIS content is the responsibility of the lead agency.

f. Consultant as meeting moderator

In some hotly contested cases, several agencies have used the EIS consultant to actually run the scoping meeting. This is permitted under the NEPA regulations and can be useful to defuse a tense atmosphere if the consultant is perceived as a neutral third party. But the responsible agency officials must attend the meetings. There is no substitute for developing a relationship between the agency officials and the affected parties. Moreover, if the responsible officials are not prominently present, the public may interpret that to mean that the consultant is actually making the decisions about the EIS, and not the lead agency.

g. Money saving tips

Remember that money can be saved by using conference calls instead of meetings, tape-recording the meetings instead of hiring a stenographer, and finding out whether people want a meeting before announcing it.

C. Pitfalls

We list here some of the problems that have been experienced in certain scoping cases, in order to enable others to avoid the same difficulties .

1. Closed meetings

In response to informal advice from CEQ that holding separate meetings for agencies and the public would be permitted under the regulations and could be more productive, one agency scheduled a scoping meeting for the cooperating agencies some weeks in advance of the public meeting. Apparently, the lead agency felt that the views of the cooperating agencies would be more candidly expressed if the meeting were closed. In any event, several members of the public learned of the meeting and asked to be present. The lead agency acquiesced only after newspaper reporters were able to make a story out of the closed session. At the meeting, the members of the public were informed that they would not be allowed to speak, nor to record the proceedings. The ill feeling aroused by this chain of events may not be repaired for a long time. Instead. we would suggest the following possibilities:

a. Although separate meetings for agencies and public groups may be more efficient, there is no magic to them. By all means. if someone insists on attending the agency meeting, let him. There is nothing as secret going on there as he may think there is if you refuse him admittance. Better yet, have your meeting of cooperating agencies after the public meeting. That may be the most logical time anyway, since only then can the scope of the EIS be decided upon and assignments made among the agencies. If it is well done. the public meeting will satisfy most people and show them that you are listening to them.

b. Always permit recording, In fact, you should suggest it for public meetings. All parties will feel better if there is a record of the proceeding. There is no need for a stenographer, and tape is inexpensive. It may even be better then a typed transcript. because staff and decision makers who did not attend the meeting can listen to the exchange and may learn a lot about public perceptions of the proposal.

c. When people are admitted to a meeting, it makes no sense to refuse their requests to speak. However, you can legitimately limit their statements to the subject at hand—scoping. You do not have to permit some participants to waste the others' time if they refuse to focus on the impacts and alternatives for inclusion in the EIS. Having a tape of the proceedings could be useful after the meeting if there is some question that speakers were improperly silenced. But it takes an experienced moderator to handle a situation like this.

d. The scoping stage is the time for building confidence and trust on all sides of a proposal, because this is the only time when there is a common enterprise. The attitudes formed at this stage can carry through the project review process. Certainly it is difficult for things to get better. So foster the good will as long as you can by listening to what is being said during scoping. It is possible that out of that dialogue may appear recommendations for changes and mitigation measures that can turn a controversial fight into an acceptable proposal.

2. Contacting interested groups

Some problems have arisen in scoping where agencies failed to contact all the affected parties, such as industries or state and local governments. In one case, a panel was assembled to represent various interests in scoping an EIS on a wildlife-related program. The agency had an excellent format for the meeting, but the panel did not represent industries that would be affected by the program or interested state and local governments. As a result, the EIS may fail to reflect the issues of concern to these parties.

Another agency reported to us that it failed to contact parties directly because staff feared that if they missed someone they would be accused of favoritism. Thus they relied on the issuance of press releases which were not effective. Many people who did not learn about the meetings in time sought additional meeting opportunities, which cost extra money and delayed the process.

In our experience, the attempt to reach people is worth the effort. Even if you miss someone, it will be clear that you tried. You can enlist a few representatives of an interest group to help you identify and contact others. Trade associations, chambers of commerce, local civic groups, and local and national conservation groups can spread the word to members.

3. Tiering

Many people are not familiar with the way environmental impact statements can be "tiered" under the NEPA regulations, so that issues are examined in detail at the stage that decisions on them are being made. See Section 1508.28 of the regulations. For example, if a proposed program is under review, it is possible that site specific actions are not yet proposed. In such a case, these actions are not addressed in the EIS on the program, but are reserved for a later tier of analysis. If tiering is being used, this concept must be made clear at the outset of any scoping meeting, so that participants do not concentrate on issues that are not going to be addressed at this time. If you can specify when these other issues will be addressed it will be easier to convince people to focus on the matters at hand.

4. Scoping for unusual programs

One interesting scoping case involved proposed changes in the Endangered Species Program. Among the impacts to be examined were the effects of this conservation program *on user activities* such as mining, hunting, and timber harvest, instead of the other way around. Because of this reverse twist in the impacts to be analyzed, some participants had difficulty focusing on useful issues. Apparently, if the subject of the EIS is unusual, it will be even harder than normal for scoping participants to grasp what is expected of them.

In the case of the Endangered Species Program EIS, the agency planned an intensive 3 day scoping session, successfully involved the participants, and reached accord on several issues that would be important for the future implementation of the program. But the participants were unable to focus on impacts and program alternatives for the EIS. We suggest that if the intensive session had been broken up into 2 or 3 meetings separated by days or weeks, the participants might have been able to get used to the new way of thinking required, and thereby to participate more productively. Programmatic proposals are often harder to deal with in a scoping context than site specific projects. Thus extra care should be taken in explaining the goals of the proposal and in making the information available well in advance of any meetings.

D. Lead and Cooperating Agencies

Some problems with scoping revolve around the relationship between lead and cooperating agencies. Some agencies are still uncomfortable with these roles. The NEPA regulations, and the *40 Questions and Answers about the NEPA Regulations*, 46 Fed . Reg. 18026, (March 23, 1981) describe in detail the way agencies are now asked to cooperate on environmental analyses. (See Questions 9, 14, and 30.) We will focus here on the early phase of that cooperation.

It is important for the lead agency to be as specific as possible with the cooperating agencies. Tell them what you want them to contribute during scoping: environmental impacts and alternatives. Some agencies still do not understand the purpose of scoping.

Be sure to contact and involve representatives of the cooperating agencies who are responsible for NEPA-related functions. The lead agency will need to contact staff of the cooperating agencies who can both help to identify issues and alternatives *and* commit resources to a study, agree to a schedule for EIS preparation, or approve a list of issues as sufficient. In some agencies that will be at the district or state office level (e.g., Corps of Engineers, Bureau of Land Management, and Soil Conservation Service) for all but exceptional cases. In other agencies you must go to regional offices for scoping comments and commitments (e.g., EPA, Fish and Wildlife Service, Water and Power Resources Service). In still others, the field offices do not have NEPA responsibilities or expertise and you will deal directly with headquarters (e.g., Federal Energy Regulatory Commission, Interstate Commerce Commission. In all cases you are looking for the office that can give you the answers you need. So keep trying until you find the organizational level of the cooperating agency that can give you useful information and that has the authority to make commitments.

As stated in 40 *Questions and Answers about the NEPA Regulations*, the lead agency has the ultimate responsibility for the content of the EIS, but if it leaves out a significant issue or ignores the advice and expertise of the cooperating agency, the EIS may be found later to be inadequate. (46 Fed. Reg. 18030, Question 14b.) At the same time, the cooperating agency will be concerned that the EIS contain material sufficient to satisfy its decision making needs. Thus, both agencies have a stake in producing a document of good quality. The cooperating agencies should be encouraged not only to participate in scoping but also to review the decisions made by the lead agency about what to include in the EIS. Lead agencies should allow any information needed by a cooperating agency to be included, and any issues of concern to the cooperating agency should be covered, but it usually will have to be at the expense of the cooperating agency.

Cooperating agencies have at least as great a need as the general public for advance information on a proposal before any scoping takes place. Agencies have reported to us that information from the lead agency is often too sketchy or comes too late for informed participation. Lead agencies must clearly explain to all cooperating agencies what the proposed action is conceived to be at this time, and what present alternatives and issues the lead agency sees, before expecting other agencies to devote time and money to a scoping session. Informal contacts among the agencies before scoping gets underway are valuable to establish what the cooperating agencies will need for productive scoping to take place.

Some agencies will be called upon to be cooperators more frequently than others, and they may lack the resources to respond to the numerous requests. The NEPA regulations permit agencies without jurisdiction by law (i.e., no approval authority over the proposal) to decline the cooperating agency role. (Section 1501 .6(c)). But agencies that do have jurisdiction by law cannot opt out entirely and may have to reduce their cooperating effort devoted to each EIS. (See Section 1501~(c) and 40 *Questions and Answers about the NEPA Regulations, 46* Fed. Reg. 18030, Question 14a.) Thus, cooperators would be greatly aided by a priority list from the lead agency showing which proposals most need their help. This will lead to a more efficient allocation of resources.

Some cooperating agencies are still holding back at the scoping stage in order to retain a critical position for later in the process. They either avoid the scoping sessions or fail to contribute and then raise objections in comments on the draft EIS. We cannot emphasize enough that the whole point of scoping is to avoid this situation. As we stated in 40 *Questions and Answers about the NEPA Regulations. "if* the new alternative [or other issue] was not raised by the commentor during scoping, but could have been, commentors may find that they are unpersuasive in their efforts to have their suggested alternative analyzed in detail by the [lead] agency." (46 Fed. Reg. 18035, Question 29b.)

III. Advice for Public Participants

Scoping is a new opportunity for you to enter the earliest phase of the decision making process on proposals that affect you. Through this process you have access to public officials before decisions are made and the right to explain your objections and concern. But this opportunity carries with it a new responsibility. No longer may individuals hang back until the process is almost complete and then spring forth with a significant issue or alternative that might have been raised earlier. You are now part of the review process, and your role is to inform the responsible agencies of the potential impacts that should be studied, the problems a proposal may cause that you foresee, and the alternatives and mitigating measures that offer promise.

As noted above, and in 40 *Questions and Answers,* no longer will a comment raised for the first time after the draft EIS is finished be accorded the same serious consideration it would otherwise have merited: if the issue had been raised during scoping. Thus you have a responsibility to come forward early with known issues.

In return, you get the chance to meet the responsible officials and to make the case for your alternative before they are committed to a course of action. To a surprising degree this avenue has been found to yield satisfactory results. .There's no guarantee, of course, but when the alternative you suggest is really better, it is often hard for a decision-maker to resist.

There are several problems that commonly arise that public participants should be aware of:

A. Public input is often only negative

The optimal timing of scoping within the NEPA process is difficult to judge. On the one hand, as explained above (Section 11. B. 1.), if it is attempted too early, the agency cannot explain what it has in mind and informed participation will be impossible. On the other, if it is delayed, the public may find that significant decisions are already made, and their comments may be discounted or will be too late to change the project. Some agencies have found themselves in a tactical cross-fire when public criticism arises before they can even define their proposal sufficiently to see whether they have a worthwhile plan. Understandably, they would be reluctant after such an experience to *invite* public criticism early in the planning process through open scoping. But it is in your interest to encourage agencies to come out with proposals in the early stage because that enhances the possibility of your comments being used. Thus public participants in scoping should reduce the emotion level wherever possible and use the opportunity to make thoughtful, rational presentations on impacts and alternatives. Polarizing over issues too early hurts all parties. If agencies get positive and useful public responses from the scoping process, they will more frequently come forward with proposals early enough so that they can be materially improved by your suggestions.

B. Issues are too broad

The issues that participants tend to identify during scoping are much too broad to be useful for analytical purposes. For example, "cultural impacts"—what does this mean? What precisely are the impacts that should be examined? When the EIS preparers encounter a comment as vague as this they will have to make their own judgment about what you meant, and you may find that your issues are not covered. Thus, you should refine the broad general topics, and specify which issues need evaluation and analysis.

C. Impacts are not identified

Similarly, people (including agency staff) frequently identify "causes" as issues but fail to identify the principal *"effects"* that the EIS should evaluate in depth. For example, oil and gas development is a cause of many impacts. Simply listing this generic category is of little help. You must go beyond the obvious causes to the specific effects that are of concern. If you want scoping to be seen as more than just another public meeting, you will need to put in extra work.

IV. Brief Points For Applicants

Scoping can be an invaluable part of your early project planning. Your main interest is in getting a proposal through the review process. This interest is best advanced by finding out early where the problems with the proposal are, who the affected parties are, and where accommodations can be made. Scoping is an ideal meeting place for all the interest groups if you have not already contacted them. In several cases, we found that the compromises made at this stage allowed a project to move efficiently through the permitting process virtually unopposed.

The NEPA regulations place an affirmative obligation on agencies to "provide for cases where actions are planned by private applicants" so that designated staff are available to consult with the applicants, to advise applicants of information that will be required during review, and to insure that the NEPA process commences at the earliest possible time. (Section 1501 .2(d)). This section of the regulations is intended to ensure that environmental factors are considered at an early stage in the applicant's planning process. (See *40 Questions and Answers about the NEPA Regulations*, 46 Fed. Reg. 18028, Questions 8 and 9.)

Applicants should take advantage of this requirement in the regulations by approaching the agencies early to consult on alternatives, mitigation requirements, and the agency's information needs. This early contact with the agency can facilitate a prompt initiation of the scoping process in cases where an EIS will be prepared. You will need to furnish sufficient information about your proposal to enable the lead agency to formulate a coherent presentation for cooperating agencies and the public. But don't wait until your choices are all made and the alternatives have been eliminated (Section 1506.1).

During scoping, be sure to attend any of the public meetings unless the agency is dividing groups by interest affiliation. You will be able to answer any questions about the proposal, and even more important, you will be able to hear the objections raised, and find out what the real concerns of the public are. This is, of course, vital information for future negotiations with the affected parties.

Appendix 6 Federal NEPA Liaisons*

Agriculture Department

Dr. Richard M. Parry, Jr.
Deputy Assistant Administrator
Office of Cooperation Interactions
Agriculture Research Service
U.S. Department of Agriculture
Room 102, Building 005, BARC-West
Beltsville, MD 20705-2350
301-344-2734
301-344-1621 (fax)

Mr. G. Tim Denley
Chief
Planning and Evaluation Branch
**Agriculture Stabilization
and Conservation Service**
Department of Agriculture
Rm 4714, P.O. Box 2415
14th and Independence Avenue, SW
Washington, DC 20013
202-447-3264
202-447-4619 (fax)

Mr. Carl Bausch
Deputy Director
Environmental Analysis and Documentation
Animal and Plant Health Inspection Service
Department of Agriculture
Room 842, Federal Building
6505 Belcrest Road
Hyattsville, MD 20782
301-436-7602
301-463-8669 (fax)

Dr. John A. Miranowski, Director
Resources and Technology Division
Economic Research Service
Department of Agriculture
Room 524
1301 New York Avenue, NW
Washington, DC 20005
202-219-0455
202-219-0477 (fax)

Ms. Susan G. Wieferich
Environmental Protection Specialist
Program Support Staff
Farmers Home Administration
Department of Agriculture
Rm 6309 South Agriculture Building
14th and Independence Avenue, SW
Washington, DC 20250
202-382-9619
202-382-9719 (fax)

Mr. Ralph Stafko, Director
Policy Office
Food Safety and Inspection Service
Department of Agriculture
Room 3812 South Agriculture Building
12th and Independence Avenue, SW
Washington, DC 20250
202-447-8168
202-447-5124 (fax)

* **Source:** Council on Environmental Quality (October 5, 1992)

Mr. John A. Vance
**Natural Resources and Rural Development
  Extention Service**
Department of Agriculture
Room 3909 South Agriculture Building
14th and Independence Avenue, SW
Washington, DC 20250-0900
202-447-7947
202-475-6489 (fax)

Mr. Charles Terrell
Environmental Specialist
Soil Conservation Service
Department of Agriculture
Ecological Science Division
P.O. Box 2890
Washington, DC 20013
202-447-4925
202-447-2646 (fax)

Mr. David Ketcham, Director
Environmental Coordination Staff
U.S. Forest Service
Department of Agriculture
201 14th Street, SW - 550
Washington, DC 20250
202-205-1708
202-205-0936 (fax)

COMMERCE DEPARTMENT

Dr. Frank Monteferrante
Senior Environmental Specialist
Economic Development Administration
Department of Commerce
Room H7019 Herbert Hoover Building
14th and Constitution Avenue, NW
Washington, DC 20230
202-377-4208
202-377-0995 (fax)

Mr. David Cottingham, Director
Ecology and Conservation Office
Office of the Chief Scientist
**National Oceanic and Atmospheric
  Administration**
Department of Commerce
HCHB, Room 6222
14th and Constitution Avenue, NW
Washington, DC 20230
202-482-5181
202-482-5231 (fax)

DEFENSE DEPARTMENT

Mr. L. Peter Boice
Deputy for Natural Resources
ODASD (E)
Department of Defense
400 Army Navy Drive, #206
Arlington, VA 22202-2884
703-695-8355
703-697-7548 (fax)

Mr. Bill Randall
**Defense Logistics Services and
  Environmental Protection**
Environmental Division
Attention: DLA-WE Room 4D489
Cameron Station
Alexandria, VA 22304-6100
703-274-6124
703-274-8650 (fax)

Mr. Dave Van Gasbeck
Chief, Environmental Planning Division
Department of Air Force
The Pentagon, 5D381
Washington, DC 20330-1000
703-695-8940
703-695-8943 (fax)

Col. Chris Conrad
Assistant for Environmental Projects
Department of the Army
Room 2E577 Pentagon
Attn: OASA (I L and E)
Washington, DC 20310
703-695-7824
703-693-8149 (fax)

Mr. John Bellinger
Office of Environmental Policy
CECW-PO
U.S. Army Corps of Engineers
20 Massachusetts Avenue, NW
Washington, DC 20314-1000
202-272-0130
202-272-1163 (fax)

Commandant of the Marine Corps
Code LFL
Attention: Mr. Marlo Acock
Washington, DC 20380
703-696-0865
703-696-1020 (fax)

Mr. Tom Peeling
Office of Chief of Naval Operations
  (OP-44EP1)
Department of the Navy
Room 10N67 Hoffman Building II
200 Stovall Street
Alexandria, VA 22332-2300
703-325-7344
703-325-2261 (fax)

Ms. Ann Anderson
SW Division Code 232AA
Naval Facilities Engineering Command
1220 Pacific Highway
San Diego, CA 92132-5190
619-532-1322
619-532-3824 (fax)

ENERGY DEPARTMENT

Ms. Carol Borgstrom
Director
Office of NEPA Oversight
Department of Energy
Room 3E-080
1000 Independence Ave, SW
Washington, DC 20585
202-586-4600
202-586-7031 (fax)

Mr. Jon Worthington
Power Marketing Specialist
Bonneville Power Administration
1000 Independence Avenue, SW
Room 8G033
Washington, DC 20585
202-586-5640
202-586-6762 (fax)

Mr. Lawrence Wolfe
Environmental Policy Specialist
Electric Staff Division
Rural Electrification Administration
Room 1247 South Agriculture Building
14th and Independence Avenue, SW
Washington, DC 20250
202-382-9093
202-382-6098 (fax)

Mr. Bill Karsell
Director of Environmental Affairs
Western Area Power Administration
1627 Cole Boulevard, A0420
Golden, CO 80401
303-231-1706 or FTS-327-1706
303-231-1748 (fax) or FTS-327-1748 (fax)

HEALTH AND HUMAN SERVICES DEPARTMENT

Mr. Richard Green
Safety Manager
Department of Health and Human Services
Cohen Building, Room 4700
200 Independence Avenue, SW
Washington, DC 20201
202-619-0426
202-619-1407 (fax)

NATIONAL INSTITUTE OF HEALTH

Mr. Thomas C. Cloutier, P.E.
PHS Environmental Officer
National Institute of Health
Parklawn Building 17A-10
5600 Fishers Lane
Rockville, MD 20857
301-443-2265
301-443-0084 (fax)

HOUSING AND URBAN DEVELOPMENT DEPT.

Mr. Richard H. Broun, Director
Office of Environment and Energy
Department of Housing and Urban
  Development
451 Seventh Street, SW
Washington, DC 20410-7000
202-708-2894
202-708-0299 (fax)

INTERIOR DEPARTMENT

Mr. Jonathan P. Deason, Director
Office of Environmental Affairs
Department of the Interior
MS 2340 Interior Building
1849 C Street, NW
Washington, DC 20240
202-208-3891
202-289-7405 (fax)

Mr. John T. Goll, Chief
Environmental Policy and Programs
  Division
Minerals Management Service
Department of the Interior
The Atrium Building
381 Elden Street
Mail Stop 4300
Herndon, VA 22070
703-787-1656
703-787-1010 (fax)

Mr. Don Peterson
Environmental Coordinator
Division of Endangered Species and Habitat
  Conservation
US Fish and Wildlife Service
Department of the Interior
400 Arlington Square Building
Washington, DC 20240
703-358-2183
703-358-2232 (fax)

Mr. Cliford A. Haupt
Chief
Environmental Affairs Program
US Geological Survey
Department of Interior
Mail Stop 423, National Center
Reston, VA 22092
703-648-6832
703-648-5704 (fax)

Mr. George R. Farris
Chief, Environmental Services Staff
Office of Trust & Economic Development
Bureau of Indian Affairs
Department of Interior
MIB 4544
18th and C Streets, NW
Washington, DC 20240
202-208-4791
202-208-3282 (fax)

Mr. Paul Petty
Environmental Specialist
Planning and Environmental Coordination
Bureau of Land Management (WO-760)
Department of Interior
2850 Youngfield Street
Lakewood, Colorado 80215
303-239-3736
303-239-3933 (fax)

Mr. William L. Miller
Chief
Division of Policy Analysis
Bureau of Mines
Department of the Interior
Mail Stop 5204, Room 627
2401 E Street, NW
Washington, DC 20241
202-634-1292
202-634-4659 (fax)

Mr. Jacob Hoogland, Chief
Environmental Quality Division
National Park Service
Department of the Interior
Mail Stop 774, Room 1210
18th and C Streets, NW
Washington, DC 20240
202-208-3163
202-208-4260 (fax)

Ms. Judith Troast
Senior Environmental Specialist
Bureau of Reclamation
Department of the Interior
Mail Code W6550
Main Interior Building
Washington, DC 20240
202-208-4442
202-208-3484 (fax)

Mr. Andrew F. DeVito, Chief
Branch of Environmental and Economic
 Analysis
Office of Surface Mining
Department of the Interior
1951 Constituion Ave., NW, Room 5415-L
Washington, DC 20240
202-343-5150
202-898-1291 (fax)

JUSTICE DEPARTMENT

Ms. Ellen Harrison
Associate Chief Counsel
Civil Litigation Section
Drug Enforcement Administration
Department of Justice
Washington, DC 20537
202-307-8040
202-307-8069 (fax)

Ms. Victoria Kingslien
Director
Facilities and Engineering
Immigration and Naturalization Service
Department of Justice
425 Eye Street, NW
Room 2003
Washington, DC 20536
202-514-4448
202-514-0579 (fax)

Mr. Gerald (Jerry) P. Regier
Acting Director
Bureau of Justice Assistance
Room 1042
Department of Justice
633 Indiana Avenue, NW
Washington, DC 20531
202-514-6278
202-514-5956 (fax)

Dr. Steven Dillingham
Director
Bureau of Justice Statistics
Room 1142
Department of Justice
633 Indiana Avenue, NW
Washington, DC 20531
202-307-0765
202-307-5846 (fax)

Mr. William M. Cohen, Chief
General Litigation Section
Land and Natural Resources Division
Department of Justice
601 Pennsylvania Avenue
8th Floor, Room 870
Washington, DC 20530
202-272-6851
202-272-6815 (fax)

Ms. Kathleen Murphy
Office of Legal Counsel
Department of Justice
Room 5224, Justice Building
10th and Constitution Avenue, NW
Washington, DC 20530
202-514-2051
202-514-0539 (fax)

Ms. Patricia K. Sledge, Chief
Site Acquisition
Office of Facilities Development and
 Operations
Bureau of Prisons
Department of Justice
320 1st Street, NW
Washington, DC 20534
202-514-6470
202-514-6466 (fax)

LABOR DEPARTMENT

Mr. Robert E. Copeland, Director
Office of Regulatory Economics
Assistant Secretary for Policy
Department of Labor
S-2312 Frances Perkins Building
200 Constitution Ave, NW
Washington, DC 20210
202-523-6197
202-523-9216 (fax)

Mr. Alan Mattes
Office of Standards, Regs. and Variances
Mine Safety and Health Administration
Ballston Tower #3, Room 627
4015 Wilson Boulevard
Arlington, VA 22203
703-235-1910
703-235-1563 (fax)

Dr. Hugh Conway, Director
Office of Regulatory Analysis
**Occupational Safety and Health
  Administration**
Department of Labor
N-3627 Frances Perkins Building
200 Constitution Avenue, NW
Washington, DC 20210
202-523-9690
202-523-0383 (fax)

State Department

Ms. Evelyn Wheeler
Office of Ecology, Health and Conservation
**Bureau of Oceans and International
  Environmental and Scientific Affairs**
  (OES/EHC)
Room 4325
Department of State
Washington, DC 20520
202-647-3367
202-736-7351 (fax)

Transportation Department

Mr. Joseph Canny
**Deputy Assistant Secretary for Policy and
  International Affairs**
U.S. Department of Transportation
Room 10228, Nassif Building
400 Seventh Street, SW
Washington, DC 20590-0001
202-366-4540
202-366-7172 (fax)

Ms. Louise E. Maillett
Deputy Director
Office of Environment and Energy (AEE-2)
Federal Aviation Administration
Department of Transportation
Room 432B
800 Independence Avenue, SW
Washington, DC 20591
202-267-3576
202-267-5594 (fax)

Mr. Kevin E. Heanue, HEP-1
Director
Office of Environment and Planning
Federal Highway Administration
Department of Transportation
Room 3212 Nassif Building
400 Seventh Street, SW
Washington, DC 20590
202-366-2951
202-366-3713 (fax)

Ms. Marilyn W. Klein
Senior Policy Analyst
Economic Studies Division
Federal Railroad Administration
Room 8300 Nassif Building
400 Seventh Street, SW
Washington, DC 20590
202-366-0358
202-366-7688 (fax)

Mr. Daniel W. Leubecker
Office of Technology Assessment
Maritime Administration
Code 840, Room 7328
Department of Transportation
400 Seventh Street, SW
Washington, DC 20590
202-366-1939
202-366-3889 (fax)

Ms. Kathleen C. DeMeter
Assistant Chief Counsel/General Law
**National Highway Traffic Safety
  Administration (NCC-30)**
Department of Transportation
Room 5219 Nassif Building
400 Seventh Street, SW
Washington, DC 20590
202-366-1834
202-366-3820 (fax)

Mr. Alfred E. Barrington, Chief
Safety and Environmental Technology
  Division (DTS-75)
Department of Transportation
**Research and Special Programs
  Administration**
John A. Volpe National Transportation
  Systems Center
Kendall Square
Cambridge, MA 02142
617-494-2018
617-494-2497 (fax)

Mr. John B. Adams, III
Senior Staff Engineer
**Saint Lawrence Seaway Development
  Corporation**
U.S. Department of Transportation
P.O. Box 520
Massena, NY 13662-0520
315-764-3233
315-764-3243 (fax)

Mr. T.J. Granito, Chief
Environmental Protection Branch
Commandant (ECV-2)
U.S. Coast Guard
U.S. Department of Transportation
2100 2nd Street, SW
Washington, DC 20593
202-267-1941
202-267-4219 (fax)

Mr. Samuel L. Zimmerman
Director
Office of Planning
Federal Transit Administration
U.S. Department of Transportation
Room 9301 Nassif Building
400 Seventh Street, SW
Washington, DC 20590
202-366-0096
202-366-7951 (fax)

TREASURY DEPARTMENT

Mr. William McGovern
U.S. Department of Treasury
Management Support Systems
1500 Pennsylvania Avenue, NW
Treasury Annex Building
Room 6140
Washington, DC 20220
202-377-9165
202-786-8455 (fax)

ACTION

Mr. Lowell Genebach
Director
Planning and Budget
Action
Suite 4100
1100 Vermont Avenue, NW
Washington, DC 20525
202-606-5137
202-606-5127 (fax)

ADVISORY COUNCIL ON HISTORIC PRESERVATION

Mr. Ronald Anzalone, Director
Office of Program Review and Education
Advisory Council on Historic Preservation
Old Post Office Building, #803
1100 Pennsylvania Avenue, NW
Washington, DC 20004
202-606-8505
202-606-8672 (fax)

APPALACHIAN REGIONAL COMMISSION

Ms. Geraldine Storm-Gevanthor
Director
**Division of Housing and Community
  Development**
Appalachian Regional Commission
1666 Connecticut Avenue, NW
Washington, DC 20235
202-673-7845
202-673-7930 (fax)

ARMS CONTROL AND DISARMAMENT AGENCY

Mr. Thomas Graham, Jr.
General Counsel
Arms Control and Disarmament Agency
Room 5534
320 21st Street, NW
Washington, DC 20451
202-647-3582
202-647-6721 (fax)

CENTRAL INTELLIGENCE AGENCY

Ms. Ellen Tidd, Chief
Environmental Issues Branch
Office of Resources, Trade and Technology
Central Intelligence Agency
Room 2G00
CIA Headquarters
Washington, DC 20505

COMMITTEE FOR PURCHASE FROM THE BLIND AND OTHER SEVERELY HANDICAPPED

Mr. G. John Heyer
General Counsel
Committee for Purchase From theBlind and
  Other Severely Handicapped
Crystal Square 5, Room 1107
1755 Jefferson Davis Highway
Arlington, VA 22202-3509
703-557-1145
703-521-7713 (fax)

CONSUMER PRODUCT SAFETY COMMISSION

Mr. Warren J. Prunella
Associate Executive Director
Directorate for Economic Analysis
Consumer Product Safety Commission
Washington, DC 20207
301-492-6962
301-492-6924 (fax)

DELAWARE RIVER BASIN COMMISSION

Mr. Gerald M. Hansler
Executive Director
Delaware River Basin Commission
25 State Police Drive
P.O. Box 7360
West Trenton, NJ 08628
609-883-9500
609-883-9522 (fax)

ENVIRONMENTAL PROTECTION AGENCY

Mr. Dick Sanderson, Director
Office of Federal Activities (A-104)
Environmental Protection Agency
Room 2119-I
401 M Street, SW
Washington, DC 20460
202-260-5053
202-260-0129 (fax)

EXPORT-IMPORT BANK OF THE UNITED STATES

Mr. Stephen G. Glazer
Deputy General Counsel
Export-Import Bank of the United States
Room 957 - Lafayette Building
811 Vermont Avenue, NW
Washington, DC 20571
202-566-8864
202-566-7524 (fax)

FARM CREDIT ADMINISTRATION

Mr. Victor A. Cohen
Acting Associate General Counsel
Office of General Counsel
Enforcement and Litigation Division
Farm Credit Administration
1501 Farm Credit Drive
McLean, VA 22102-5090
703-883-4023
703-734-5784 (fax)

FEDERAL COMMUNICATIONS COMMISSION

Ms. Holly Berland
Staff Attorney
Legal Counsel Division
Office of General Counsel
Federal Communications Commission
Room 621
1919 M Street NW
Washington, DC 20554
202-254-6530
202-632-0149 (fax)

FEDERAL DEPOSIT INSURANCE CORPORATION

Mr. James A. Watkins
Assistant Director
**Division of Accounting and Corporate
    Services**
Federal Deposit Insurance Corporation
Room PA-3030
550 Seventeenth Street, NW
Washington, DC 20429
202-898-3605
202-898-7160 (fax)

FEDERAL EMERGENCY MANAGEMENT AGENCY

Ms. Brenda Groanflo
Federal Emergency Management Agency
Room 840
500 C Street, SW
Washington, DC 20472
202-646-3543
202-646-4536 (fax)

FEDERAL ENERGY REGULATORY COMMISSION

Mr. Michael Schopf
Associate General Counsel
**Enforcement and General and
    Administrative Law**
Federal Energy Regulatory Commission
825 North Capitol Street, NE
Washington, DC 20426
202-208-0597
202-208-2115 (fax)

Mr. Richard R. Hoffmann, Chief
Environmental Policy Branch
Office of Pipeline and Producer Regulation
Federal Energy Regulatory Commission
Room 7312
825 North Capitol Street, NE
Washington, DC 20426
202-208-0066
202-208-2853 (fax)

Mr. Dean L. Shumway
Director
Division of Project Review
Office of Hydropower Licensing
Federal Energy Regulatory Commission
HL-20, Room 1027, 810 UCP
825 North Capitol Street, N.E.
Washington, DC 20426
202-219-2770
202-219-0125 (fax)

FEDERAL MARITIME COMMISSION

Mr. Edward R. Meyer
Office of Information Resource Management
Federal Maritime Commission
Suite 11305
1100 L Street, NW
Washington, DC 20573
202-523-1930
202-523-3782 (fax)

FEDERAL RESERVE SYSTEM

Mr. Gerald Bechtle
Board of Governors of the Federal Reserve
    System
20th and Constitution Avenue, NW
Stop 192
Washington, DC 20551
202-452-3971
202-452-6474 (fax)

Federal Trade Commission

Mr. Jerold D. Cummins
Deputy Assistant General Counsel
Federal Trade Commission
Room 582
6th Street & Pennsylvania Avenue, NW
Washington, DC 20580
202-326-2471
202-326-2050 (fax)

General Services Administration

Mr. Anthony E. Costa
Chief
**Environmental Policy and Planning Branch
 (PL&P)**
Office Planning
General Services Administration
Room 6037
18th and F Streets, NW
Washington, DC 20405
202-501-3695
202-501-2300 (fax)

International Boundary and Water Comm.

Mr. Conrad G. Keyes, Jr.
Principal Engineer
Planning
International Boundary and Water
 Commission
United States Section
4171 North Mesa, Suite C310
El Paso, TX 79902-1422
915-534-6703
FTS-570-6680 (fax)

Interstate Commerce Commission

Ms. Vicki Dettmar
Staff Attorney
Section of Energy and Environment
Interstate Commerce Commission
Interstate Commerce Commission Building
Room 3115
12th and Constitution Avenue, NW
Washington, DC 20423
202-275-7316
202-275-7564 (fax)

Marine Mammal Commission

Mr. Michael L. Gosliner
General Counsel
Marine Mammal Commission
Room 512
1825 Connecticut Avenue, NW
Washington, DC 20009
202-606-5504
202-606-5510 (fax)

National Academy of Sciences

Dr. James Reisa
Director
**Board of Environmental Studies and
 Toxicology**
National Academy of Sciences
Mail Code HA354
2101 Constitution Avenue, NW
Washington, DC 20418
202-334-3060
202-334-2752 (fax)

NASA

Mr. Kenneth Kumor
Environmental Management Branch (NXG)
National Aeronautics and Space
 Administration
Room 5031
400 Maryland Avenue, SW
Washington, DC 20546
202-453-1956
202-755-2468 (fax)

National Capital Planning Commission

Mr. Maurice Foushee
Environmental Specialist
Technical Planning Services Division
National Capital Planning Commission
801 Pennsylvania Avenue, NW
Suite 301
Washington, DC 20576
202-724-0179
202-724-0195 (fax)

NATIONAL CREDIT UNION ADMINISTRATION

Mr. Michael J. McKenna, Esquire
Staff Attorney
Division of Operations
Office of General Counsel
National Credit Union Administration
1776 G Street, NW
Washington, DC 20456
202-682-9630
202-682-9620 (fax)

NATIONAL SCIENCE FOUNDATION

Dr. Julian Shedlovsky
Chairman and Staff Associate
Committee on Environmental Matters
Directorate for Geosciences
National Science Foundation
Room 641, 1800 G Street, NW
Washington, DC 20550
202-357-9752
202-357-9629 (fax)

NUCLEAR REGULATORY COMMISSION

Mr. Seymour H. Weiss
Director
Office of Nuclear Reactor Regulation
Nuclear Regulatory Commission
11-B-20
Washington, DC 20555
301-492-0170
301-492-0259 (fax)

Mr. Richard E. Cunningham
Director
Division of Industrial and Medical Nuclear Safety
Nuclear Regulatory Commission
Mail Stop GH3
Washington, DC 20555
301-492-3426
301-492-0259 (fax)

Ms. Maria Lopez-Otin
Federal Liaison
Nuclear Regulatory Commission
Mail Stop 3D23
Washington, DC 20555
301-504-2598
301-504-2395 (fax)

OVERSEAS PRIVATE INVESTMENT CORPORATION

Mr. Harvey A. Himberg
Director
Development Policy and Environmental Affairs
Investment Development Department
Overseas Private Investment Corporation
1615 M Street, NW
Washington, DC 20527
202-457-7139
202-331-4234 (fax)

PENNSYLVANIA AVENUE DEVELOPMENT CORPORATION

Mr. Jerry M. Smedley
Assistant Director of Development
Pennsylvania Avenue Development Corporation
Room 1220N
1331 Pennsylvania Ave., NW
Washington, DC 20004
202-724-9068
202-724-0246 (fax)

SECURITIES AND EXCHANGE COMMISSION

Mr. David G. LaRoche
Staff Attorney
Public Utility Regulation
Securities and Exchange Commission
Room 10227, Stop 10-6
450 Fifth Street, NW
Washington, DC 20549
202-272-2073
202-504-2395 (fax)

SMALL BUSINESS ADMINISTRATION

Mr. Michael Dowd
Acting Director
Office of Business Loans
Small Business Administration
8th Floor
409 3rd Street, SW
Washington, DC 20416
202-205-6570
202-205-7591 (fax)

SUSQUEHANNA RIVER BASIN COMMISSION

Mr. Robert J. Bielo
Executive Director
Susquehanna River Basin Commission
1721 North Front Street
Harrisburg, PA 17102
717-238-0422
717-238-2436 (fax)

TENNESSEE VALLEY AUTHORITY

Mr. M. Paul Schmierbach
Manager
Environmental Quality
Tennessee Valley Authority
400 West Summit Hill Drive
WT 8B
Knoxville, TN 37902-1499
615-632-6578
615-632-6855 (fax)

UNITED STATES INFORMATION AGENCY

Ms. Jacqueline Higgs Caldwell
Assistant General Counsel
United States Information Agency
Room 700
301 Fourth Street, SW
Washington, DC 20547
202-619-6975
202-619-4573 (fax)

US AGENCY FOR INTERNATIONAL DEVELOPMENT

Mr. Laurence R. Hausman
Environmental Coordinator, C/AID
US Agency for International Development
Department of State
Room 508, SA-18
Washington, DC 20523-1810
703-875-4203
703-875-4053 (fax)

US POSTAL SERVICE

Mr. Edward Wandelt
Environmental Coordinator
Facilities Department
US Postal Service
Room 4130
475 L'Enfant Plaza West, SW
Washington, DC 20260-6421
202-268-3135
202-268-3878 (fax)

VETERANS AFFAIRS

Mr. Jon E. Baer
Director
Landscape Architectural Service
Department of Veterans Affairs
Code 088B4
810 Vermont Avenue, NW
Washington, DC 20420
202-233-8453
202-233-3968 (fax)

APPENDIX 7   SOURCES OF *NEPA* INFORMATION

BOOKS AND REPORTS

- *CEQ Environmental Quality Annual Reports.* U.S. Government Printing Office. Washington, DC.

    - U.S. Department of Transportation: Procedures for Considering Environmental Impacts, Order 5610.C.

- Mandelker, *NEPA Law and Litigation.* Callaghan & Company, Willmette, Illinois, 1984 with updates.

    - This treatise is a comprehensive legal review of NEPA's requirements. It covers NEPA case law in detail.

- Environmental Law Institute, *NEPA Deskbook.* Washington, DC, 1989.

    The deskbook includes a legal analysis of NEPA by Nicholas Yost, former Chief Counsel of CEQ, copies of NEPA, CEQ NEPA regulations, and federal agency NEPA procedures.

- Fogleman, V. M., *Guide to the National Environmental Policy Act: Interpretations, Applications and Compliance.* Quorum Books, New York, New York, 1990.

    - This guidebook contains thorough, well-cited coverage of NEPA theory and practice.

    - CEQ's annual reports typically contain a review of NEPA developments over the preceding year and a summary of recent NEPA statistics.

FEDERAL AGENCY REGULATIONS AND OTHER GUIDANCE

- **CEQ Regulations.** The CEQ regulations implementing NEPA are found at 40 C.F.R. Sec. 1500.1 et seq.

- CEQ, **Preamble to Proposed CEQ NEPA Regulations**, 43 Fed. Reg. 25230, June 9, 1978.

    - This document contains CEQ's detailed explanations of the proposed NEPA Regulations.

• CEQ, **Preamble to Final CEQ NEPA Regulations**, 43 Fed. Reg. 55978, November 29, 1978.

  – This document contains CEQ's detailed explanations of the final NEPA regulations and discusses the comments raised during the regulatory review process.

• CEQ, **NEPA Implementation Procedures: Appendices I, II, and III**, 49 Fed. Reg. 49750, December 21, 1984.

  – These appendices list agency NEPA contacts and agencies with jurisdiction by law or special expertise on environmental issues.

• **CEQ Informal Advice**. CEQ has issued the following informal advice on NEPA implementation:

  – **Memorandum: Questions and Answers About the NEPA Regulations ("40 Questions")**, 46 Fed. Reg. 18026, March 23 1981, as amended 51 Fed. Reg. 15618, April 25, 1986.

  – **Memorandum: Scoping Guidance**, April 30, 1981.

  – **Memorandum: Guidance Regarding NEPA Regulations** 48 Fed. Reg. 34263, July 28, 1983.

• **Federal Agency NEPA Procedures**. Each federal agency has issued procedures for applying NEPA to its activities. Citations to selected federal agency NEPA procedures are as follows:

  – U.S. Department of Agriculture: 7 C.F.R. Secs. 1b.1 et seq.

  – U.S. Army Corps of Engineers: 33 C.F.R. Secs. 230.1 et seq.

  – U.S. Environmental Protection Agency: 40 C.F.R. Secs. 6.100 et seq.

  – Federal Highway Administration: 23 C.F.R. Secs. 771.101 et seq.

  – U.S. Department of the Interior: Departmental Manual, Part 516 (includes appendices for individual agencies and bureaus within the Department of the Interior).

• **U.S. Environmental Protection Agency. Policy and Procedures for the Review of Federal Actions Impacting the Environment**, October 23, 1984.

  – This document establishes EPA's procedures for review of EISs.

Laws

• **The National Environmental Policy Act**. The Act is found at 42 U.S.C. Sec. 4321 et seq.

Glossary and Acronyms

Glossary

CEQ – The President's Council on Environmental Quality is the agency responsible for the oversight and development of national environmental policy. Created by NEPA, CEQ also shares this responsibility with EPA.

Categorical Exclusion – A category of project actions, which a federal agency identifies in its NEPA procedures, that do not individually or cumulatively have a significant effect on the environment.

Cooperating Agency – A federal agency, other than the lead agency, that has legal jurisdiction or special expertise to comment on the project actions of a lead agency.

Cumulative Effects – Effects that are the result of incremental impacts of an action, when added to other past, present, and reasonably foreseeable future actions, regardless of which agency (federal or nonfederal) or person undertakes such actions.

Direct Effects – Effects that are caused by an action and occur at the same time and place as the action.

Environmental Assessment (EA) – A concise public document that analyzes the environmental impacts of a proposed federal action and provides sufficient evidence to determine the level of significance of the impacts.

Environmental Impact Statement (EIS) – The detailed statement required by NEPA when an agency proposes a major federal action significantly affecting the quality of the human environment.

Finding of No Significant Impact (FONSI) – A public document that briefly presents the reasons why an action will not have a significant impact on the human environment, and therefore, will not require the preparation of an environmental impact statement.

Indirect Effects – Effects that are caused by an action and occur later in time, or at another location, yet are reasonably foreseeable in the future.

Lead Agency – The agency or agencies that have taken the primary responsibility for preparing the environmental impact statement.

National Environmental Policy Act (NEPA) – Federal legislation that establishes environmental policy for the nation. It provides an interdisciplinary framework for federal agencies to prevent environmental damage and contains "action-forcing" procedures to ensure that federal agency decision-makers take environmental factors into account.

Notice of Intent (NOI) – The first formal step in the environmental impact statement process, consisting of a notice with the following information: a description of the proposed action and alternatives; a description of the agency's proposed scoping process, including scoping meetings; and the name and address of the persons to contact within the lead agency regarding the environmental impact statement.

Record of Decision (ROD) – A public document that reflects the agency's final decision, rationale behind that decision, and commitments to monitoring and mitigation.

Scope – The types of actions to be included in a project, the range of alternatives, and the impacts to be considered.

Tiering – The process of preparing multiple levels of environmental review, typically including general matters in broad environmental impact statements with subsequent narrower environmental impact statements.

ACRONYMS

ACHP	Advisory Council on Historic Preservation
AEC	Atomic Energy Commission
BLM	Bureau of Land Management
CDBGs	Community Development Block Grants
CERCLA	Comprehensive Environmental Response Compensation and Liability Act
CEQ	Council on Environmental Quality
Corps	U.S. Army Corps of Engineers
DOD	U.S. Department of Defense
DOI	Department of Interior
DOT	Department of Transportation
EA	Environmental Assessment
EIA	Environmental Impact Assessment
EIS	Environmental Impact Statement
EPA	U.S. Environmental Protection Agency
FAA	Federal Aviation Administration
FHWA	Federal Highway Administration
FONSI	Finding of No Significant Impact

HUD	U.S. Department of Housing and Urban Development
NEPA	National Environmental Policy Act
NOI	Notice of Intent
NPS	National Park Service
RCRA	Resource Conservation and Recovery Act
RI/FS	Remedial Investigation/Feasibility Study
ROD	Record of Decision
USFWS	U.S. Fish and Wildlife Service
USMC	United States Marine Corps

INDEX